POLICING SHROPSHIRE 1836 – 1967

By DOUGLAS J. ELLIOTT.

A year by year account of the Shropshire
Constabulary and the police forces of the
Boroughs of Bridgnorth, Ludlow, Oswestry,
Shrewsbury, and Wenlock.

To Christina, David,
Jonathan & Siân.

HELMET
PLATE

COLLAR

BADGES

CAP
BADGE

POLICING SHROPSHIRE

1836 - 1967

Douglas J. Elliott

K.A.F. BREWIN BOOKS. 1984

First published in 1984 by
K.A.F. Brewin Books, Studley, Warwickshire.

Text Copyright 1984 © Douglas J. Elliott

ISBN 0 947731 00 8 HARDBACK

ISBN 0 947731 01 6 PAPERBACK

Typeset in Baskerville and printed by
Supaprint (Redditch)Ltd., Worcestershire, England

Made and printed in Great Britain

'I Thomas Abel Wilmot of Birmingham late a Private in the 2nd Dragoon Guards and Constable in the Birmingham Police. Do swear that I will well and truly serve our Sovereign Lady the Queen, in the Office of Constable for the County of Salop, without favour or affection, malice, or ill-will; and that I will, to the best of my power, cause the Peace to be kept and preserved, and prevent all Offences against the Persons and Properties of Her Majesty's Subjects; and that while I continue to hold the said Office, I will to the best of my skill and knowledge discharge all the duties thereof faithfully according to Law.   So help me God.'

Attestation of Constable Thomas Abel Wilmot.
Dated 31. March. 1840.
Shropshire County Constabulary.

Contents

List of Illustrations

The illustrations are reproduced by the courtesy of — The West Mercia
Constabulary, Salop Record Office, Shrewsbury Chronicle, The Police Review,
North Wales Newspapers Ltd., The Illustrated Sporting & Dramatic News,
Shropshire County Library (Local Studies), Mr. Stanley Davies, Mrs. Betty
Pickering, Mr. Thomas Goodman.

Mr. R.W. Cozens, Q.P.M. Chief Constable
West Mercia Constabulary

Foreword

by ROBERT W. COZENS, Q.P.M.

Chief Constable of the West Mercia Constabulary

It is with particular appreciation of the timeliness of this history that I recommend the painstaking research of the author, who has brought the past to life so vividly. Crime prevention has been the central aim of the police force since its establishment. Successful achievements towards this goal require a far-sighted application of knowledge of human behaviour.

A localised history filled with anecdotes of individual characters and their often courageous responses to dangerous incidents offers much food for thought.

The evolution of the police force has followed a series of steady responses to changing social conditions and attitudes. To continue with a balanced development which will best serve our society in future we need to learn from similar times of rising crime rates and violence in the past.

The extraordinary gift which Douglas Elliott has of clothing dry accounts with a wealth of detailed lively and often humorous information makes this book a source of fascinating knowledge to police and public alike.

Acknowledgements

It is with pleasure that I record my indebtedness to the many police officers, both serving and retired, who have given of their time and knowledge to answer my many queries. In particular thanks are due to Mr. R.W. Fenwick, C.B.E., Q.P.M., Chief Constable of Shropshire 1962 – 1967; Ex-Det/Supt: Sam Evans; Police Sgt: John Ray, and Miss Ellalene Parton who so generously put at my disposal her collection of police newspaper cuttings.

My special thanks are also due to Mr. Stanley Davies, who so kindly allowed me access to his collection of papers and photographs of the Shrewsbury Borough Police Force, of which his father had been Chief Constable.

I am grateful to Mr. W.F. Mumford for making available the records of the Wenlock Corporation, and Mr. R. Peart, Town Clerk of Oswestry Town Council for similarly making available the records of the old Corporation of Oswestry.

Mention must be made of the kindness of the staff of 'The Police Review' who supplied information from their files.

The helpfulness of the County Archivist, Ms Marion Halford, M.A., and her staff at the Salop Record Office has been considerable. Also that of Mr. Anthony Carr, M.A., Mrs May Ion and the late Ms Honor Williams, A.L.A., of the Local Studies Library, Shrewsbury, who have attended to my innumerable requests with the greatest of patience and good humour.

And last, but not least, thanks are due to Superintendent Jack Lloyd of the West Mercia Constabulary, and previously of the Shropshire Constabulary, for his painstaking reading of the typescript of this book.

Chapter One

The instrument by which regular, paid police forces were ordered to be established within the boroughs of England and Wales was the Municipal Corporations Act, 1835. However, the Act was not exclusively, nor even primarily promoted for the purposes of establishing police forces.

Its main concern was to extend the franchise of local government to a wider number of electors. From it was to extend an age of municipal enterprise and local self-government.

Thus it was to these new democratic forms of borough administration that the Act assigned amongst other duties, that of maintaining a police force.

Immediately after the election of the new town councils, the members were charged to appoint and elect a sufficient number of their own body (subsequently restricted by the Municipal Corporations Act, 1882, to not more than one-third of the council) to form a watch committee, together with the mayor, who whilst holding office, was declared a justice of the peace. It was then ordered that the watch committee should (within three weeks of its establishment), appoint a sufficient number of fit men, to be sworn in to act as constables, for preserving the peace by day and night.

It was not uncommon for watch committees to appoint existing watchmen as members of the new police force. In some cases these men may have been the best choice available, but generally speaking it must have meant the continuation of old habits which would not be conducive to efficiency.

It was a practice followed for a number of reasons — perhaps from a charitable thought for old servants, maybe to avoid the expense of compensating them for loss of office, or perhaps the watch committees saw in the old watchmen and constables a ready and convenient, cheap source of labour.

At Shrewsbury the new reform council held its first meeting on New Year's Day, 1836. Promptly they appointed a committee to report upon the present state of the constables and night watch. The report of the committee was read out at the second meeting of the council, when they declared that they could do nothing about the situation, so it was ordered that their report — 'be kept amongst the records.' It was at this second meeting of the council that a watch committee was elected from the council members, as was ordered by the Reform Act.

One could say that the real history of the Shrewsbury Borough Police Force commences with this first meeting of its watch committee. However, this does not mean that 1836 saw in Shrewsbury, or in any other borough in the land, a sudden rash of blue uniformed policemen. Far from it. Many boroughs carried on with the old system of unpaid parish constables, appointed yearly, and at night, with perhaps a beadle in charge, would be the night watch.

A decision was made by the watch committee to appoint four police officers, who would be expected to give up the whole of their time to the performance of their duties. They were also to superintend the night watch, which was to be kept on. The watch committee reported on the 5 February 1836, to the Mayor and council, that they had appointed thirteen constables. Four to act as police officers during the day, and nine to be night watchmen.

The Recorder of Shrewsbury, John Bather, spoke out very strongly, in July 1836 on the subject of the unlit and unwatched suburbs of Shrewsbury. It should be pointed out, that the policing of the town of Shrewsbury was confined to the area within the bridges, as was the lighting of the streets. The suburbs were left to fend for themselves, as they did not

2

contribute towards these services. John Bather's speech is most illuminating —

'I would not slander any classes or divisions of our fellow-townsmen; But I am only speaking facts, which the records of this Court will but too clearly prove, when I state that Frankwell and Coleham have usually been the main haunt and resort of the profligate gangs of juvenile offenders, and their still more wicked abettors, who infest the town, pilfering from the honest and heedless tradesmen — the hole-and-corner boroughs, if I may so express it, to which these noxious vermin run for refuge, when pursued. I need not tell you that, in Frankwell particularly, are whole rows of houses, tenanted by shameless and wretched females, to which thieves and robbers have been frequently traced; or that the Castle-Foregate abounds with lodging-houses, in which a miserable class of vagabonds, without any apparent means of honest subsistance, are constantly housed.

But I would ask any man of plain sense, whether it is fitting that those places which want watching most should go un-watched altogether? and, as economy is the order of the day, I would ask its staunchest advocate, whether he thinks it cheap to breed up and foster a race of thieves in darkness and security, that they may afterwards be laboriously hunted out and prosecuted at an expence which absorbs a great part of the local taxation of the town?.'[1]

Little notice was taken of the Recorder's wisdom, although one councillor did put forward a motion at the next council meeting, that they should both light and police the suburbs. The motion was opposed, as calculated to throw an additional burden of taxation upon the poorer inhabitants of the suburbs.

In 1837, one of the four policemen, John Owen, resigned, having found a better post as Governor of the Atcham Union Workhouse. The watch committee made a careful examin-ation of the receipts of the police officers and found that the sum of fifteen shillings and twopence, which included salary and fees, had been the low weekly average paid to them for

3

the last eleven months.   Which they thought very inadequate for their services.   With the resignation of John Owen, the watch committee came up with the suggestion that if they did not replace Owen, they could then divide the four salaries between the remaining three officers.   The only alternative would be to replace Owen, and put up all four salaries.   The council resolved, unanimously to adopt the recommendation of the committee.   Thus the Shrewsbury police force took the seemingly retrograde step of dropping in number from four to three.   The remaining three gained a rise in pay, but, at the cost of sharing between them, the duty of the fourth.

On the 22 April 1838, one of the police officers, Zachariah Price, died.   For the next four months, Richard Evans and William Badger, the two remaining police officers were forced to shoulder his duty as well.   This time without a rise in pay.

It was decided early in 1838, to vacate the old Watch-House, and find more convenient premises for a Police Station. A suitable property was found in Gullet Passage.   The house was converted to the special needs of the day.   The ground floor housed the Watch room, whilst below, the cellar was divided into cells.   The first floor contained the Street Act Committee of Management office.   While above all on the top floor, resided one of the police officers, who was considered to have charge of the building.

A committee was set up by the Shrewsbury town council, on the 2 May 1838, to consider the state of the borough police, and as to the propriety of adopting a new and improved system of policing the town.   In the following August, the committee made their recommendation that the watch committee should employ a more efficient set of men as watchmen, until October next;   and that the age of these men should not exceed thirty.   This was to be a trial, in order to try out a better system within the town, previous to it being suggested for the suburbs.   No more was heard of this committee's recommendations.

The Grand Jury of the Shrewsbury Borough Sessions made a representation to the Recorder of the Borough, in January

1839, referring to the state of the town and suburbs. They expressed themselves quite satisfied that the present police officers (as far as they were able), discharged their duties quite competently. But, declared that from information received, their number was insufficient for the preservation of property, or in general for the peace of the town. And further, that their remuneration was totally inadequate.

Turning their attention to the suburbs of the town, they noted that three of them — Coleham, Frankwell and the Abbey-Foregate now had street lights, but were still not policed. An evil which they thought could not be remedied too soon. The suburb of Castle-Foregate was neither lit nor policed, and was considered by them to be the nucleus of all local crime. This suburb afforded the greatest facilities for the disposal of stolen property of every description. To remedy this evil, they suggested the lighting of the whole of the suburbs together with an extention of the jurisdiction of the police, and their better remuneration.

Later, in May 1839, the investigating committee, gave further findings on the policing of the town. They recommended that the numbers of day and night constables should be twelve. Of these, two should be Superintendents. Notably, their last recommendation was that the whole of the force should be clothed in uniform. The latter suggestion was not accepted until 1844. The expense of the new system would, with the adoption of the recommendation, and the decision to watch the suburbs, be borne by both the town and suburbs.

In 1838, John Thomas of Shoplatch, a tailor by trade, was appointed a Sergeant at Mace to the Shrewsbury corporation. At the same time the corporation recommended Thomas to the watch committee as a police officer. This man stayed with the borough force until 1851, when with the rank of superintendent, he was dismissed for misconduct.

William Badger, sergeant at mace, and police officer of the town of Shrewsbury, resigned his offices in August 1839, leaving Shrewsbury to end the decade, once more down to just two police officers to keep law and order within the town, during the hours of daylight.

The Borough of Bridgnorth

The Corporation of Bridgnorth reacted quickly to the Municipal Reform Act, holding the first meeting of its newly elected Whig council, on New Year's Day 1836. One of its first decisions was to declare the Mayor and the entire council, a Watch Committee for the borough.

During the proceedings of this meeting, Edward Goodall was appointed Chief Constable of the borough, at a salary of eighteen pounds three shillings per annum.

At a second meeting, held a week later, Goodall and nine other men were sworn in as constables for the borough. The commencement of their duties was Monday, 18 January, 1836. Later, Goodall and one of his constables, George Evans were additionally appointed Inspectors of Weights and Measures. Evans was also elected Sergeant for the execution of process in the borough court of record. He was Town Crier too, and later in the year succeeded Edward Goodall as Chief Constable. Goodall died on the 19 May, at the early age of 45. A further two of the constables were appointed by the Justices of the borough to serve summonses issuing from their Petty Sessions — ' and that they be appointed alternately to do those duties.' [2]

Side by side with the day constables, who appear to be unpaid, except perhaps for the perquisites of the courts, appear the night constables, or watch. At a meeting of the Watch Committee held the 15 January 1836, Hezekiah Pinner, Richard Shaw and Richard Felton were appointed night constables. They received fifteen shillings weekly for their trouble and expenses, but were required to buy their own

6

clothes. Their duties were to start as soon as the watch houses were constructed. One was delegated constable for the Low Town, and two to act in the High Town. The three men taking the Low Town watch alternately.

The prison called 'The Cribb', at the North Gate, was designated the Lock-up House, and the gaoler was ordered to prepare and clean it out for that purpose, whilst the watchman nearest to the North Gate was to take charge of the keys. The Night constables were ordered to commence their rounds at ten o'clock in the evening, finishing their nocturnal duties at five in the morning; proclaiming the time every half hour throughout the night. Giving comforting knowledge (to those awake) that the watch were about and alert. That is, if the watchmen kept awake to perform this part of their duty. Many of the watchmen were old and ailing, employed mostly out of charity, or as an alternative to having them a charge on the poor rate.

The Night Watch was only employed during the winter months. In 1836 the tour of duty lasted to the seventh of May only. The watch resuming their duties on the following first of October, found that the watch committee had reduced their wages to twelve shillings per week, and given them the extra duty of maintaining the lamps in the Stoneway.

Coal was provided for the fires in the watch-houses, and presumably many a watchman would be loath to leave his snug retreat on a cold winter night, to make his rounds of the town.

The watch committee meeting of the 17 November 1837, was to be a memorable one, radically changing the police establishment of the borough.

It was ordered that the allowance, out of the borough fund, paid to the Day constables and Beadle, was to cease from the first of December. In lieu of those officials, there would be appointed, under the authority of the Municipal Act, two police constables to act by day. Their individual salaries were not to exceed thirty-five pounds per year. For this, they were expected to give up the whole of their time to the duties of their office.

7

The two constables commenced their duties on the 1 December 1837. Beginning at six a.m. in the morning and ending at ten p.m. in the evening. Of course in such cases as riot, felony or other great emergency, they could be called upon outside these hours, by a magistrate or night constable.

Each constable was alloted a respective district, which he was expected to perambulate at least four times each day, with such variation of hours, as to render it uncertain when they could be expected. Apart from regular police duties they were required to attend the Quarter and Petty Sessions. They executed all summons and warrants, obtained signatures to petitions and addresses, circulated handbills, and all other duties belonging to the Mayor's office. They were required to visit each public-house and beer-shop every Sunday, Christmas Day and Good Friday, during the hours of Divine Service; and visit all Lodging-houses when directed by the borough magistrates.

It was unanimously agreed by the Watch Committee that the two constables should not be local men, but selected from a distance. Two of the committee were then requested to write and make application to the heads of the police forces of — Birmingham, Shrewsbury and Worcester, to recommend fit and suitable persons for the office.

On the 1 December, the Bridgnorth Watch Committee having read the satisfactory testimonials of Thomas Barker and Luke Edwards, declared them constables for the Borough of Bridgnorth. Despite the agreement not to appoint local men, Thomas Barker is on record as being one of the ten local men chosen as constables on the 8 January 1836, but who then declined the office. This time he found the post of constable more to his liking, now that it carried a salary of thirty-five pounds per annum.

The old engine-house, which adjoined the Savings Bank, was converted in January 1838, into a police station, for the use of both the Day police, and the Night constables.

The Bridgnorth watch committee of the late 1830's concerned themselves with the welfare of their police constables. Consideration was given by them to the fact that the heavy material, which constituted the coats of the constables, while ideal for keeping them warm in winter, would prove most uncomfortable in the warmer weather of the summer period. Therefore a coat of much lighter texture was ordered to be provided in time for the summer season.

The Borough of Ludlow

The new reform council of the Ludlow borough met the 5 January 1836. Their first act was to remove from office the old sergeants-at-mace — Richard Jolley and Richard Cooke. Prior to this date they had been responsible for policing the town.

The next act of the new council was to appoint a watch committee, who put in hand the construction of three new cells at the gaol, for use by the new police. The lack of minute books of this watch committee leaves us rather in the dark about most police matters within the borough. The size of the borough police force is not shown, nor the names of the officers. That they were dressed in uniforms we do know, for accounts for these appear in the council minutes, but what colour was chosen for the uniforms is not recorded.

William Davis became the first superintendent of the Ludlow Borough Police Force. His tenure of office was brief. On the 10 August 1837, the council decreed that he no longer hold the post of superintendent of their police force. It would appear that the Inspector of Prisons had paid Ludlow a visit of inspection. He found William Davis holding the dual posts of gaoler of the Ludlow Gaol, and also that of superintendent of the borough police force. The inspector pointed out that William Davis should confine his duties to the former post. The council complied with his recommendation.

Though Davis lost his salary as superintendent of police, his wife was appointed as Matron of the Gaol. It was her duty to attend to the female prisoners, for which she received a salary of five pounds per annum, offsetting part of Davis's loss of salary.

It had been the custom to allow prisoners in the Ludlow Gaol sixpence per day for food. Now it was decided to discontinue the allowance, and substitute the following diet —

'½lb of best bread, 1lb of Potatoes or mixed vegetables, to such prisoners not on Hard Labour or ½lb if on Hard Labour, with three pints of Gruel per day — three different times, and warm if so desired — this allowance to each prisoner.'[3]

It was the matron's duty to cook the food in the gaoler's house. The magistrates also directed that a sufficient number of Bibles and Prayer books be furnished for the use of the prisoners.

A brief note in the Ludlow corporation minutes, dated 9 November 1839, informs us that the borough police required new clothing. With that small crumb of information, our scanty knowledge of Ludlow's borough police force during the period 1836 - 1839, closes.

The Borough of Oswestry

With the passing of the Municipal Reform Act 1835, the new Whig council at Oswestry made a show of discharging all the old officers of the late corporation. Most of these were immediately re-appointed. A watch committee was then formed on the 12 February 1836. Jacob Smith and Richard Jones being re-elected Sergeants at Mace. Jacob Smith was the police officer for the borough, an old soldier from Leicestershire. General handyman to the corporation, he included amongst his many duties those of — Collector of the Borough Rate; Clerk of the Markets; Collector of the tolls called the Mayor's Tolls, and of the money paid for the public standings at 'The Cross'.

It was not intended that the police officer should idle his time. In payment he was awarded the salary of forty-one pounds per year, plus a house, rent free, and the fees from the weighing machine at 'The Cross'.

The second Sergeant at Mace, Richard Jones, also re-appointed, doubled up as Gaoler for the borough gaol.

One of Jacob's tasks was to caution the several local coach proprietors, to cease the furious and dangerous manner in which their coaches were frequently driven through the town. It is not hard to imagine a coach and four rumbling at speed through the streets of Oswestry, with the pedestrians crouching in doorways, to evade being run down. On a repetition of the offence Jacob would lay information against the offender, and the magistrates would then proceed to enforce 'the utmost penalties'. The 1838 equivalent of a modern speeding ticket sounds horrific.

With the ending of the third decade of the nineteenth century, we find Oswestry taken care of by Jacob Smith, the police officer, helped out by Richard Jones the gaoler. At night the watch would perambulate the town. On riotous occasions special constables could be sworn in. This then was law and order in the town of Oswestry.

The Borough of Wenlock

Wenlock borough under its charter of 1468 comprised within its bounds most of the lands held by the Priory of Wenlock, and included some twenty civil parishes. Even with many reductions it was until 1966, the largest non-county borough in the country.

As most of this large area was rural, it was not affected by section 76 of the Reform Act of 1835; only the small urban districts being concerned. Although the minute books of the

11

watch committee appear to have been lost, it is known that the borough was divided into three wards, (Broseley, Madeley and Much Wenlock). Each of which had its own watch committee, consisting of the Mayor of the borough, and such councillors as represented that particular ward. Again each ward had its own 'Police Office', which was used for the purpose of transacting the business of the borough justices, in that ward. Each of the wards appointed a constable, but beyond that nothing of a contemporary nature has survived to extend our knowledge of the police force of this large borough. One could say that John Johnson had his eye blacked, several teeth knocked out, and generally came off worse in an attempt to stop a fight on Wenlock Edge in September 1837. Johnson was constable of Much Wenlock, and had been to Shrewsbury to attend the Assizes, returning along the Edge with a companion, they heard shouts for help. Attempting to part the fighters, he and his companion found themselves assaulted by both parties.

Despite their injuries they succeeded in hauling the offenders back to Wenlock, where they were suitably fined.

But only such isolated incidents exist to show that there was a police force at Wenlock during the latter half of the 1830's.

The Rural or Shropshire Constabulary

The establishment of the Metropolitan, and other municipal police forces, resulted in many habitual criminals migrating in fairly large numbers from London, and such other large towns where an improved police force had superceded the old parish watch.

Moving out to the unprotected rural areas, where they could employ their nefarious trades with less chance of detection and capture.

County magistrates reported that the bulk of the more serious offences committed within their jurisdictions, were 'the work of strangers from the great towns'. By this time, highwaymen, the terror of the previous century, had been practically suppressed, but footpads were still common enough to make travellers very apprehensive on lonely country roads. Countrymen returning from town markets, would wait until a party of them were gathered, rather than face the journey home alone. Commercial travellers would often as not arm themselves with a pistol, and be accompanied by a large dog, in the hopes of scaring off would be robbers.

Riots breaking out in the industrial parts of the county, left the parish constables unable to cope with the numbers concerned. At times the local authorities called in the army (and because the army was paid by the government it cost them nothing). But the use of military methods increased the discontent, and the soldiers did not like being used against their fellow countrymen.

As early as January 1831, at the Shropshire quarter sessions, an opinion was given by the court —

'that the formation of a Constabulary Force throughout the County of Salop with a view to the preservation of the Peace and security of property should be adopted, and that this court strongly recommends the Magistrates in their respective districts to take immediate steps with a view to its organisation.' [4]

A year later, the Earl of Powis, as Lord Lieutenant of the county, was asked to communicate with the Home Secretary, informing him of the magistrates wish to form a paid police force throughout the rural parts of the county. Here the matter appears to have rested, pigeon-holed perhaps, in the dusty files of the Home Office.

The next move to obtain rural policing did in fact come from the government, but not until 1836, when a Royal Commission was appointed — 'For the purpose of Inquiring as to the best means of establishing an efficient constabulary

13

force in the countries of England and Wales'. The commissioners spent nearly three years hearing and sifting evidence from all sorts of people, not only the law-abiding, but also from the law-breakers. All the evidence pointed the same way, that there could be no security in the country districts without a trained, full-time police force.

While the deliberations of the commissioners were taking place, the magistrates of Shropshire, sitting in December 1838, passed the following resolution —

'That in consequence of the present inefficiency of the constabulary force, arising from the great increase of population, and the extention of the trade and commerce of the country — It is the opinion of this Court, that a body of Constables appointed by the Magistrates, paid out of the County Rate, and disposable at any point of the Shire where their services might be required, would be highly desirable, as providing in the most efficient manner for the prevention as well as detection of offences, for the security of persons and property, and for the constant preservation of the public peace.' 5

Copies of the above resolution were sent to the Home Secretary, the High Sheriff of Shropshire, and the Chairmen of neighbouring quarter sessions. Sir Baldwin Leighton optimistically suggested that twelve or fourteen men, with the aid of the paid police of the several Shropshire boroughs, would be quite sufficient. In which case the additional expense of an improved system of policing would not be so great as many persons had anticipated.

In the Hundred of Ford, an experiment had been tried out with one efficient paid officer. A man named William Baxter. The result was that since the previous September, only five or six felonies had been committed, whilst in the six months previous to his appointment, about sixty felonies had occurred. Several known thieves, who had been placed under the observation of this officer, had been detected and convicted. The officer recovered an amount of stolen property equal to his own salary.

The copy of the resolution, which had been sent to the Home Secretary, was very favourably received, and moreover he used it to outline the main points —

'a body of constables appointed by the magistrates, paid out of the county rate and disposable at any point of the shire where their services might be required.'[6]

in a circular letter sent to all the magistrates of the country. Canvassing them on his own account, as to the best means of organising a rural police force.

About half of the magistrates warmly supported the resolution put forward by the Shropshire bench.

The Royal Commission closed its report at the end of March 1839. There it would have hung fire for some considerable time, but for the Chartists.

The Chartist movement had started the year previous. The unrest and disturbances which this body caused, and which accelerated during 1839, soon made it obvious that the government lacked the resources to deal with the situation.

On the 20 July 1839, Major-General Sir Charles Napier, Officer Commanding the Northern District, wrote to the Home Secretary —

'My belief is that concession must be made to the people's feelings, or the establishment of a strong rural police force hurried on. I would do both thinking them absolutely necessary; if the police force be not quickly increased we shall require troops from Ireland.'[7]

The Home Secretary, Lord John Russell, saw that no time was to be lost. Within four days he introduced into Parliament his bill entitled — 'An Act for the Establishment of County and District Constables, by the Authority of Justices of the Peace'. The bill, despite a very stormy passage through parliament, received the Royal Assent a month later, on the 27 August 1839.

The Shropshire magistrates acted just as quickly. At a sessions held on the 14 October 1839, the chairman, Thomas Kenyon, read out a letter, dated the sixth of that month, to the Marquess of Normanby, now Home Secretary, in which he

15

had asked for a copy of the rules and regulations of the Metropolitan Police to be forwarded to him. And he pointed out that he would be grateful to know the wishes of the government, relative to the numbers required in such a force —

'preparatory to our consideration of the duties imposed upon us by the County Police Act.' [8]

The letter also queried the amount of salaries to be paid to the officers of the intended force, and particularly that of its superintendent, —

'which would of course very greatly assist us in our decision.' [9]

The Marquess though new to the post, shrewdly realized that he could not allow the Shropshire bench; who had originally led the idea of county police, to hesitate and waver over costs. Once the leader hesitated on the brink, the other counties might have second thoughts, and the whole scheme, so important to the nation, come to nought.

A reply was dictated, and sent post haste —

'Sir,   Whitehall. 9 Oct: 1839.

I am directed by the Marquess of Normanby to acknowledge the receipt of your letter of the 6th instant, and to inform you that his Lordship would prefer that the Magistrates should themselves take the initiative step of resolving to adopt the County Constabulary Act, before he interferes in the matter. Immediately on learning that the Magistrates have resolved to adopt the Act, Lord Normanby will trsnsmit copies of a set of Rules which have been compiled in this Department for the guidance of Magistrates in the formation of the Constabulary Force, which convey his ideas; but before adopting finally, Lord Normanby will be glad to receive any suggestions from the Magistrates as to their application to different localities.' [10]

One cannot really blame the magistrates for being cautious. Even at this late stage. Discussions held by them as to the numbers of constables needed, and the total cost of financing such a force had been wildly speculative. Sir Baldwin Leighton had spoken most optimistically in December 1838,

16

that twelve or fourteen men would be quite sufficient. At the other end of the scale J.A. Lloyd now pointed out that if the Act were to be carried out in its fullest extent, then 200 constables would be needed in proportion to the population of the county. With a salary of one pound per week each, this would make the cost One thousand pounds a year. Doubling the county rate. (standing at that time, at one halfpenny in the pound).

R.A. Slaney reminded his fellow magistrates that in Hertfordshire, which was so near as to be subject to the depredations of the London thieves, the commissioners had thought one policeman to one thousand six hundred inhabitants to be quite sufficient. Therefore the number of constables in Shropshire might be further reduced in proportion to the population.

As against this, it was shown from various returns, that the population of this county had, between 1792 and 1832, increased only 60%, whilst crime had been trebled.

William Ormsby-Gore rose to remind his fellow magistrates that, — 'as the suggestion of a constabulary force had, as it were, emanated from this county, they were bound to adopt the provisions of the act to such extent as might be required.'

The proceedings ended with a committee being formed of one magistrate from each petty sessions. They were to enquire into the circumstances required by the act, and. to report their opinion and information to the next sessions.

December 1839, the decision was made. The magistrates of the Shropshire Quarter Sessions formerly adopted the County Police Act. A certain amount of opposition was shown at the crowded court, but on the chairman's motion, a substantial majority voted to establish a County Police Force. It was to consist of one Chief Constable, six Superintendents, and forty-three constables.

The following rates of pay was agreed upon — Chief Constable £300 per annum, Superintendents £78 per annum (with power to raise two of them to £104), and Constables to be paid eighteen shillings a week, with twenty-one shillings a week, as a maximum for not more than ten such constables.

A petition stating this, was sent to the Home Secretary, signed by thirty-three Shropshire county magistrates.

A two man committee was then formed, consisting of Sir Baldwin Leighton and W. Wolryche Whitmore. It was their task to advertise for candidates for the office of Chief Constable of Shropshire.

And so the third decade of the nineteenth century came to a close, with the county magistrates of Shropshire having taken a determined step towards the establishment of a county police force; while the various boroughs still struggled to attain efficiency within their own small police forces.

Chapter Two

1840 — 1849

Eighteen hundred and forty, the third year of the young Queen Victoria. A year which opened with great activity on the part of the police authorities of Shropshire. In London, the Secretary of State had received the resolution of the Shropshire county magistrates, and in reply had sent on the rules and regulations which they had requested.

The testimonials of the thirty-eight candidates for the office of chief constable had been read. From a short list of four, the choice was made of Captain Dawson Mayne, R.N. He was appointed on the 25 January 1840, as the first chief constable of the county of Shropshire.

Mayne soon settled into the duties of his new command. His first task required him to divide up the county to the best advantage of the new force. By the 3 March he made his intentions known of dividing the county into six police divisions. Each division to have a superintendent in charge.

The First Division had the river Severn at Shrewsbury as the southern boundary, from there along the Wem road to Whitchurch as an eastern boundary, and extended north and west to the adjoining counties. The superintendent residing at West Felton.

The Second Division used the Wem road as a western boundary, and extended north and east to the adjoining counties, and south to the Newport and Shifnal areas. The superintendent to reside at Hodnet.

The Third Division included the industrial areas of Wellington, Newport and Shifnal. The superintendent residing at Wellington.

The Fourth Division included Bridgnorth, Broseley, Cleobury Mortimer and Overs Hundred. The superintendent residing at Bridgnorth.

The Fifth Division extended through the valley between the line of hills east and west of the turnpike road from Shrewsbury to Ludlow. The superintendent to be at Church Stretton.

The Sixth Division to extend from the river Severn north, and from the extremities of the county south and west to the district allocated to the superintendent of the Church Stretton division. The superintendent to reside at Bishopscastle.

After outlying his plan, Captain Mayne made the provision that —

'I may perhaps find it desirable to take off a portion from the last two divisions, to form a small one immediately around Shrewsbury to be under the charge of a Senior Constable on a reference to the map it will be found, that this will give to each Superintendent such an extent of ground to travel over, that it will be impossible for them to perform their duties efficiently without being mounted. I therefore beg to suggest that provision be made for this purpose accordingly.' [1]

Mayne also suggested that he be allowed to enage, at the expence of the county, an experienced policeman. The idea being that he should instruct the force for two or three weeks in their several duties. Having a lack of police experience himself, this was a judicious move.

Eighty-five hopeful applicants came forward to join the new police force, as candidates either for the post of superintendent, or as constables. Of the six men appointed as superintendents on the 9 March there were — John Sing MacMichael (who also became deputy chief constable). A Shropshire man, born at Bridgnorth in 1806. Already with police experience, having served with the Birmingham Police Force, as a sub-inspector.

Richard James of Chalford, county Gloucester, took up post as superintendent of 'B' Division.

William Baxter of Edge, county Salop, ex-police officer of the Hundred of Ford, took charge of 'C' Division. A native of Birmingham, his smartness soon gained him the nickname of 'The Brummagem Button Stick'.

Philip James, reputed to have been an inspector of the Birmingham Police, took charge of 'D' Division.

Stephen Surman of Shrewsbury, a native of Oxfordshire and formerly a horse keeper, was sworn in as superintendent of 'F' Division.

The sixth superintendent was Charles Lewis, a draper of Oswestry, who took over command of 'E' Division at Church Stretton.

Thirty-one constables were sworn in by the county magistrates, not nearly as many as were needed, but over half of the applicants had proved unsuitable. Even so, some of those chosen only lasted a month or two before being dismissed. Mainly for drunkenness and neglect of duty. Edward Butler, as constable number one, was caught and convicted of poaching, and dismissed the force, after only nine days service. All told 13 men were dismissed in the first year, and a further five resigned. To obtain a force of 43 constables there had been sixty-one appointments, constituting a wastage of 18 men. Of the men recruited in the first year (including the six superintendents) forty-one were natives of Shropshire; five of Montgomeryshire; two of Denbighshire; one from Glamorganshire; one from Gloucestershire; one from Oxfordshire; one from Staffordshire; one from Worcestershire and fourteen from the City of Birmingham.

The trades and occupations of these early entrants read like a trade directory —

One Baker; one Book-keeper; one Bookmaker; two Butchers; one Carpenter; one Currier; one Draper; one Dyer; four Farmers; two Gardeners; one Gilder; one Gilt-ornament maker; two Grocers; one Horse-keeper; two Innkeepers; one Japanner; one Joiner; six Labourers; one Maltster; one Pump-maker; five Shoemakers; one Silver-plater; one Stonemason; five Tailors and one Yeoman.

Seven men came from the Birmingham Police Force including two inspectors. From the army came a further nine men — two from the 2nd Dragoon Guards; one from the 8th Hussars; two from the Royal Horse Guards; two from the Royal Marines; one from the Life Guards and one from the 38th Regiment. From this list it can be seen that although the new force had a nucleus of sixteen men who had been used to discipline, it would be an uphill task needing much patience to instil discipline and order into such a mixed bag of tradesmen.

The raw recruits had to undergo a three months probation period, wearing their own clothes. Later their uniforms were issued, and a picture of the well-dressed constable of the day emerges —

Clad in his rifle-green frock-coat and trousers, topped with a black (Stove-pipe) hat, a leather stock wound around his neck, a leather belt around his waist, plus an Oxford-grey overcoat, to don when it was cold, he would present quite a smart figure. For his protection he would carry a staff or truncheon, a little longer than the modern type. And at night a cutlass would be swinging from a frog on his belt. A large wooden rattle, which when swung energetically, hopefully brought assistance. A lanthorn was also provided for use at night. The cutlass was a weapon, I suspect more intended to give him courage on his lonely beat, and frighten would be attackers, than to be put to any serious use.

It was recorded at the June Sessions, 1840, that during the first quarter of the year, the rural constabulary had apprehended and charged before the magistrates, two hundred and ninety five persons. The following quarter, a further five hundred and twenty-nine offenders were brought before the bench, showing clearly that the green-clad constables were rapidly becoming efficient, and pouncing on offenders when and where ever found. Little wonder that they had gained the nickname of 'Paddy Mayne's Grasshoppers'.

In the meantime the Shrewsbury watch committee had decided to vacate the old watch house in Gullet Passage, and drew up an agreement with the committee of the public rooms, whereby the borough police could establish a new police station and cells, on their premises.

At Bridgnorth the watch committee held a meeting in January, 1840, appointing a sub-committee of six to investigate the police and night watch expenses. They were to report such arrangements that they might agree upon, for establishing the police of the borough upon a more efficient system. With the cautionary reminder, that it had to show a financial saving as against the present cost. Within a short time the six man committee had handed in their report to the watch committee. They proposed sweeping changes in the policing of the borough. The chief constable was to be made redundant, and the night watch done away with altogether — 'as entailing a serious expense without adequate advantage'. They suggested that two efficient policemen would amply provide for the security of persons and property within the borough. they recommended that one man be appointed chief constable, with a weekly wage of one guinea; and that the second man, as a subordinate under the control of the chief constable, should receive eighteen shillings per week. The former, while taking his full share of duty, both by day and night, should consider himself responsible for the peace of the town. Should any circumstances occur to render a larger force necessary, the committee suggested that one or more of the special constables, appointed annually might be employed in aiding the police force, under the direction of the chief constable. Their opinion was that such occasions rarely occurred, and that such extra force should only be used when sanctioned by a borough magistrate. Then recalling the cautionary instructions given them, they went on to speak of costs — their proposals, they estimated, would save up to £50 per annum. On the 3 February 1840, Luke Edwards was appointed Chief Constable of the Borough of Bridgnorth, whilst Thomas Barker was appointed as the subordinate officer on the same day.

A second rural police act was now put through parliament. (County Police Act. 1840. 3 & 4 Vic.c.88). Amongst many improvements it optimistically provided for the consolidation of borough and county police forces by mutual agreement. The members of the Ludlow Corporation disagreed with the Act. A petition was hurriedly drawn up, and presented to parliament. It asked them to delete the consolidation clause, of the Act. But, despite many boroughs being against the clause, the Act was passed. Later in the year, Oswestry showed its solidarity with Ludlow by entering a resolution in its minute book —

'that it was not expedient to make any alteration in the Constabulary of the town, as regards its incorporation with the County Force, under the provisions of the new Constabulary Act'.[2]

Wenlock took advantage of the new Act. At a meeting of the Wenlock Borough Council, held on the 17 October 1840, it was resolved that in the interests of the borough, it was advisable that their police establishment should be consolidated with that of the county. Contact was made with the county magistrates to effect such a merger. The Wenlock council outlined the necessity of there being at least three constables supplied by the county police force, for the policing of the borough. It was pointed out that the borough consisted of three wards — Wenlock, Madeley and Broseley. That the ward of Wenlock consisted of 17,540 acres, with a population of 3,331, chiefly employed in agriculture. Madeley extended over 5,210 acres, with a population of 6,879 chiefly employed in the Iron, Coal and China Works.

Broseley with 6,870 acres, and a population of 5,473, who were mainly employed in the Iron and Coal works. Therefore the council were strongly of the opinion that not less than one constable for each ward would be effective in policing the borough. The agreement was signed on 4 January 1841, and from thereon the tiny police force of Wenlock borough (three men only) ceased to exist, and the borough was included within the boundaries and jurisdiction of the county constabulary. (See Appendix 1 for full transcript of the agreement).

The first anniversary of the Shropshire County Constabulary was mentioned at the January Sessions 1841. The foreman of the grand jury handing the chairman of the

24

magistrates the following note —

'The Grand Jury cannot separate without congratulating the County upon the apparent efficiency of the Rural Police, and to add the satisfaction they have experienced in receiving the very straight forward evidence in the many cases that have been brought before them'.[3]

The chairman, Thomas Kenyon added his comments —

'that he attributed much of the decrease of crime to their exertions. The Constabulary Force had been established twelve months, and had done all that was expected. They had protected the poorer farmers and cottagers, and the decreased number of tramps was to be attributed to their activity'.[4]

Praise was merited by the rural constables, alone in country districts they often suffered greatly whilst trying to uphold the law, as the following incident illustrates —

The New Year festivities at the 'Old Three Pigeon's', at Nesscliffe, nearly ended in tragedy. To Constable Thomas Griffiths it must have seemed like a nightmare. He had been called out in the early hours of the morning, to quell a disturbance at the 'Old Three Pigeon's'. On entering the house, he found himself surrounded by a drunken crowd of men, who were in a most unfriendly mood. When he tried to execute his duty and clear the inn, he was repeatedly struck from all sides. At one time he was lifted bodily in the air, and to his intense horror, thrown upon the great open fire. Jammed in by the hostile mob, he was unable at first to draw his staff. Finally being knocked and kicked under a large cupboard, he was able to free his staff. He then laid about him with considerable energy, and succeeded in felling the ringleader, a character named Edward Wilde, who was the most violent of his attackers. It would appear to be nothing short of a miracle that Thomas Griffiths escaped with his life. It had been necessary to fight his way through the mob, and had it not been for the landlady and her servants thrusting him into the safety of the cellar, the consequences for the lone constable could well have been fatal.

Three months passed before the constable, or his prisoner

were in a fit state to appear before the magistrates. The bench expressed their sorrow that they could not punish Wilde with more severity, and fined him the maximum, thirty shillings and costs.

The prisoner insolently replied that he would go to gaol first. The magistrates thereupon kindly indulged his wish, with two months hard labour. Wilde gave vent to a series of taunting insults, which the bench told him could further endanger his liberty. He then cheekily thanked the police for their kindnesses, and hinted what he would do at a future time. He was then handcuffed, and Constable Bromley was directed to take him to gaol.

Before the constable had got him to the turnpike he had turned restive, and the constable had to call for assistance. Mr. Kenyon, chairman of the Bench, driving up at this moment, ordered that a vehicle should be procured, in which this desperado was driven off. It was not without difficulty that he was finally lodged in gaol.

At Bridgnorth the subordinate officer, Thomas Barker, resigned his office on the 2 February 1841, leaving the chief constable, Luke Edwards, to police the borough on his own. This impossible situation was slightly eased when the watch committee ordered one of the special constables to assist him, but only on the Saturdays and Sundays of each week. It was not until May that Barker was replaced. Luke Edwards handed in his own resignation as chief constable in the August. He had decided that 18s. 0d. as an ordinary constable in the county constabulary would no doubt give him more peace of mind, and less work, than one guinea as Chief Constable of Bridgnorth. He remained with the Shropshire constabulary until 1848, when once more he resigned. The Bridgnorth watch committee soon met and appointed Richard Evans and Thomas Hinckesman constables for the borough, at a wage of 18s. 0d. per week. It will be seen that the new chief constable, Richard Evans was to receive three shillings less than his predecessor, and the same rate of pay as his subordinate officer. Thomas Hinckesman was an ex-constable of the county force, to which he had been appointed in April 1840. His stay with the Bridgnorth Borough Police was equally short, for he resigned in the October of 1842. He then returned to the Shropshire Constabulary in April, 1843, remaining with that force until July 1844, when he was ignominiously dismissed. Caught making false entries in his journal, regarding duty performed, (or perhaps in his case, not performed) and also for what was regarded as more serious in the eyes of his superior officers — 'for incurring debts with publicans.' In September 1841, new regulations were drafted for the guidance of the Bridgnorth Borough police, and agreed upon. (See Appendix II).

A police committee was appointed at the June County Quarter Sessions 1841, to investigate the working of the Shropshire Constabulary since its inception in 1840. The completed report was produced at the following October Sessions. It would appear from the evidence gathered, that the constabulary had no means of tracing suspicious characters or vagrants from one police district to another. The constables not being in the habit of writing anything concerning them in their diaries. It was found that although the force as a whole was controlled by the Chief Constable, there was no cohesion. The men did not appear to have any knowledge of adjoining police districts. Or indeed of local bad characters, and, unfortunately, the same could be said about the superintendents. The constables made no entries in their diaries as to the times when they visited public-houses and beer-shops on their beats, nor did they mention any bad characters who might have been there.

The Bad Character books (with the exception of those belonging to the Wellington Division) were very badly kept. In several, produced for the committee's inspection, merely the name of a bad character was written down, without any description of his person, residence, or any account of the crimes he had committed. There were no means for the Chief Constable to ascertain whether the superintendents had examined these books, with a view to seeing whether they were correct, and indeed it appeared that the Chief Constable himself had not been in the habit of inspecting them. In one instance a constable had been transferred from one district to another, and although he had been there three weeks, the bad character book of his predecessor had not been handed over to him. In another instance a list of bad characters in a district had been given to the Chief Constable, but he had made no use of it, either in showing it to the superintendent concerned or to the constables of that district, or even using it to test the accuracy of their books.

With regard to robberies, the Chief Constable and the superintendents had no means of knowing how the constables conducted their enquiries. No evidence was written down, and in many instances no description or marks of the stolen property were entered in their books.

The returns of offences were also found to be inaccurate.

In all fairness it should be pointed out that in these early days recruits to the constabulary received no training other than by direction and example from their superintendents. They had to learn by experience as had their superintendents.

It was pointed out that the Chief Constable was not sufficiently aware of the importance of frequently inspecting the operations of his force, at their different stations. He was informed by the committee that he should do so at least four times a year.

It was a sad recital of the shortcomings of the county force. It also showed that the police committee had a greater knowledge of what a police force should be doing, than the Chief Constable had. One must take into consideration that prior to his appointment, Mayne had no experience of police work at all. His life had been spent in the Royal Navy and the Coastguard service.

Mayne stated his readiness to carry into effect any suggestions, for the better working of the force, which might be made by the committee. He assured them that he was most anxious to render the Shropshire Constabulary as efficient as possible — indeed they were happy to find that since the report, the Chief Constable had circulated amongst his men, a manual of instructions in the case of robberies, which appeared to be well calculated to facilitate the apprehension of offenders.

In the Wellington Division, Superintendent William Baxter, the only officer to come out favourably in the police committee's report, was being maligned by the local press. Possibly because he was so efficient at his work. The Salopian Telegraph & Border Review was a scurrilous sheet which sold largely because of the amount of slanderous gossip which it printed. It made Baxter, and the county constabulary in general, its number one target. The campaign started in November 1841, when the newspaper went to town on the 'Brummagem Button-stick' as he was nicknamed —

'CORNER FOR THE RURALS.

These muckworms have not been quite so busy of late. The Brummagem Button-stick is not quite so fast since the check at the Quarter Sessions a short time ago; but he is still as fond of his brandy and pipe, and people generally know where to find him in the evening.

As for his underlings they are seen dragging their lazy carcasses about the streets and lanes like so many spies habited in a coarse workhouse livery. Only for their mawkish looks and the absence of fire arms, you would take them for Italian brigands. How these fellows do their duty is well-known eating and drinking at the expense of hospitable farmers, beer shop keepers, and old public houses, instead of looking after the poultry stealers, bad houses, and those ale house keepers who really keep disorderly houses — all these matters are not considered when their bellies have been well stuffed. In short, they are considered a useless burthen on the country, which we hope soon to be rid of'.[5]

After a while the paper left him alone and focused their whole attack on the entire Shropshire Constabulary Force. —

'Is it true — that Mayne's useless green brigade are to be tried by a district court-martial, on the 1st of April next, before the rate-payers of Shropshire?

The charges — which are very numerous — to be brought against them, are — incapacity — and rascality — immorality — credulity — inebriety — infidelity — duplicity — and stupidity: also, with being ignorant, base, and cowardly.

As not the least doubt exists but that the rural delinquents will be brought in guilty, the following is said to be the sentence and punishment to be awarded them by their judges: viz., first bastinadoed, after which, they are to be divested of their green toggery, which is already contracted for by a certain rag-man, and reduced to a state of nudity; then to be tarred and feathered, and marched off in double quick time, to the devil, pro bono publico.

In order to cheer these ragamuffins on their route to pandemonium four drummers and fifers, belonging to his Satanic Majesty's brimstone regiment, and who are said to be hell-ish good uns, are to accompany them playing alternately, the Rogues March and Nix my Dolly; the whole to be under the immediate command of Jonathan Wild, whom John Stones, the mighty magician of Watling Street — whose power in "calling spirits from the vasty deep" is well known — has engaged to resuscitate for the above purpose.

Upon their arrival in the infernal regions, the green incapables are to be distributed as pioneers among the Devil's own.'[6]

One must admit that the author of the above article had a most picturesque imagination. A pity that it was wasted in such efforts, or perhaps those that enjoyed such a newspaper would not agree.

The year 1842 started with an exciting chase after a criminal. A tale of extreme endurance, extending far beyond the limits of the county.

It took place when Superintendent Charles Lewis and Constable Andrew Corden of the County Constabulary, set to pursue and capture John Jones, who had committed a 'violent outrage and attempt at murder' upon Diana Biggs at Stokesay. The would be murderer fled. The two officers hot on his trail. Superintendent Lewis reported that throughout the whole route travelled by them, in this case, a distance of 170 miles out of the county of Shropshire. He was pleased to say that he had received every assistance from the police forces of the counties of Hereford, Brecon, Worcester and Monmouth. The police committee highly commended the successful two man posse for having — 'used great exertions, activity, zeal and intelligence to discover and apprehend John Jones'.

Massive unemployment was the keynote of 1842. By March there were well over one million persons in receipt of poor law relief, out of a total population of about sixteen millions. Many of those that still held jobs in the industrial areas were told that they would have to face wage reductions. The disturbances in Shropshire were similar to those in other parts of the industrial Midlands. They were not initiated by the Chartists, but came into being as a protest against the wage reductions and the truck system, existing at that time in the coal fields of the Midlands.

Although there were Chartists in eastern Shropshire, they played little part in the troubles of 1842. They were neither powerful nor numerous enough to give the miners any lead.

Towards the early summer the gravity of the depression had become widespread in all of the industrial areas of the country.

Feelings came to a boiling point in the neighbouring county of Staffordshire, leading to riots at Dudley and Stourbridge. Over 3,000 Special Constables had to be sworn, in and around the Potteries area. It was not until late July that any disturbances broke out in Shropshire.

The Duke of Sutherland held the Lieutenancies of Shropshire, and of the Scottish county which gave him his title, in plurality. He had been absent from the latter when riots broke out there in 1841.[7] Now he was absent in Scotland for the duration of the disturbances in Shropshire.[8] His deputy in Shropshire was the Earl of Powis, who was Lord Lieutenant of Montgomeryshire. The Earl of Powis had distinguished himself by the vigor with which he had suppressed the Chartist riots of 1839, in Montgomeryshire.

Now he handled the situation not only in Montgomeryshire, but also in Shropshire. Powis clearly showed that he possessed the necessary ability and energy to cope with the crisis. He demonstrated that he could work for public order on the one hand, yet soon showed an instinctive sympathy for discovering and attempting to correct the worker's grievances on the other.

On the 20 July several gangs of Staffordshire miners marched into the Wellington and Shifnal areas, where they commenced attacking the machinery at the pits, a great deal of which they broke, cutting ropes etc, and so keeping the men down the pits, who would not strike and join them.

Considerable damage was done at Donnington Wood, Prior's Lee and Old Park. From Donnington Wood they proceeded to Wrockwardine Wood, and from there through Pain's Lane to Snedshill and Prior's Lee. Their numbers increasing as they went. It would appear to have been a preconcerted plan, for a party went ahead calling at houses and levying contributions of food and money, which if not offered freely, was obtained by threats of violence.

The fight against reduction in pay was on in earnest. The magistrates of Wellington had a public notice hurriedly printed — 'To Colliers and Miners', warning them against further violence, and inviting them to return peaceably to their work. At the same time making known their firm determination to use the powers vested in them to check violence, and to protect and preserve the persons and property of the peaceable part of the community.

On Wednesday evening the mob dispersed, and in the course of the night, the yeomanry and the county police contrived to arrest five of the ringleaders.

The next morning a party of the South Shropshire Yeomanry left Shrewsbury bound for Wellington, while yet another party of the same cavalry proceeded from Bridgnorth to help in quelling the disturbances.

Thursday morning the rioters re-assembled, and gathered in the London road, just above Oakengates. Despite the arrests of the preceding evening, they marched in a determined manner to the 'Old Park Works', where the pitmen stopped working, and joined them. The Salopian Journal gives a very melodramatic picture of what happened next —

'they came round to Ketley Bank, when, as they were about to stop the pits lying between the "Bank House" and the "Schools", a body of police appeared in sight, and put a stop to their further progress. It was then about nine o'clock, and there were supposed to be not less than two or three hundred. The police were dexterous, armed with sword and pistol, and, rushing up the Mounts, took the multitude by surprise; so much so, that there was a general helter-skelter-tumbling over one another down the Mounts, and they made off in all directions, separating into the multitude of passages and roads thereabout, and so far, the most part escaped being taken. It was a very skilful manoeuvre of the police, and all was quiet after. Being Wellington market day, many made off in that direction, and mingled with the crowd to prevent detection.'⁹

The disturbances died down, and by the 22 July the magistrates were able to announce that the miners were returning to work.

But the peace was short lived. On the 15 August the colliers came out on strike again. Dawson Mayne had to recall his force and concentrate it in the Wellington area. The pits were idle for nearly a fortnight, but towards the end of the month the men had started to drift back to work.

Work however, was restricted to three or four days a week for most.

The whole episode had put a great strain on police resources while it lasted. The Shropshire Constabulary Force was so small that the disturbances of the August had necessitated the concentration of more than 80 per cent of the force (50 constables out of 58) in the Wellington district, while other parts of the county were left at the mercy of bands of beggars.

Special Constables were appointed to assist the regular police in keeping order at this difficult time, but it was not easy to find dependable men in the industrial area of Shropshire, who were not on the opposing side.   Thomas Eyton wrote to Sir James Graham at the Home Office —

'We have sworn in some special constables, but the fact is that in the collieries few, if any, can be depended upon in that capacity.'[11]

In his report to the magistrates of the quarter sessions in October, Dawson Mayne referred to the conduct of the force having been exemplary, with not one case of irregularity having been brought to his notice, or to his knowledge, having occurred.

Both the Lord Lieutenant of the county, and the Home Secretary wrote to Dawson Mayne, expressing their approval of the steps adopted, and of the good conduct of the force. A troublesome time ended, with the Shropshire Constabulary having proved themselves capable of handling, and handling well a very serious situation.

Of course you cannot please everyone, and the Salopian Telegraph took delight in making disparaging remarks about the conduct of the constabulary.   An article appeared on the 27 August, which was headed —

'FROM THE SEAT OF WAR.

Captain Mayne's brigade head-quarters, the George:

All quiet — the greenhorns patroling about the works — brave fellows eat a lot of mutton and drink a quantity of drink, when it can be got cheap — have a fine martial appearance when girt with their stab beggars.   Old Buttonstick fancies himself quite a hero, a knight-errand, or cavalier, and the poor half-famished colliers salute him as he passes by their idle groups.

Their station is visited every day by either old or young Tom Shallow, in company with Paddy Mayne.   Since the rurals have been stationed here, soap has advanced 2d per lb. In Wellington, we hear, since those valiant heroes, the Wellington cavalry, have been under marching orders, the above article has rose 1½d per lb, and doctors are much in request.   What the end of these things will be no tongue can divine'.[12]

The next issue from this newspaper gives the impression that they had been well and truly reprimanded for their slanderous printing, for there is a long and very flowery retraction of all that they had written against the Rural constabulary, and their favourite target, Superintendent Baxter. Apologies are profuse. Forgiveness is craved. Then, having got it off their chests, the paper proceeds to re-villify the constabulary. However, let it be clear, this was a paper which only sold by reason of the scandals, or pretended scandals which it published. High and low suffered, not just the police alone.

A distressing accident which nearly proved fatal, happened to Superintendent Philip James, of 'D' Division, stationed in the Bridgnorth area. It was the Monday after Christmas, and James had set out on his horse and gig to attempt to recapture an escaped prisoner. At Chelmarsh he passed close to the Haybrook, which at that time was greatly swollen and in flood. His horse slipped on the muddy bank, and within seconds the gig was upset into the swiftly flowing stream, and being carried rapidly downstream for some considerable distance. The unfortunate horse was drowned. The superintendent had the presence of mind to grasp the low branch of a tree as he whirled past in the swift current, but that breaking under his weight, he was once more plunged into the stream. After considerable exertion he managed to reach the bank, where he shouted loudly for help. His cries were at length heard by a passer by who succeeded in rescuing him from his perilous situation. He had been severely bruised by knocking against trees before he managed to get out. Further pursuit of the prisoner would be cancelled out for that day. Such an incident shows only too clearly the hazards and dangers of a police officer's life.

While speaking of dangers, January 1843 opened with a particularly blood-thirsty attack on a constable, at Upton Magna.

In consequence of an extensive robbery of carpenter's tools at Smethcote, from a man named Benjamin Burgwin, suspicion fell upon Richard Freeman of Upton Magna, and complaint made to Superintendent Lewis of the Shropshire Constabulary; who directed Constable Jeremiah Smith to obtain a search warrant, and seek for the missing tools at Freeman's house.

On the Saturday evening Smith accompanied by Burgwin proceeded to Upton Magna to execute the warrant.

When they reached the prisoner's residence they saw him in the fold-yard. The constable climbed over the stile and laying his hand on Freeman's shoulder said 'You are my prisoner, you are charged with felony'. Freeman replied — 'I'll be damned if I am', and tried to escape. In the struggle all three fell over the hedge, and on getting up again Smith tried to handcuff him, but Freeman wrenched them away and threw them into an adjoining garden. Burgwin went after them and brought them back. A second scuffle ensued during which the accused once again threw the handcuffs away, and Burgwin went once more to retrieve them.

The constable then took a firm grip of Freeman's neckerchief.

Freeman finding that he could not overcome the policeman, gave in, asking Smith to go into his house with him, and tell him what charge he had against him. The constable thinking that Freeman meant to give himself up quietly, went with him. Freeman had by this time laid hold of Smith by the collar. When they got to the door, the prisoner pulled Smith into the house, and suddenly stooping down seized a chopper which was lying under a table; saying 'Now damn your eyes, will you loose me'. The constable still kept his hold, nothing daunted by Freeman's menaces, when the prisoner lifted the chopper again in a threatening position, and said 'Damn your eyes, if you don't loose me now, I'll knock your brains out'. He then aimed a violent blow at the constable with the chopper, hitting him across the head, and felling him to the ground. He afterwards wounded him in other parts of the head and face, nearly severing his nose. By this time Smith and Freeman were covered in the constable's blood.

36

Burgwin then entered the house, snatching up a stick he struck out at Freeman which had the effect of making him loose his hold on Smith, he then ran out of the house, and made his escape. When the badly wounded constable was fit enough to stand, he pluckily carried on with his duty and searched the house. The stolen property was found hidden away.

Burgwin then helped Smith to the Elephant and Castle, at Upton Magna, where every means was resorted to, to stop the flow of blood. He was then set upon a pony to ride back to Shrewsbury to have his wounds dressed. He was so badly cut about that it took the local surgeon two hours to patch him up.

On the following morning a gamekeeper and his assistant were making their rounds of the grounds of Acton Reynold, when they perceived two men hiding in a covert; suspecting them to be poachers, the gamekeepers attempted to capture them, when one of them drew a six inch bladed knife, and said he would run it through the first one who attempted to take them. Undeterred one of the keepers quickly knocked him down, and both men were secured. They were taken before the magistrate at Wem, when it was noticed that the one with the knife had a lot of blood splattered about his person. He refused his name, but said that he had been fighting at Shrewsbury. The magistrate was very suspicious and sent off a description of the man to Shrewsbury. It was soon found that the description matched that of Richard Freeman, wanted by the Shropshire Constabulary.

Freeman was escorted from Wem to Shrewsbury Gaol. His companion was allowed to go free. Freeman described as — 'a young man of great muscular power, and very forbidding appearance' was committed to the next Assizes. When brought to trial the jury found the prisoner 'guilty of wounding with intent to disfigure and do grievous bodily harm, and to prevent his lawful apprehension'. The judge in passing sentence, said 'Richard Freeman, the Jury have taken a very merciful view of your case. It was your duty to submit to the officer when he told you that he had a charge against you, and your resistance was at your own peril; instead of which you had recourse to that conduct which might have ended in murder, and then your life would have been forfeited. As it is, I think an example necessary to prevent your frequent recourse to the use of sharp weapons, and your case is a proper one for that purpose. The sentence of this Court is therefore, that you be transported beyond the seas for the term of twenty years'. Constable Jeremiah Smith was confined to his home for ten days, the local newspapers giving him the greatest praise for his undoubted courage. Smith remained in the Shropshire constabulary until his superannuation in 1858.

A sad and solemn occasion was witnessed at Church Stretton in February 1843, when the funeral of Constable Charles Henry Ellis took place. His was the first death of a serving member of the Shropshire Constabulary. It must have been an impressive sight. As a member of the Loyal Caradoc Lodge of Oddfellows, his remains were attended to their resting place, by thirty members of that Lodge. Each wore a black scarf with white rosettes and gloves. The coffin was carried by four of his brother officers, whilst Superintendents Lewis and Surman, with Inspectors Wilmot and Corden, walked in full uniform as pall-bearers.

The local press reported that —

' A more solemn and imposing scene has rarely, if ever, been witnessed in this town.'[13]

The Shrewsbury Council decided in August 1844, to appoint a committee to consider generally the present state of the police of the borough. Particularly with reference to the protection of property in the suburbs. Also the committee were to take into consideration the method of paying the police, whether by salaries only, or otherwise. In giving their findings one month later, the committee found that the police force of the borough was inadequate for the proper preservation of the peace, and the protection of property. This remark applied especially to the suburbs of the town, where during the day, no police officer had been employed to check vagrancy and enforce compliance with the Bye-Laws. During the night there was no watch whatsoever in the suburbs. A considerable number of cases of breach of the peace had arisen, and the allegations in the memorials which had been presented to the council, of the necessity of police in those districts were fully supported.

It further appeared to the committee, that the system in use of nightly watch only, was by no means as desirable as the employment of Day and Night Constables, as directed to be appointed under the Municipal Act, who would be adequately paid, and required to devote their whole time to the duties of their office.

The system of paying officers partly by salary, partly by fees and allowances as witnesses, was open to abuse.

The committee were decidedly of the opinion that no police officer employed by the borough should receive any fees or allowances whatever, but shall be paid wholly by salary.

The old police force at Shrewsbury consisted of the three sergeants at mace, and ten night watchmen, one of the sergeants doubling up as Marshall. Special constables were employed on such occasions as they were needed, i.e. the Shrewsbury Races etc. The committee gave their opinion that to adequately police the borough, they would need —

One Superintendent or Chief Constable, at a salary of thirty shillings per week; with three sergeants to be kept on, at one guinea per week, with such clothing as is required by the Secretary of State for County Constabulary Forces. It was thought that thirteen constables plus the three sergeants, and the chief constable, would constitute a sufficient force to police the town and suburbs; and that it should be distributed in the following manner —

'Three in the Castle Ward Without, Three in the Stone Ward Without, and Three in the Welsh Ward Without, that out of each of these three Constables for each Ward two should watch by Night and one perambulate by day.

Considering the distance, the extent of population, and the

property contributing to the Rate, possibly the services of one of the Constables in Frankwell may if requisite, be called for within the town portions immediately adjourning their district. That the four remaining Constables be employed within the Town to watch principally by night.

The day duty being done by the Sergeants, one of whom would also sit up each third night as he does now.'[14]

It was suggested that the pay of the constables should be fourteen shillings per week, with clothing supplied to each man.

The committee ventured to suggest their earnest hope that great care would be taken in the selection of a Chief Constable or Superintendent. Upon his efficiency must depend the due working of the force. And they proposed to name as his salary a sum rather greater perhaps than might be considered requisite, but they had done so under the impression that some party of experience in the management of a police force, with habits likely to give weight and authority, might be induced to take the situation. The Shrewsbury council adopted its committee's findings in full. The situation of chief constable for the town of Shrewsbury was duly advertised in the press.

A wag at Wellington wrote to the local paper, applying, in a most hilarious manner for the post —

'TO JOSHOE PEAL, ESQ., TOWN CLARK A SOESBERRY.

Sur, — I see'd a hadvertesement for a superhintendant of the New perlease, and i beggs to hoffer miself for that ere sitivation, mi qualefecation his, has, How, i can do henny thin from bying of beddsteds, toe keepin BARNESES PIGGS, i shal gyv hup awl bad cumpenney hand nevver go toe they plow, hand i nevver hintends a tellin Eddows abboute A penney, if yew gets me they pleace.

Now do trye that's a good un, yew nose how i ham a good usband, and That i hintends givin hup Fridays partnurship, hin those are ship pens awl hin a fortnnet,

Yewers hever, awl the way from Wellinton,

JON PHILIPS.'[15]

Amongst the serious applicants was Lieutenant Edward John Blake, late of the Royal Marines Light Infantry. He was chosen at the November meeting of the council, to be the first Chief Constable, of Shrewsbury's new Borough Police Force.

The Watch Committee faced with the recruiting of constables for the new force, found in the old night watchmen and sergeants at mace, a cheap and convenient source of labour. Here was a ready made nucleus from which to build up the new police force. It was also a chance to improve their image by showing their loyalty to past employees of the borough, by their retention. Seven of the old watchmen were appointed as constables.

The uniforms of the Shrewsbury Borough Police Force were to be blue in colour, to distinguish them from the County Police Force, who were dressed in green. Dressed in single-breasted coats with Prussian collars.

Trousers of the same cloth and colouring. Greatcoats of a dark grey Oxford mixture. Stovepipe tall hats; black stocks around their necks. Boots. Numbers in cloth, each separately fastened, from 1 to 13, to be fixed on each side of the coat collars, and brass buttons, made from a mould in the possession of the watch committee.

The uniform chosen for the Superintendent was very similar, although the coat was of a better quality, and was double-breasted. Gilt buttons instead of brass, and no number on the collar. The coats were Frock-coats.

On the 3 May 1845 the new chief constable made his first report —

'Circumstances considered. I have every reason to be satisfied with the general conduct of the Men placed under my Orders I feel confident that when the arrangements now under the consideration of the Watch Committee shall be matured.

The Force will become as efficient as the Numbers will admit and give satisfaction to the well disposed Inhabitants of the Town. In making the Return of expences I beg to state that savings are effected by keeping the Court at the Quarter Sessions, Fees on Committments and the Moiety of fines for

informations.   Edw. Jo.Blake. Lieut. R.M.
                                 Chief Constable.'[16]
All of which sounded a note of confidence, but in view of
subsequent happenings a couple of months later — well let
events speak for themselves. The story which appeared in the
local press centres around two geese, who were found wander-
ing around the streets of Shrewsbury, one night.

A constable escorted them to the police station, and there
they stayed for some ten days, in custody. It was then
decided by the Chief Constable, that the Town Cryer should
make proclamation throughout the town — that unless the
geese were immediately claimed, they would be sold to defray
the expences of their keep. Consequently the owner not
appearing, the Chief Constable invited the landlord of one of
Shrewsbury's inns, to inspect the geese, with a view to
purchasing them. On his arrival at the police station, it was
found to the amazement of all concerned, that the geese had
disappeared. A handbill was quickly issued by the indignant
Chief Constable —

'SHROPSHIRE TO WIT. STOLEN OR STRAYED.
FROM THE SHREWSBURY POLICE OFFICE.
TWO FAT GEESE.

Whoever may apprehend the said Geese, if strayed, or the
offenders if stolen, and will restore them to Captain Blake,
shall be handsomely rewarded for their trouble and no
questions asked; and who ever may kill and eat the said
geese, after this notice, will be considered as receivers and
consumers of stolen goods.
Shrewsbury Police Office. July 28th. 1846.'

Of course the geese were never seen again, at least by the
police. But the local press made much of the story. They
put out a rumour that on the following Tuesday, the chief
constable was to journey from the police office to the Angel
Inn, in a special carriage, built for the occasion. It was to be
drawn by the ghosts of the two geese stolen from the police
office. But, the press had to admit, that they had a strong
suspicion that the rumour had not, like the geese, a solid

SHROPSHIRE TO WIT.

Stolen or Strayed,

FROM THE SHREWSBURY POLICE OFFICE,

TWO FAT GEESE.

Whoever may apprehend the said Geese, if strayed, or the offenders if stolen, and will restore them to Captain Blake, shall be handsomely rewarded for their trouble and no questions asked; and whoever may kill and eat the said police geese, after this notice, will be considered as receivers and consumers of stolen goods.

SHREWSBURY POLICE OFFICE

July 28th. 1845.

foundation.

Another report circulated by the press, who claimed not to know how true it was, is just as amusing — it was that Bernado Eagle, the great magician of the south, would produce the identical geese on Monday next, during one of his performances, and that he intended to transform them into — two superintendents of the borough police. All of which was good natured fun, but hardly designed to show the efficiency of the Borough Police Force, or its Chief Constable.

In the same month of July, the Royal Agricultural Show held its 7th Annual Meeting at Shrewsbury. The chief constable and his force soon showed that despite the fun that was being enjoyed at their expence, they were in truth very efficient. Blake was aware that pick-pockets and thieves would attend the meeting from most of the cities and large towns. Writing to the police chiefs of London, Birmingham, Manchester and Liverpool, he asked for detachments of their forces to help in recognizing criminals from their towns. The results of this strategy was most gratifying. Sixteen criminals were recognised and apprehended by the officers from the cities.

Notwithstanding the immense crowds that assembled, the chief constable was able to report to his Watch Committee, that not one case of robbery had occurred during the meeting. This statement, and the knowledge of his strategy would make the inhabitants realize that their chief constable was not just a figure to make fun of. Memories are short, and his good work was soon to be forgotten. On the 10 November the Watch Committee sent in its report condemning the expence of having a chief constable —

'That it is the deliberate Opinion of this Committee on due consideration; and after observing the relative utility and expence of the present Police Force, that the management thereof calls for a strict revision of the system, that the beneficial results which had been calculated on have not been demonstrated to the Committee, nor experienced by the Public.

That several large ratepayers have often and extensively complained that the efficiency of the Force has not been in proportion to the expenditure which it entails on the Borough; and this Committee representing the Council, as the Council represents the Public feel themselves called upon to recommend that the Office of Chief Constable be superseded and that Superintendent Harper should be appointed to the duties of the Post at an advanced Salary of 24/- per week.

That the Committee anticipate from the change an additional benefit from the appointment of two extra Men for the Town duty; an increase of force indispensible to a due efficiency of the Constabulary corps. Which efficiency may be thus promoted in a different application of the funds now appropriated in maintaining the Office of Chief Constable.'[17]

Blake, his brilliant handling of the Royal Agricultural Show forgotten, was summarily dismissed. Superintendent William Harper was put in charge of the borough police force. At the age of twenty-nine it was a promotion to be proud of, although his pleasure would be a little soured by the thought, that he was taking over Blake's office, at a far less salary, and without the prestige of its title. He was subsequently to prove a bad choice.

The police had often to deal with characters of great local renown. One such was Joseph Hughes, much better known by his nickname of 'Joe Thunder'.

Joe had a wooden leg, and was employed about the coal wharfs of Ketley. He was what was termed 'a queer customer' when in drink, certainly not a man to tangle with. One Saturday in September 1846, Joe Thunder had become very rude and noisy at Mrs. Dolphin's beer-shop. Constable Weaver of the Shropshire Constabulary was called in to restore some order, and he interfered to prevent a row. But Joe brought down the constable like lightning, and disposed of several others who came to his assistance in a similar way. Making a conductor of his wooden leg, 'Thunder' distributed his bolts in rapid succession, flooring his assailants as if struck with lightning.

45

It finally required the united efforts of four constables and several of the bystanders, to secure this son of Jupiter. In fact nothing could be done with him until they had deprived him of his formidable wooden-leg.

It was never a dull life for the constabulary, with such characters as 'Joe Thunder' to regularly enrich it.

The building of the railways across Shropshire, as in other parts of the country, created a great many headaches for the police authorities.

The influx of thousands of navvies, many of them Irish, was not conducive to peaceful co-existence. Pay-days led to nights of drunken riotousness with the navvies only too happy to take on the odd constable or two, who in vain tried to keep the peace. A typical Saturday night in Shrewsbury is illustrated by the following story which happened in the November of 1847. Constable Farmer of the Borough Police Force was patrolling his beat in the Abbey Foregate, between 11.00 p.m. and midnight. All had been reasonably quiet, when he heard a disturbance outside the Crow Inn.

Hurrying to the scene he found ten or twelve men fighting in the street. Even with the assistance of several of the public, it took half an hour to stop the fight. As it finished a second fight started lower down the street. Farmer arrived on the scene just in time to collect a blow to the eye, which stretched him out on the ground. Eventually he secured his attacker. Then several Irish labourers came out of a nearby house, one of whom cried 'By Jasus, but the b. . . . . . policeman has got him,' whereupon they all ran to the rescue. One of the would be rescuers attacked Farmer with two knives, but a smart blow from the constable's staff soon cooled his fighting spirit. The disturbance then died down. The officer started back towards the town and the police office, when at the English Bridge he heard another noisy disturbance down Coleham. Proceeding there he spotted the man who had attacked him in Abbey Foregate, promptly arresting him, he took him to the police office.

While all this was going on, Constable Finch was on Wyle

Cop, keeping an eye on a number of Irish navvies who were trying to get a drink at the Coffee House. Failing there, they saw a light in the bar of the Unicorn, and went down the passage at the side, exclaiming 'Health to ye soul, we shall git some here.' Finch stopped them and sent them on their way.

On the English Bridge they met two English navvies, and proceeded to beat them up, one of whom they lifted up and threatened to throw into the 'Big Say,' as they called the Severn. Just at this moment several Englishmen came out of the Abbey Foregate, and a general fight took place, which ended in the Irishmen running away towards the Abbey Foregate, with the English in full pursuit. Such was a Saturday night at Shrewsbury in the winter of 1847.

Of course riots and disturbances were part of life in Victorian England, the railway navvies were just an added ingredient, whether Irish or just native English. A few months previous in June 1847, it would appear that the Shropshire Constabulary were having similar trouble with the navvies. Dawson Mayne reported to the Constabulary Committee that the peace of the county had, on more than one occasion, been disturbed by the workmen employed on the railways, particularly on pay-days. On such occasions the constabulary stationed in the vicinity had used their utmost exertions to preserve the peace, and would of course continue to give every assistance in doing so, but feared that it would be necessary to appoint additional men for that purpose. Not only to preserve more effectually the peace of the county, but also to prevent the necessity of calling the constabulary from other and equally important duties.

It became necessary in January 1848 to appoint two special constables to act in the Shifnal area, solely on the Shrewsbury and Birmingham Railway.

Complaint had been made by some of the inhabitants that tumults and riots had taken place, amongst the labourers employed on that part of the railroad.

At Wellington the magistrates had to appoint six special constables in consequence of the serious riots that had taken place amongst the railway labourers in that town. In February a disturbance of a serious nature occurred, between the English and Irish labourers employed on the line from Wellington to Shifnal. This resulted in Dawson Mayne concentrating the whole of the Shropshire Constabulary in that locality for upwards of ten days, and it was only by such extreme measures, plus the arrival of a detachment of the 87th Prince of Wales Own Irish Fusiliers, that order was restored.

Superintendent William Baxter, was a courageous man, always to the front of his men when there was a disturbance. On Good Friday 1848, he was set upon by a crowd of Irish navvies, near the King's Head, at Wellington. It was not to be a good Friday for Baxter, for he came off worst, with a broken rib. Some of the navvies were formidable figures, and when full of liquer, showed some remarkable feats of strength. Such a one was a man named Reilly, who in the July, was put away in Shrewsbury Gaol for a month, for 'riotous and disorderly conduct at Admaston.' It took the united efforts of eight constables to take him into custody.

Also in July, a Saturday night riot flared up near Parton Square, Wellington. Superintendent Baxter with a party of constables endeavoured to disperse the mob of navvies (armed with staves) who put up a great resistance. In the struggle, Baxter and one of his constables were severely beaten about the head and body. Baxter had no time to recover from his injuries, for on the following afternoon, he was attacked once again, by a party of drunken navvies. He courageously resisted them for a time, but was at last overpowered, knocked to the ground, and severely kicked. But for the interference of some passers by, the consequences would have been very serious. It is the bravery and determination of such men as William Baxter that makes them stand out as courageous examples of the type of men who were needed to keep law and order in such turbulent districts.

A special meeting was held at the Sun Inn, Wellington, between the local magistrates and the Chief Constable. Decisions were made to increase the number of constables, for the protection of the public. Several people had been dangerously molested and robbed by, what was referred to, as these 'railway savages' in the neighbourhood of Wellington. Stationed in the town were two officers and 45 men of the 31st Huntingdonshire Regiment of Foot, who could be called upon to give assitance to the county police, as and when required. The outcome of the meeting was to appoint twenty-seven special constables to keep the peace amongst the railway labourers in the Wellington area. The railway contractors, Messrs. Hammond and Murray, were of course liable to pay for the services of all such special constables. (As was required by Act of Parliament). As the tension eased the specials were gradually discontinued, but the final body of specials did not stand down until April 1849.

Great indignation and horror was expressed around the county when Charles Colley, aged 40, a labourer, was charged with having (on the 2 January 1849) 'wilfully, and of malice aforethought, killed and murdered one John Micklewright, a police constable, stationed at Acton Burnell.' John Micklewright holds a sad place in the history of the Shropshire Constabulary, for in the hundred and twenty-seven years of its existance, he was the only officer to have been murdered.

At the trial, the jury took just two minutes to return a verdict of manslaughter. The judge in sentencing the prisoner, remarked that when parties resisted the police they deserved to be punished severely, and from what he had seen of the case, the conduct of the prisoner showed a very depraved and brutal mind. He felt it his duty to sentence the prisoner to be transported for ten years.

Chapter Three

1850 — 1859

The amalgamation of the Bridgnorth Borough Police, with that of the Shropshire Constabulary, took place in the year 1850. The Bridgnorth Corporation had insisted that their sole officer, Chief Constable Richard Evans, should be transferred into the county force.

Captain Mayne was quite agreeable to his transfer, subject to his being efficient. However, on examination it was soon found that Richard Evans was practically illiterate. He made a poor attempt at writing, and it was proved that the poor man could not read at all. Mayne was adamant in refusing to accept him into the ranks of the Shropshire Constabulary.

The Mayor of Bridgnorth then reluctantly asked to break the engagement to unite with the county, despite the fact that the agreement had already been signed. This was agreed, and the amalgamation was formerly cancelled. Bridgnorth remained loyal to their Chief Constable, who had given them such faithful service over the past nine years.

Six months later, the impasse was happily solved. The Bridgnorth Corporation found another post for Richard Evans. A second application to the county magistrates for an amalgamation of police forces was accepted. This time it was carried out without a hitch.

Superintendent William Baxter (The Brummagem Buttonstick) was ignominiously dismissed from the Shropshire Constabulary in March 1850. This officer had maintained since 1840, an excellent record of keeping law and order in a very difficult area; during which time he had suffered many injuries in the exercise of his duty. He was charged with having embezzled from the county, various sums of money, totalling a very large amount, and was sentenced to three months imprisonment. The police committee, with this scandal fresh in their minds were highly critical of the Chief Constable in their report.

Mayne was possibly saved from more serious repercussions only by his wife's relationship with the Hill family. But even this proved to be a double-headed weapon. Sir Baldwin Leighton, J.P. an early critic of the force's command and administration, became convinced that no chief constable ought to have personal connexions with the magistracy. In 1858 as chairman of the Court of Quarter Sessions, he made a point of making Mayne's position as chief constable, untenable.

At Oswestry, Jacob Smith informed the Corporation, in November 1850, that he wished to retire as chief police officer of the borough. He volunteered to stay on until such time as the council could obtain a suitable person to replace him. This was to be far longer perhaps, than he thought, for it was not until September 1851, that the suitable person could be found. The choice fell upon John Donald, a former member of the Liverpool City Police.

Also on the short list of three for the post of superintendent was John O'Donnell, late of the Denbighshire Constabulary. Failing to obtain the higher post, he made the best of a bad job, and took the lesser paid post of constable, which was also vacant. An Irishman from Tipperary, he commenced his duties at a weekly wage of 17s. 0d. a week. Three shillings a week less than he would have got as superintendent. O'Donnell only stayed at Oswestry for a year, but while he was there, the inhabitants must have found it confusing to have two officers with such similar names. O'Donnell went on to join the Shrewsbury Borough Police, in which force he served until 1859. By this time he had seen service in three separate police forces.

The Oswestry corporation decided in August 1851, that it

was high time that their small police force was dressed in uniform. In the following February the new uniforms were issued to the superintendent and three constables who made up the borough force.

After the dismissal in March 1850 of Superintendent William Baxter from the Shropshire Constabulary, Robert Jones (Constable First Class) was promoted to superintendent. Two of this man's brothers were superintendents in the Derbyshire Constabulary; while his father had been Head Constable of the borough of Stafford for thirty years. Robert Jones had served as a constable in the Shropshire Constabulary since 1841. After a year as superintendent he resigned, to take up the vacant post of superintendent of the Ludlow borough police force. While in charge of this small force, he was joined by yet another of his brothers, Edward Jones, as constable. A family which had made the police service their way of life.

Internal troubles rocked the Shrewsbury Borough Police Force in mid-summer of 1851. Superintendent John Thomas preferred charges against his superior officer, Chief Constable William Harper. The Watch Committee made a full investigation of the matter, finding a great want of discipline, and laxity of duty in the force. They reported that they would re-organize the force entirely. As a first step Superintendent Thomas was discharged. The chief constable was suspended for a fortnight, and then cautioned.

The rules and regulations of the borough police force were revised and amended, and the watch committee trusted that by a stringent enforcement of them, that the efficiency of the force would be firmly established. At this time the Shrewsbury Borough Police Force consisted of — One Chief Constable; one Superintendent, two Inspectors and twelve constables.

The Chief Constables of boroughs in the mid nineteenth century, were expected to fill a number of odd posts, which their councils had found necessary to create, due to various acts of parliament requiring them to so do.

At Shrewsbury, the Chief Constable had the added post of

Inspector of Weights and Measures. He was also Inspector of Common Lodging Houses, with these duties he was also expected to supervise the town Fire Brigade.

The Ludlow Superintendent of Police held the triple appointments of Inspector of Common Lodging Houses, Inspector of Nuisances and Inspector of Weights and Measures. And like his Shrewsbury colleague he was Superintendent of the Borough Fire Brigade. At Oswestry the Chief of the Borough Police was Collector of the Market Tolls, Inspector of Nuisances, Inspector of Provisions and Inspector of Weights and Measures. The Gaoler ranked as Inspector of Nuisances at Bridgnorth, while the Chief Constable and his sole constable, served in the inferior rank of sub-inspectors. The Chief Constable in addition was Inspector of Tramps, Inspector of Weights and Measures, and Inspector of Common Lodging-houses. These duties were commonly assigned to the police, as a contribution towards finding them sufficient employment to justify their cost.

Superintendent John Sing MacMichael, Deputy Chief Constable of the Shropshire Constabulary, resigned in December 1852. He went to Lancashire, where he had been appointed Chief Constable of the Borough of Warrington, a post which he held until 1866, when he was forced to retire through ill-health.

In Shropshire the post of Deputy Chief Constable was filled by Superintendent Richard James, who had been in the force since its inception in 1840.

The first half of 1853 witnessed many conferences between the Chief Constables of Shropshire and Montgomeryshire. Their talks were in connection with the exchanging of certain areas of each other's counties, for the better policing of those areas. It was proposed that those parts of the parishes of Mainstone, Lydham, Churchstoke, Hyssington, Shelve and Snead, situated in the county of Montgomery, and on the Shropshire side of a line to be drawn from Proll-y-Piod, nearly north, to cross the main road from the Snead to Churchstoke (about halfway between Broadway and Church-

Samuel Farlow, Chief Constable
of Shrewsbury 1840. Died 1857.

stoke), dividing the Corndon Hills, to Grit Marsh and Priest Weston, to be attached to Shropshire for policing purposes. Those parts of the parishes of Chirbury and Churchstoke, situated in Shropshire, and to the south of the road from Priest Weston to Chirbury, and from thence to Shirebridge, to be attached to Montgomeryshire for policing by their county force. The Shropshire constabulary committee recommended the Court of Quarter Sessions to sanction these arrangements, providing the magistrates of Montgomeryshire also acquiesed to the arrangements. Nothing more is recorded of this exchange, but no doubt as this would be to the mutual benefit of both parties, the Montgomeryshire magistrates would be agreeable.

The Shrewsbury Watch Committee reported on the 8 May 1854, that they had been induced to adopt a long contemplated change in the management of their police force. They were of the opinion that they should place the force under the command of a thoroughly practical and experienced officer, at a higher salary than had hitherto been paid. As a result they had inserted an advertisement in the press, offering £100 per annum, and in reply received thirty applications. The committees choice fell upon Joseph Shackell, a former Inspector of the Metropolitan Police. The ex-chief constable, William Harper was demoted to chief-superintendent.

Lord Palmerston, as Home Secretary, tried to introduce his Rural Police Bill in 1854. It was to the effect that all counties would be obliged to maintain police forces. Government inspectors would be appointed to ensure uniformity. Boroughs with less than 20,000 inhabitants would lose their local police forces (this clause would effect 120 out of 180 boroughs with their own police). Boroughs so affected would in fact be surrendering the powers held by their watch committees to the county magistrates. Regarding those boroughs who would escape the net, the Home Secretary would have the power of making rules for their police forces, as he already could for the county forces. The selection of the borough chief constables, would be subject to the approval of the Home Secretary. The final humiliation was the statement that there would be no financial aid from the government.

A few days after the bill's introduction into parliament, the storm broke. An angry meeting was held in London by some seventy representatives of the cities and boroughs, headed by the Lord Mayor of York. Petitions against the bill, were sent by the corporations of Shrewsbury and Bridgnorth, to the House of Commons. It was pointed out that the bill had the effect of entirely throwing the authority and regulation of independant boroughs, and their rights, into the hands of the county police, and the authorities of the Home Department. A bill striking at once at the liberty and independance of the country gentlemen as magistrates, and making mayors and town councils a nullity in the administration of their own police.

Palmerston bowed before the storm which he had created. He decided that —

'he would not consider it rendering a good service to the country to force it upon boroughs against their own will'[1]
and he then withdrew the offending bill. Some time later Palmerston tried a second police bill, of a less contentious measure, which was confined to the counties only. As its predecessor, it was doomed to fail at the second reading. Like so many others, Palmerston had underestimated the political strength of the boroughs.

A new headquarters for the Shrewsbury borough police was opened in March 1854, in the Market Hall. It had the added attraction of an officer of the borough force always being in attendance. Presumably the building was found unsuitable, for later in July, there is reference to the lower part of the right wing of the old Talbot Hotel, being converted into a police station for the borough force.

In the August of 1855, John Joyce, an Irish vagrant knocked on the door of a house in Oakengates. With his arm in a sling, he solicited charity. Too late he realized that he had unwisely chosen a police house. P. C. Edwards of the

Shropshire Constabulary demanded that Joyce unwrap the dirty covering about his hand. Reluctantly he was compelled to show, what he had just described as a stump, from which his fingers had been amputated, after a terrible accident, 'somewhere'. Strange to say, a miracle appeared to have been affected since it was wrapped up, for the fingers were now firmly and properly fixed in place where they should be. Whole, well and remarkable only for their plump strength.

He was committed for fourteen days as a dire warning to all pseudo cripples.

In February 1855, Edwin Morgan, a tailor of Ludlow, was commissioned to supply the first uniforms for the Ludlow Borough Police Force. Whilst at Shrewsbury a change was made in their police uniforms, by substituting a frock coat for the previously used swallow-tailed coat.

A historic council meeting was held in the Guildhall at Bridgnorth, on the 12 of January 1855. The main item on the agenda was the policing of the town. Four years of being policed by the Shropshire Constabulary appeared to have caused a great deal of dissatisfaction. It was pointed out by Alderman Jones, that the public disturbances on the Bridge, and in the Lower Town, were worse than ever. Rarely was a constable to be found on duty there. He had himself sent repeatedly in such cases of tumult for the police, but no officer ever came. It was noted that the continual disturbances created by the Irish, were ignored by the constabulary. The Mayor then remarked that he had given orders to Constable Ross respecting the nuisance on Castle Hill, committed by boys and others playing bandy (hockey), to the annoyance of parties promenading there. Ross had done nothing to alleviate the nuisance. The Rev. Marshall of St. Mary's, had repeatedly requested police assistance to put down the noise and rioting in front of the School house Chapel of Ease, on preaching nights; but the police had taken no notice of his requests. Councillor Deighton observed that he had consented four years ago, to the establishment of the county police within the borough, but could now only say it had proved a failure, it had been a source of aggravation to the townsfolk. In his opinion it formed a link in the evils of centralization, a system which he abominated. And so the long list of grievances went on.

There was a great deal of talk about the privileges of the borough. Councillor Phillips saying 'he was the last to propose change for change sake. It was a matter purely of a local nature.' The question was — 'are we able to manage our own affairs and appoint our own officers, or are we to submit to be led by the nose by Sir Baldwin Leighton or any other constituted chairman of quarter sessions at Shrewsbury who may choose to define our privileges?'

One sees from all this that the main grievance of the corporation was its lack of control over the police. A control which they themselves had, voluntarily, signed over to the county authorities in 1850.

The outcome of the meeting was a recommendation for a withdrawal from the constabulary force of the county, and a re-establishment of their own borough police force. The recommendation was carried. The Town-Clerk sent notice to the County Constabulary Committee that his council wished the present contract with the county constabulary to expire at the termination of six months, from the date of the notice. It was then agreed by both parties that a convenient date would be the 1st of July, it being the end of the half year.

And so the experiment of amalgamation at Bridgnorth came to an end.

Bridgnorth now had the task of recruiting a new police force. Their choice for Chief Constable was George Ross, a constable of the Shropshire Constabulary. It was a surprising choice, for Ross had been the county constable who had been complained about, when the council were busy breaking the agreement with the county. John Jackson of Birmingham was appointed second constable of the tiny borough force. With the personnel settled, a decision had to be made regarding uniforms and equipment. It was resolved that the new borough police be accoutred similarly to the county constabulary, in rifle-green frock-coats, but ornamented with gilt buttons, bearing the corporation arms. The collar of the Chief Constable's coat to be distinguished by a gold-lace loop and badge. The rest of the uniform was similar to the county constabulary. Smartly turned out, all that was now required of them, was to prove their mettle.

A change of superintendent at Ludlow, took place in July 1855. Robert Jones resigned from office, to make way for Henry Biggs, who came from the Gloucestershire Constabulary.

At Oswestry the Chief Constable, John Donald, was having his share of trouble. One Saturday night, Donald accompanied by one of his constables, came across William Baverstock, in a very drunken state. He refused to go home peacefully, and when the two police officers tried to seize him, he attacked the Chief Constable with a knife. Happily no damage was done.

Superintendent Thomas Abel Wilmot of the county constabulary, resigned in October 1855. A native of Fulham, Middlesex, he had served at one time in the 2nd Dragoon Guards, followed by service in the Birmingham Police Force.

When the county constabulary was first established in Shropshire, Wilmot was one of the first men to join. Six years later he was promoted to the rank of superintendent. Wilmot had been very badly injured in 1849, whilst on duty at the Wenlock Races, when he had endeavoured to capture a notorious and vicious criminal, named William Broadfield. It was due to this assault that his health had been impaired for the rest of his service. The county granted him a pension of twelve shillings a week.

It was poetic justice that in the month following the resignation of Wilmot, that William Broadfield was at long last captured, and made to pay for his many crimes. Warrants without number had been issued for his apprehension. The first on account of the bloody onslaught which he, in company with others of the same brutal mind, made on the police at Wenlock Racecourse, as far back as July 1849. Up

59

until the present time (1855) he had very cleverly avoided capture.

Time after time he visited Bridgnorth surreptiously returning safely to his hideout. Thinking doubtless, that he might continue the game safely, and emboldened by success, he came once too often to Bridgnorth. His presence was made known to Superintendent W.H. Baxter, as also all particulars of the vengeful and daring cove that he had to deal with.

The superintendent, accompanied by four of his men, slipped quietly into the kitchen of the Britannia public-house, in the Cartway. There sat the notorious Broadfield, enjoying himself. On his being pointed out to Baxter, the capture was quickly made. Baxter walked over and arrested him, whereupon he slipped down from his seat to the floor, putting up a terrific resistance. Kicking and struggling most violently. Swearing he would not be taken. Baxter stood no nonsense from him, two or three taps on his head with a baton, and the application of a pair of steel bracelets settled his business.

Broadfield sullenly submitted to fate. Later in the police station he threatened Baxter, saying that he would kill him for having taken him, he did not care about the gallows, he would have his revenge even if it took forty years.

The Chief Constable of Shrewsbury, resigned his post, the 22 February 1856. His stay in office had been short a mere two years. His successor was Inspector John Hughes, a Shrewsbury man. The choice was very popular and was backed by a testimonial signed by practically everyone who was anyone in Shrewsbury.

Another police bill was introduced into parliament in 1856, entitled – 'A Bill to render more effectual the Police in Counties and Boroughs in England and Wales.'

Once again the corporate towns of the country were up in arms to defend their privileges. A petition was sent from the Shrewsbury corporation –

'That your petitioners consider that the proposed alteration in the regulation of the Police Force is an expedient and uncalled for interference with the privileges of Boroughs; and that it would unjustly deprive the local Authorities of their useful and beneficial influence over the Police, and control over the organization of an expenditure in respect thereof, and is a violation of the principal of local self-government established by the Municipal Corporation Act.

Your petitioners therefore humbly pray your Hon: House not to pass the said Bill as it now stands into a Law.'[2]

This time there was to be no weakening at the Home Office. Sir George Gray, the Home Secretary, had dropped the proposal to abolish the smaller police forces, but now insisted that all counties be compelled to establish rural police forces. County policemen were to have the same jurisdiction in the boroughs that the borough police had always had in the counties. The crown was empowered to appoint two inspectors of constabulary, to test the efficiency of all police forces. Such forces as the inspectors found to be efficient, were to be paid a government grant, amounting to one quarter of the cost of the pay and clothing of the men. No grant would be paid to forces serving populations of under five thousand. This was putting the screw on the smaller borough forces, for they were faced with the choice of amalgamating with their county constabularies, or of paying the full cost of their own police forces.

The bill included provisions which safeguarded the amalgamation agreements. Once entered into, these agreements could not now be broken without the Home Secretary's consent. The bill also enabled an Order in Council to impose an agreement on an unwilling county authority. Another clause compelled all police authorities to submit statistics of local crime to the Home Secretary.

The bill was to sail a stormy passage through parliament. As previously in 1854, a meeting was held in London, consisting of Mayors from all over the country, Members of parliament, and other influential people; and once more it was chaired by the Lord Mayor of York.

The bill was furiously denounced as dangerous and unconstitutional. A deputation waited on the Home Secretary. He

61

was told bluntly that they were not interested in having the bill amended, but demanded its withdrawal. He was told —

'After the examples the country had had of the perfect inability of the public departments to conduct the affairs of war, they must have only brought forward this measure to show their inability to manage the peace of the country.'[3]

In the House of Commons the members for the boroughs outdid each other in stormy abuse. The government was depicted as showing an indecent lust for power, the boroughs they said, should not be subject to 'the degradation of inspectorship:' the Home Secretary was likened to a second Fouche, with spies all over the kingdom. But, despite all the rantings and ravings against the bill, it received the Royal Assent on July 21st 1856. In retrospect this bill turned out to be a very successful experiment in central supervision over local management.

The new pattern of administration established by this bill, was to survive for more than one hundred years.

Little time was lost in appointing the first Inspectors of Constabulary. Two were appointed, and at first they divided the country into two halves, each taking a half as their area. But it was soon found that they were unable to cope successfully with such large areas. A third division was then made, and a third Inspector appointed. The areas being designated North, Midlands, and South. The northern area was put in charge of Lieut. Colonel John Woodford, who had previously held the post of Chief Constable of Lancashire. Captain Edward Willis, formerly Chief Constable of Manchester became the Inspector of Constabulary for the southern area. Both men with police experience. To the midland area came Major-General Cartwright, a veteran of Waterloo and the Peninsular War, who appears, unlike his colleagues, to have had no previous police experience. The inspectors resided within their own districts, corresponding with the Home Office; and dealing directly with the Chief Constables, and the police authorities in their areas.

It was due to their inspections of the forces, that were duly reported on, to the Home Secretary, in their annual reports, that national policies for the police began to emerge.

There were two hundred and thirty seven police forces in England and Wales in 1856, and if the Exchequer grant was to be paid to them, then the inspectors had to inspect each and every one of them. It being necessary that they should be certified as efficient in discipline and numbers, before the grant could be made. Despite the great hostility which had been shown towards the idea of inspectors in Parliament, the inspectors themselves were generally cordially welcomed. Mainly most local authorities co-operated in an affable manner.

Ludlow corporation discussed the new Police Act, relative to amalgamating the borough police force with that of the county. The discussion ended with the resolve that they would retain their own force. Oswestry was more inclined to favour a union with the county, and sent a deputation early in 1857, to discuss the matter with the County Police Committee. The meeting ended in disagreement, and Oswestry retained their own police force.

The majority of the county forces passed the first inspection by the Inspectors of Constabulary with credit. Only seven of the fifty-nine county constabularies were disqualified from receiving the government grant at the end of the first year (1 October 1857). Sad to relate Shropshire was one of the seven.

General Cartwright had pointed out earlier in the year, that the Shropshire Constabulary was greatly lacking in numbers. He suggested that the number of 1st class constables should be raised from nine to twenty. That there should be a new 3rd class constable's rank for recruits, at sixteen shillings per week, in which class they should remain for at least six months. Also the pay of inspectors should be raised by one shilling per week. His opinions went unheeded by the County Police Committee, so after his official inspection, his report to the Home Office declared the Shropshire Constabulary — 'inefficient in numbers.' No grant was forthcoming for that year.   The County Police Committee were deeply shocked, but their reaction was swift.   An increase of twenty-six men was ordered for the force, namely — one inspector, five sergeants and twenty constables.   This would bring the force up to a total of eighty-four men.   The salary of the sergeant, which was a new rank in this force, was set at twenty-three shillings per week.

At the same meeting Dawson Mayne's suggestion of 1840, was resurrected, when the committee came to the conclusion that it would facilitate the detection and prevention of crime if a new police division was formed around the town of Shrewsbury.   It would be put in charge of an Inspector, and subject to the immediate control of the chief constable.

The committee also recommended that application be made to the Staffordshire Court of Quarter Sessions, to ascertain whether an arrangement could be made by which the townships of Woore and Mucklestone may be, for police purposes, placed under the charge of the Staffordshire Constabulary.   In lieu of which, the Shropshire Constabulary would take over the policing of the Staffordshire portion of the parish of Drayton-in-Hales.   A meeting was held the following January, when both county chief constables agreed to the exchange.

General Cartwright had also suggested alterations to the Shrewsbury Borough Police Force.   These he thought the watch committee would be wise to consider, and implement, before his official visit in July 1857.

The Shrewsbury watch committee were anxious to reduce the heavy expenses which they were already shouldering, but they also had an eye on the government grant.   Discussions comparing the police salaries of other borough forces took place, after which it was decided that the present salaries were sufficient; with the exception of that of the chief constable. He was voted an increase of ten pounds per annum to his salary.   The committee also concluded that three more men would be advantageous, bringing the strength of the force to twenty-three.

At the official inspection of the force, General Cartwright

"Two Superintendents and Prisoner c.1858"
Shrewsbury Borough Police

65

found that the alterations and additions, suggested by him, had been adopted. Thereupon a favourable report was returned to the Home Office, and Shrewsbury received the grant.

At the end of 1856, Superintendent John Donald, head of the Oswestry Borough Police Force, resigned his post. Moving back to his home county, he was appointed to the rank of superintendent in the Cumberland County Constabulary. He died in 1861, whilst on a visit to his old force at Oswestry. His post at Oswestry was filled by one William Sykes, whose only claim to fame is that he was the last superintendent of the Oswestry Borough Police Force, and perhaps, that he bore the same name as the infamous Dickensian burglar.

Wanderlust was in the air, for a month later, in the January of 1857, George Ross, chief constable of the tiny two man borough force at Bridgnorth, decided to better himself. He resigned his post at Bridgnorth, to become an inspector with the Devon County Constabulary. His police career ended with his retirement from that force, on the 18 October 1870, with the rank of superintendent.

There were some thirty to forty candidates for the post of Chief Constable of Bridgnorth. The successful contender John Cole, a sergeant in the Stafford Borough Police Force.

The name of a person does not always reflect their nature, as is clearly shown in the following anecdote.

William Gentle, a travelling hawker, was charged in January 1858, with fighting and creating a public disturbance near the White Horse Passage, Frankwell. A borough constable was called to quell the noisy disturbance, and found that the defendant had been fighting with his father, and that these 'gentle' people, father, mother and defendant were all drunk. On the officer ordering 'Gentle' away, he commenced abusing him, and when he attempted to take 'Gentle' to the Police Station, 'Gentle' commenced kicking him. When a bystander came to the officer's assistance, he too was in turn assaulted. This 'gentle' individual nearly succeeded in biting off one of the officer's fingers.

66

Sir Baldwin Leighton had always been very critical of the chief constable's command and administration of the Shropshire Constabulary. Later, in 1858, when he was appointed chairman of the Shropshire Court of Quarter Sessions, he was in a position to make Dawson Mayne's position most uncomfortable. The fact that Mayne had married a cousin of Sir Rowland Hill, a county magistrate, annoyed him still further. Sir Baldwin did not approve of chief constables having personal connections with the county magistracy. An inquiry was held in 1858, into the efficiency and discipline of the county constabulary. The county magistrates found, that in a number of cases investigated by them, that there did not appear to have been the intelligence and activity displayed, which they had a right to expect from the chief constable and his superintendents.

This criticism came at a time when derogatory letters were appearing in the local press —

'Sir, — A week or two ago I was much struck by the perusal of a letter in your paper upon the iniquitous system of espionage pursued by the police of this country.

Such conduct on the part of police authorities is miserably mean; and I am glad to observe that both Judges and magistrates are beginning to view it in its proper light.

"You should be very cautious," said Baron Watson, in his charge to a grand jury at Shrewsbury, "in taking evidence of a police officer, unless borne out by respectable corroboration." [4]

The detection rate in Shropshire was at this time one of the lowest in the country. General Cartwright suggested that the force required the assistance of a Detective Officer, to be employed in all serious cases.

The police committee were unwilling to employ yet another man on the force, and found a way around this, by suggesting in their turn that —

'if the Chief Constable should need a Detective then he be authorised to obtain such assistance from London or elsewhere with the approval of the Chairman of this committee and the costs allowed by the Court.' [5]

Although General Cartwright had no previous police experience, he appears to have had an astute mind, quick to find the faults and errors of the forces in his area. He soon found that there was a lack of co-operation between the county constabulary and the borough police force of Shrewsbury.

The county police committee agreed with him that it was detrimental to the working of both police forces. To remedy this defect, they recommended the court to appoint several of their members to arrange a meeting with a like number of members of the corporation of Shrewsbury, for the purpose of framing a number of regulations for the improvement of the present system.

Not all of Cartwright's suggestions were taken kindly by the police authorities, some of his suggestions were rejected year after year by the magistrates. It was an uphill fight to convince them to spend even small sums of money to improve the force. Even in 1861, Shropshire was the only county in the country with a police rate less than one penny in the pound.

Later in 1874, the chairman of the quarter sessions felt that he could boast that the police rate was only one penny, when the national average was twopence farthing, and that therefore the county had nothing to grumble about.

The magistrates appear to have been lost in a little world of minimizing the expenditure. Blind to the fact that the lack of manpower made for a lower efficiency of the force, and a resulting higher rate of crime, and uncaught criminals.

The chairman of the Shropshire Quarter Sessions received, the 3 January 1859, a letter of resignation from the chief constable. Dawson Mayne offered to stay until the court found it convenient to place the duties in other hands. The police committee recommended the court to accept Mayne's resignation, and for it to take effect from the 1 April.

Out of one hundred applications, the choice was made of Captain Philip Henry Crampton, Deputy Chief Constable of Somerset. Like his predecessor, Dawson Mayne, he was Irish born.

Crampton brought new ideas with him from the Somerset force. It was his idea to number General Orders, number one being dated 26 April 1859. He also created a new rank of unpaid acting sergeant. A change in appearance was also made, by having the brass plates and numbers removed from the collars of the police coats, and sewn on the left breast of the coats.

In mediaeval times an armed escort was a real necessity for the Sheriff, if he was to protect the judges satisfactorily whilst in the county. Later the escort became more of a ceremonial unit, dressed in the sheriff's livery, and carrying javelins. It was from the latter weapon that they became known as 'Javelin Men.' In 1859 an act was passed which transferred this responsibility to the police. Here in Shropshire the police committee recommended the chief constable to employ a number of his constables for that purpose. So from 1859 it became customary for the county constables to ceremoniously escort the judge on his walk to St. Chad's Church, Shrewsbury, for the Assize Service.

At Oswestry, the watch committee established a superannuation fund for the benefit of their small police force. They also did away with the cumbersome wooden rattles, carried by the constables, and in the December of 1859, supplied metal whistles in their stead.

In return for a very low wage, a constable worked a seven-day week. His average duty would be ten to twelve hours, generally split into two shifts.

All of his patrolling would be on foot, and constables would tramp upwards of twenty miles a day, for weeks on end. A few coppers a week would be paid to him for the upkeep of his boots, which in many forces he was expected to supply. Oswestry supplied boots as did Ludlow, the latter until 1859, when they gave an allowance instead. Five shillings would be deducted from a constable's pay when he left the force, to cover the cost of altering his uniform to fit the next recruit. Compulsary attendance at church on a Sunday, generally in his

Shropshire Constabulary 1859   Capt. P.H. Crampton, Chief Constable. Centre foreground.

best uniform, was the rule. They were also expected to be non-political, and were not allowed to vote in parliamentary elections until 1887, and in municipal elections until as late as 1893.

For all this the policeman of the mid nineteenth century received a weekly wage that left him, and in particular the married constable with a family, close to the breadline.

Chapter Four

1860 — 1869

The two man Bridgnorth Borough Police Force were having a nightmare time with the numerous Irish navvies working on the railroad in 1860. Saturday and Sunday nights, mobs of two hundred or more of these labourers congregated about the streets of the town. Their attitude to say the least was always pugnacious towards anyone, and to the local police in particular. John Cole, as Chief Constable of the Borough, asked the magistrates for additional constables, for he found it extremely dangerous, both for himself and for Constable Edward Butler, to try and keep the peace.

The situation had followed much the same pattern since 1857, when parts of Bridgnorth had become notorious as the locale of the Irish families. In particular the frequent brawls, disturbances, fights and rows which occurred late on Saturday nights, had become unbearable to the inhabitants of the area, in and around Listley Street. One must admit however, that the Irish looked after their own, for after being paid, they would club together to put up a sum of money, in order to extricate such of 'the unfortunate boys' as were caught by the police, and brought before the magistrates.

Progress had called for railroads all over the country, and without the mechanical aids of later times, hordes of navvies were needed to build them. Irishmen were hard workers, and came over in droves from their native land, glad of the work and money, but as with most manual workers of that time, they also liked the bottle, and at weekends with money jingling in their pockets, were inclined to raise merry hell wherever they had settled.

Edward Butler had been appointed a constable at Bridgnorth in March 1860, however, his conduct had not been all that was desired.   An investigation was made into the many irregularities which he had been charged with, ending with the Mayor stating that — 'it would be better for him to go at once.'

In his place was chosen John Instone, hardly a better choice, for he had just been dismissed from the county constabulary for drunkenness, and neglect of duty.   His stay with the Shropshire Constabulary had been brief, only lasting from February 1859 to September 1860.   Now he was given a month's trial at Bridgnorth.

It is interesting to note the form of oath sworn by a constable, at this period —

'You swear to execute the Office of Constable on behalf of our Sovereign Lady the Queen for the Borough of Bridgnorth according to the best of your skill and judgement — in preserving the peace by day and by night and preventing Robberies and other Felonies and apprehending offenders against the Peace.   John Instone.
Sworn the 8th dy of September 1860.
Before me R.O. Backhouse.   a justice of the peace in the Borough of Bridgnorth.'

John Instone did not change his ways, and John Cole (Chief Constable) mentions him in his journal under the date — 'Sat. 11 October 1863 — Found P.C. Instone drinking in the Fox after 12-0 a.m. also smoking a long pipe.'   Then in the following year — 'Sat. 19 November 1864. P.C. John Instone. Suspended from duty for being found in a brothel.'   Instone realised that he had gone too far, and sent in his resignation.

Policemen as a rule are not apt to believe in ghosts, but, one dark and dreary evening in the February of 1861, P.C. Broughall, of the Shrewsbury Borough Police felt that he was being personally haunted.

As he walked down Pride Hill, a tall gaunt figure closely followed him, when the constable crossed the road to return up the hill, the figure still clung close behind him. In fact wherever he went, his mysterious shadow silently glided after him. It came to the witching hour of twelve, when even churchyards yawn, and the constable had become extremely nervous. Plucking up courage he turned and accosted his ghostly shadow, demanding his name. The tall figure said his name was Michael, now the constable had read of Michael the Archangel in the Bible, but had never heard of a ghost of that name, so he then asked for the reason of his strange behaviour. Michael requested his protection. 'From whom' enquired the astonished constable. 'From myself', was the lugubrious reply. The constable began to wonder if this was some perturbed spirit from the netherworld, which had presented itself before him. Perhaps doomed for a certain term to walk the night. But finding his nocturnal walker to be flesh and blood, he ordered him to be off to his bed, threatening the vengeance of the law upon his refusal. Putting the vision aside, it turned out that Michael was no ghost, but an inebriated traveller, who on returning to his lodgings had become obsessed with the idea that he would be murdered if he remained there, and had therefore gone out into the darkened streets to seek the protection of the police.

The Inspector of Constabulary, General Cartwright, made his annual inspection of the police forces of Shropshire, in the August of 1860. His remarks paint an excellent picture of the state of the forces, and what they had to cope with at that time. He first dealt with the Shropshire Constabulary, whose inspection started on the 21 August.

'This force consists of one chief constable, one chief superintendent, one first class and four second class superintendents, one inspector, six serjeants, 20 first class, and 50 second class constables.'[1]

Three hundred and forty-six indictable offences had been reported to the police during the previous year, for which one hundred and seventy persons had been apprehended, and one hundred and forty-four committed, a low average of detection. Twelve constables had resigned during the year, and three had

74

been dismissed. He notes that the superintendents were allowed thirty nine pounds per annum to find and keep a horse, but deplores the fact that no carts were in use, which he considered detrimental to the working of the force, and also false economy, as they might be made useful in conveyance of prisoners and other county duties. They would also be of great advantage for use in the night supervision of the patrols. He goes on to say, that Shropshire was almost the only county in his district without carts. In his view the police stations were much improved. Three new ones had been erected at Whitchurch, Wem, and Ironbridge; one was required at Wenlock, but the authorities had assured him that one was about to be built. The Shropshire Constabulary passed his test and was reported efficient.

The following day it was the turn of the Shrewsbury Borough Force to be examined.

'This Force consists of one head constable, two first class, and one second class serjeants; one first class, nine second class, and nine third class constables.'[2]

Sixty-one indictable offences were reported to the police during the year, for which 40 persons were apprehended, and 38 committed, a good average. The large number of 299 persons were proceeded against as drunk and disorderly, and 244 were fined. Three constables resigned during the year, and two were dismissed. He said that the force had been much improved, and that the constables were very superiour to those formerly in the force. The determination of the watch committee to rid themselves of any men reported drunk on duty had had a very beneficial effect, and was a good example for all forces. He noted that a superannuation fund had been established 29 October 1859. The cells he thought good, and kept clean, the force was efficient.

It would appear that the General did not inspect the Ludlow Borough Police Force, but did make a report.

'This force consists of one head constable and two constables.'[3]

Ludlow was more of a peaceful town, and only twelve

75

indictable offences had been reported to the police during the preceding year, of which 11 persons had been apprehended, and five committed. Only 39 persons were taken up as drunk and disorderly, of which 24 were fined. Which speaks well for the character of its inhabitants. One constable had resigned during the year. No superannuation fund had been established. The cells, which are large, and part of the old prison, were in good order. But the force was inefficient, due to weakness.

The Oswestry Borough Police Force was inspected on the 25 August, Cartwright having very little to say about it.

'This force, which has been inefficient from weakness, is about to consolidate Borough with the County Force. Pay — No details. Population to one constable = 1,049. Strength of Force 4.'[4]

At Bridgnorth the borough police force was examined, and the General had this to say about it.

'This force consists of one head constable and one other constable.'[5]

Twenty-three indictable offences were reported to the police during the year, for which nine persons were apprehended, and only five committed. Fifty persons were proceeded against as drunk and disorderly, of whom 45 were fined. One, the only constable, resigned last year. This force of two constables has to protect a population of 6,189 persons, and have to cover an area of 2,987 acres with the small assistance of supernumery constables occasionally. A superannuation fund was established 9 December 1859.

The lock-up is part of an old prison; the cells are clean, and used by the county. Population to one constable = 3,094. The force is inefficient from weakness.

All of which shows the County Constabulary and Shrewsbury borough force as efficient, which means they would receive the government grant.

But, leaves Bridgnorth, Oswestry and Ludlow with inefficient police forces, and no government grant.

The Oswestry Council met on the 9 November 1860, once

more to enquire into the possibilities of amalgamating their borough police force with that of the county. After some discussion it became apparent that most of those present found it a desirable move. A committee was formed of the Mayor and two aldermen to negotiate with the county authorities. On the 22 February 1861, the Town Clerk explained to a full meeting of the borough council, the amicable result of the negotiations between their committee and the county authorities. A report from the County Constabulary Committee had been put before the Justices of the County Quarter Sessions, who had given their approval to the terms proposed for the amalgamation. This report was now read out by the Town Clerk to the Oswestry Corporation, who likewise approved the same. The agreement was drawn up and signed by both parties. (See Appendix IV).

With the Shropshire Constabulary taking over the policing of the Borough of Oswestry, the Night-Watch ceased to exist. Until this late period the Borough Police had only patrolled during the daytime, the Night-Watch carrying on through the night period. Now the Shropshire Constabulary would take over both day and night policing.

It was found necessary to compensate Superintendent William Sykes and his two remaining constables – John Jones and John Turner for the loss of their posts, in view of the fact that they were not being transferred into the Shropshire Constabulary.

It was agreed in 1861 to increase the Shropshire Constabulary by twenty men, to make a total force of one hundred and nine men. When the Inspector of Constabulary made his inspection in 1862, he was able to express his satisfaction with everything that came to his notice. He stated –

'The increase is a step which places the force on a par with other county forces, and I have no doubt now the Chief Constable's hands are so strengthened he will zealously carry out the duties imposed upon him, which would have been almost impracticable under the weakness of the force before the addition of twenty one constables.

Sergeant Thomas Caswell c.1862
Shropshire Constabulary

Superintendent Thomas Caswell c.1890
Shropshire Constabulary

78

The appearance of the young constables is very promising, and they generally come from the best class that is from agricultural employment for permanent policemen.'[6]

It was not always the constables who suffered violence from criminals and roughs. Sometimes the higher echelons of the force came under fire.

At Oswestry in 1862, an Irishman named Daniel Welsh, was brought before the magistrates, charged with assaulting Superintendent Joseph Ivins of the County Constabulary. It would appear that Ivins had been called to the ironmonger's shop of a Mr. Lacon. Here he had found Welsh, who was very drunk, flourishing a large iron saucepan over his head. As soon as the Superintendent approached, Welsh struck him over the head with the heavy saucepan, which cut his head open. Before Ivins had time to recover from this savage blow, Welsh dealt him another, a blow not quite so severe as the first, but still with this unusual weapon. The dazed Superintendent then managed to disarm Welsh, and after a bit of a struggle marched him off into custody. It would seem that the prisoner had attempted to borrow money from the ironmonger, who had refused, knowing that he would spend it all on drink. Welsh had then taken up the iron saucepan, and swore that he would smash everything in the shop.

His escapade with the law cost him a month in Shrewsbury Gaol.

Co-operation with other police forces appears to have come into being in the early 1860's. In the neighbouring county of Montgomeryshire, trouble flared up, in July 1862, at a parliamentary election at Llanidloes. The Montgomeryshire Force being a very small one, was unable to cope. A plea for police assistance was received at Shrewsbury. In a very short time Captain Crampton, Chief Constable of the Shropshire Constabulary, had forty officers gathered, and under his own command, proceeded by train to the trouble spot.

However on arrival they were found not to be needed, and returned home.

The following year, 1863, there were disturbances at Leeswood, Flintshire, when the colliery manager, Dougan by name, evicted local families in favour of his fellow Lancashire miners. The Flintshire authorities sent to Denbighshire and Shropshire for assistance. Crampton once again headed a party of twenty officers to assist the neighbouring force. Prompt measures were taken by the combined force of the three counties preventing any further trouble. And the Shropshire contingent returned home with the thanks of the Flintshire magistrates.

On the 30 July 1864, a letter of resignation was read to the magistrates of the County Quarter Sessions, from Captain Crampton, the Chief Constable of Shropshire. After acceptance, the constabulary committee advertised for candidates for the post. The man chosen was, Lieut-Colonel Edward Burgoyne Cureton, who with twenty-five years in the army was expected to be a man of great experience in the handling of men.

Elections of members of parliament continued to cause disturbances, which put a great strain on police resources. In 1865 Cureton had his first taste of civil riots. Serious disturbances occurred on the occasion of the county elections of members of parliament, at Church Stretton, Pontesbury, Wenlock, Shifnal and Bishopscastle. Warned of what might happen, Cureton borrowed forty men from the Staffordshire Constabulary, and a further ten men from the Shrewsbury Borough Police Force. A number of special constables were also sworn in for the occasion. On the day, at Church Stretton, the crowd rushed the thin green line of constables, and their superintendent, William Henry Baxter, was thrown to the ground, and trampled on. At Shifnal the rioting was caused by a number of colliers, who attacked the police. Sergeant Beeston received a dangerous wound to the head, delivered by a nailed boot. Three other constables were all seriously hurt. At Wenlock, one of the Staffordshire constables received a wound on the head, from a stone. There was a great deal of stone-throwing and fighting at Pontesbury, but no serious hurt. At Clun and at Cleobury Mortimer the polling passed off quietly.

Bridgnorth Borough Police Force were kept very busy at their election time, but the small force of two men could not hope to cope. Fifty-nine specials were hurriedly sworn. And as well they were, for a party of so called 'fighting men' were brought from Wolverhampton with the intention of assaulting the unfavourable voters. But, the tables were turned, and the local people thrashed the 'fighting men', and it became necessary for the police to see them safely out of the town, before the indignant townsfolk seriously maimed them.

Ludlow turned out the full borough force, plus twenty specials for the borough polling day. A week later, when it was polling day for the county, they thought it necessary to swear in eighty-nine specials to assist the borough force. The show of strength had the desired effect on both occasions, peace reigned.

But not all disturbances and riots were caused by elections. A few days before the above happenings, rioting broke out at Market Drayton. A parochial meeting had taken place at the Corbet Arms. Its subject the Local Government Act, and whether it should be adopted by Market Drayton. If so, then it would mean bringing a sewage system to the town. Incredible as it may seem, there were those who did not favour such a move. Agitators harangued gatherings of the townsfolk, and stirred them to action. When the parochial meeting came to an end, it was to find a very irate mob of some five hundred men, women and children outside the inn, who proceeded to abuse and stone those coming out, including their own vicar. The local county police sergeant, John Smith, had shrewdly forseen the trouble, and had promptly applied to the Chief Constable for an extra force of officers. These were sent, in charge of Superintendent Gough. Even then there were only twenty men to face the mob of five hundred.

With the odds at 25 to 1 the police became the target for every loose brick or stone that could be found. The violence went on until the early hours of the next morning. The police battered and bruised retired into the Lion Inn, to patch

81

1868. 'B' Division, Oswestry, Shropshire Constabulary.   Supt. Geo. Gough & Constables.

82

up their wounds, and to try to get a few hours rest before facing the mob, when daylight dawned.

Half of the police reinforcements were due to return to Shrewsbury on the following day. When they emerged from the Lion Inn, it was to find a great concourse of the townsfolk waiting for them. Bell Lane and Cheshire Street became battlegrounds. The police were abused and pelted with stones all the way to the railway station. After the police had boarded the train, the crowds lined the track for several hundred yards, and stoned the moving train.

The remainder of the police were besieged in several buildings. The windows of the police station, county court and magistrates offices were all broken.

On Tuesday evening it was deemed advisable by the authorities to telegraph for military assistance, as it was evident that no force of police would be sufficient to control such a belligerent crowd.

Wednesday morning a detachment of seventy men of the 64th Foot (2nd Staffordshire Regiment) arrived by special train from Manchester. An additional body of the county constabulary joined them. The combined efforts of military and police soon had the ringleaders under lock and key. Such riots, although a familiar sight in the Victorian era, were quite vicious while they lasted, and tested the endurance of the police officers to the extreme.

A change in police control was made at Ludlow in 1865. Superintendent Biggs, who had been appointed head of the borough force in 1855, died at the early age of 48. As his successor it was decided to appoint Police-Sergeant George Henry Brooks, of the Herefordshire Constabulary. The new superintendent was sworn into office on the 25 March 1865.

A letter of resignation in the January of 1866, from Colonel Cureton, left the office of Chief Constable of Shropshire, vacant. His stay had been short, a mere fifteen months. It was with regret that the magistracy accepted his resignation. It had been usual for the county magistrates to advertise for candidates. However since the last appointment had been so recent, it was thought to be a needless expence. Enquiries were made to see if their second choice of 1864 was still available. Not only was he available, but he had taken great pains to acquaint himself with the duties of the office of Chief Constable.

Colonel Richard John Edgell, had spent some considerable time in the county of Essex, making himself fully acquainted with the arrangements and the system of that county's constabulary. A letter from the chief constable of that county, sent as a testimonial remarked that —

'I have no hesitation in stating that I consider you in every sense of the word eminently qualified for the Office of Chief Constable, and I shall deem any county fortunate that may avail itself of your services.'

Colonel Edgell was appointed the fourth chief constable of Shropshire on the 12 April 1866.

Edgell deplored the smallness of the county force, and in a letter to the Police Committee makes the statement — 'With exception of the Counties of Rutland and Montgomery, the Police Force in this County is weaker than in any other in the United Kingdom.' His statement was not entirely correct. Had he just looked at the Welsh county forces he would have found them all smaller than the Shropshire Constabulary, both in numbers and with regard to the ratio of constables to the population. A letter from the Home Secretary in December 1867, approved the addition of six more constables, making a total force of 122.

The chief constable also showed concern about recent incidents where there had been armed interference directed against the police. He pointed out that there were only 54 cutlasses to share between the 122 officers of the force, permission was granted for the purchase of a further thirty-six cutlasses.

With respect to a reserve party of constables, this was something that did not exist. A small party of six men could on an emergency be assembled together, after due warning — but no sudden requisition for the immediate services of a body of

84

police, whether small or large could be met.

This then, was the background of the Shropshire Constabulary, when in late December 1867, a sizable riot occurred at Wellington.   It was a political fracas between mobs of Conservative and Liberal partizans.   A fight started between them — and interference by the police was immediately met with a shower of stones.   After an hour of ineffective preventative measures, Chief Superintendent Richardson telegraphed to his headquarters, at Shrewsbury, for assistance.   His telegram arrived with another one, requesting assistance at Whitchurch.   Orders were sent to Market Drayton and Oswestry to reinforce the police at Whitchurch, but the Chief Constable was at a loss what to do about Wellington, for there were no spare men available.   Finally he caught a train and went himself.   He found seventeen constables trying to control a mob of over 200 people.   By 5.0 p.m. it was getting dark, and he had two constables severely injured, requiring two men to hold each wounded comrade up.   Reduced to 13 effective men, the Chief Constable withdrew his force to the safety of the police station.   Soon the mob dispersed from the Square, and quiet reigned once more.

Edgell recorded that the constables had behaved well —

'with much good temper and steadiness under great provocation.'

Meanwhile, at Church Stretton a similar riot was taking place.   During the afternoon a mob had broken the windows in 'The Hotel', which was the quarters of the Conservative candidates and their supporters.   Captain Lovett of the Shropshire Militia was severely assaulted.   Police were as a matter of course stoned.

Superintendent Baxter assisted by a detachment of the Staffordshire Constabulary, under the direction of Superintendent Garnham, dispersed the mob.   Information of this disturbance reached the Chief Constable by telegram — but no train being available for another three hours, he went on horseback to Church Stretton.   A quick concentration of the police forces there, and the mob was driven out of the village and public houses, where many had taken shelter.

It must have been a disturbing experience for Colonel Edgell, who, with 23 years in the army (which included being present at many battles), to find his small force in action against hostile mobs, with only wooden truncheons to retaliate with.

1867 was the year of the great 'Fenian' scare. This brotherhood was formed by Irishmen in the United States of America in 1858. Its purpose to promote revolution, and to overthrow the English government in Ireland. In February 1867 an attack on Chester Castle and armoury was feared. Later in September, a policeman was killed by the Fenians in Manchester, while in December, the attempted rescue of prisoners at Clerkenwell Prison, kept the London authorities on the alert. A circular letter was sent out to all chief constables from Whitehall, marked 'Confidential' it was dated 28 September 1867 —

'I am directed by Mr. Secretary Hardy to inform you that as a precaution against any sudden outbreak and with a view of obtaining correct information as to any Fenian Organization that may exist in your District it is desirable that a system should be established by which a constant Watch should be kept on Persons believed to belong to such Organization, and regular information transmitted to this Office.

To effect this object your best plan appears to Mr. Hardy to be to tell of such a number of discreet men in your Force as you may deem advisable, whose sole business shall be, for the present, to Watch the Irish Population and to report to you any information they may obtain of suspicious movements or Persons, which information they will, of course report to this Office. Strict orders must be given to the Police so employed to keep secret all such information.

It will be for you to see that this duty is assigned only to your most intelligent and trustworthy Men, and to take care that it is conducted in such a manner as, if possible, not to attract the attention of the Suspected Persons.

This communication is for your guidance, but not meant

for publication, which would, in fact, tend to defeat its object, and Mr. Hardy therefore requests that you will act upon it without making any Public reference to it.'

It was addressed to the Chief Constable of Salop, and signed by James Fergusson.

At Wellington, there were numerous rumours that the Irish there, were contemplating a disturbance. A report circulated that a top man of the Fenian brotherhood had visited the town, for the purpose of swearing in volunteers for the Fenian army, and that he had administered the oath to something like 300 Irishmen. In actual fact there was nothing like that number of able-bodied Irishmen in the town of Wellington.

At Shrewsbury a vast number of special constables were in the process of being sworn in. By the 15 January 1868, some 800 specials had been sworn, a month later the number had swollen to 1,105. The terms of service was to be three months.

The Catholic inhabitants of Shrewsbury held a meeting in the School-room of the Catholic Chapel, for the purpose of expressing their loyalty to the throne, and their detestation of Fenianism. The outcome of this meeting was a deputation, to the Mayor of Shrewsbury, bearing an address, signed by nearly 200 Irishmen and Catholics, a large number of whom had already been sworn as special constables. Cutlasses were dealt out to the Shrewsbury Borough Police, who exercised the use of them in the Quarry, to the consternation and alarm of the more nervous of the inhabitants. Bridgnorth Corporation agreed to three cutlasses being ordered for the borough police, and a six-chambered revolver, for the use of John Cole, the Chief Constable.

Oswestry swore in 60 special constables, including the Mayor, George James Saunders, who acted as their superintendent.

By the early part of February the total number of special constables sworn in for the whole country was 113,674, of whom 52,974 were in London, and the remainder 60,700 in the provinces. The mere fact that so many special constables came forward, made it highly improbable, that any of them would have been called upon to do any real duty at all. However the effect of such overwhelming numbers was to stun the plotters into awe. They lost heart, courage, and determination, and were filled with an anxiety to disown all complication in the outrages which had been committed. By April the panic was over, and the vast number of special constables were able to stand down.

The Ludlow borough police were to change their image in January 1868. The public were now to see them with the new felt helmets, a great change to the old top-hats which had been formerly worn. The change had been brought about by a suggestion of H.M. Inspector of Constabulary. The badges for the new helmets were supplied by Messrs. Dowler of Birmingham.

It was noted in 1869 that the 'practice of running bicycles through the streets' had become very prevalent at Shrewsbury. A serious accident had happened in the Abbey Foregate, in consequence of a horse being frightened by a passing cyclist. At Wolverhampton, several persons had been fined, as it was an offence against the bye-laws of that town to run bicycles through the town. There was no bye-law as such, at Shrewsbury to curb this menace. Poor horses, they had yet to meet the motor car.

The year closed with the Bridgnorth Watch Committee finally allowing a constable to be stationed at Quatford. The inhabitants of Quatford and Quatt Jervis had for several years applied for a constable to be stationed between those places 'for their protection and security.' They had even sent a memorial to the Secretary of State, and now at long last their prayer was granted.

Chapter Five

1870 — 1879

During the 1870's the spirit of radicalism was rampant. To quote Trevelyan's picturesque language —

'Democracy, bureaucracy, collectivism are all advancing like a silent tide making in by a hundred creeks and inlets.'

But it was typical of the cautious attitude long adopted towards police reform that it alone should languish until the reform of local government was undertaken in the next decade. In 1874 it was decided by the government to increase the exchequer grant towards the cost of all forces from one quarter to one half of the cost of clothing and pay. In the following year a Select Committee on Police Superannuation was brought into being. But in general it was a time when police history and reform moved very slowly.

In Shropshire there was a growing strain between the county magistrates on the one hand and the Chief Constable and the Government Inspector on the other. Many of the Inspector's ideas to improve the efficiency of the force were rejected year after year by the county magistrates. The county force at this time consisted of 117 men, which was 19 men short of the authorised strength of 136. The Chief Constable mentions in his report of 26 Dec: 1872 —

'I have to report that the strength of the police force in the borough of Oswestry is inadequate to the duties required, and that the constables are overtasked, have not sufficient intervals of rest, and are therefore not so efficient as they ought to be.'[1]

The force was one of the weakest in the Midlands, and, after talks with the Government Inspector (Lt.-Col: Cobbe) it was agreed to add 14 men to the strength of the force. Many of the magistrates were openly hostile to such increments of men, forced upon them through fear that refusal might endanger the government grant. In 1872 the well attended Easter Sessions had its mood expressed very pungently by John Bather, who declared 'that it was beneath the dignity of gentlemen to meet and have the management of the police and. . . . to be bribed over by a government inspector. . . to go beyond our right judgment'. The agreed increase of 14 men was not recruited until April 1875, and so in 1874 the Government Inspector once again reported the county force insufficient in numbers. It was not until 1875 that the county magistrates could persuade the Home Secretary to authorise the government grant for 1873-4.

At the October Sessions 1873, the pay of 2nd class constables was increased, in the hope that such a step would bring in more recruits. Recruiting was a chronic worry, the neighbouring county forces all had a higher scale of pay. Shropshire had become the Cinderella of the Midland forces. Recruiting had become so bad that in 1874 bounty money was being paid, under the name of 'Bringing in Money'. Ten shillings was paid to any officer bringing in a suitable recruit. Also an increase of pay was to be granted after seven years service, although this would be of little interest to a new recruit.

The problems of the undermanned force in the 1860's and early 1870's, were further aggravated by the build up of extra duties assigned to the police, by both the magistrates and the government, though the Home Office kept a check on these, and sometimes prohibited them. After 1875 the main difficulty, the recruiting problem, appears to have eased off.

The image of the constables of Shropshire was greatly changed at the turn of the decade, when they exchanged their tall top-hats for cloth helmets. Ludlow led the way by making the change in 1868, followed by the county constabulary late in 1869. The following year it was the turn of the

90

Shrewsbury Borough Police. Late in the autumn of 1870, Bridgnorth Borough Police decided to follow suit, and so the last constables in the county reluctantly put away the headgear which had so distinguished their calling for near on half a century. For awhile longer the county superintendents remained dignified in their tall, silk top-hats.

The Chief Constable of Shrewsbury, John Hughes, resigned his post in May 1870. He had been a member of the borough police force since 1846, and had held the rank of chief constable for 15 years. His long period of office had been noted as one councillor remarked —

'by the careful and conciliatory way in which he had discharged his duties to the public, and by the considerate and efficient manner in which he had controlled the police force, and maintained good discipline among the men'.[2]

His successor was chosen from amongst the ranks of the force. Sergeant John Davies, a native of Welshpool, who had been a member of the force for nineteen years, during fifteen of which he had held the rank of sergeant.

A brave and meritorious act was brought to the attention of the Court of Quarter Sessions by the County Chief Constable. It had taken place on the ninth April 1872, when P.C. Michael Leader was taking two prisoners by the Severn Valley Railway to Shrewsbury. Shortly after leaving Ironbridge station one of the prisoners, Henry Norton, managed to slip out of his handcuffs. Quickly opening the door nearest to him, he jumped out of the train. The constable immediately jumped after him, and once more secured his prisoner. This brave action took place on the river side of a viaduct half a mile from Ironbridge. Both prisoner and constable had jumped at the risk of their lives. It is a nice thought that Constable Michael Leader received a gratuity in money for his act of bravery.

Photography had been first adapted to police purposes in 1854, when the governor of Bristol Gaol began to make daguerreotype photographs of the prisoners who passed through his hands. Gradually what had been at first but the experimental hobby of an amateur developed into the officially recognised system. A circular letter was sent out from the Home Office early in 1870, to all county and borough police authorities. The Home secretary requesting that the Commissioner of the Metropolitan Police be furnished with photographic likenesses of all habitual criminals convicted within their jurisdictions. At Bridgnorth the corporation instructed Chief Constable Cole to obtain photographs of such persons convicted within the borough, and to transmit them in accordance with the request of the Home Secretary. At Ludlow the borough police employed the artistry of Thomas Jones, a local photographer, to take their mug shots. At county level we read that the Home Secretary's request was referred to the consideration of the Police Committee and the visiting justices of the prison. This great step forward in the nation wide recognition of habitual criminals came about through the passing of the 'Habitual Criminals Act'.

The Bridgnorth Watch Committee drew up a very clever plan in 1870, whereby they worked out that they could employ five policemen at a less cost than the current cost of the force, which consisted of only three officers.

It had all come about through correspondence with Colonel Cobbe, the Inspector of Constabulary. The Colonel had emphatically stated that he could not certify the Borough as deserving the police grant unless they increased their establishment to six men. A meeting between Cobbe and the Bridgnorth Watch Committee was held, at which the Colonel was persuaded to agree to five officers being sufficient for the borough establishment — so long as the population did not exceed the numbers taken at the census return of 1861. The Bridgnorth Watch Committee then outlined their financial juggling trick to the members of the Corporation —

'Present cost of three Police Officers.

Wages.	Chief Constable	78. 0. 0.
Wages.	Police Constable No. 1.	52. 0. 0.
Wages.	Police Constable No. 2.	52. 0. 0.
		182. 0. 0.

Clothing.		19. 2. 0.
Rent of Cottage		8. 0. 0.
Present cost of three Policemen.		209. 2. 0.
Annual cost of four Police Officers.		
Three as above.		209. 2. 0.
Wages of a fourth.	52. 0. 0.	
Clothing for do.	5. 3. 0.	
Cottage for do.	8. 0. 0.	
		65. 3. 0.
		274. 5. 0.
Annual cost of five Police Officers.		
Four as above.	274. 5. 0.	
A fifth as above.	65. 3. 0.	
		339. 8. 0.
Deduct Government allowance.		84. 17. 0.
		254. 11. 0.
Deduct cost of Special Constables (		
(		25. 1. 4.
on an average of ten years. (		
		229. 9. 8.
Deduct wages of Inspector of Nuisances (		
(		
it being proposed to appoint a Police (		
(		20. 16. 0.
man to perform those duties. (		
Net cost of Five Policemen.		£.208. 13. 8.'[3]

As can easily be seen from the above statement the Watch Committee could propose two extra constables on the borough establishment, and yet save eight shillings and four-pence per year on the cost. This brilliant proposal was, need-less to say, adopted by the Bridgnorth Corporation.

The following month (October) the Bridgnorth Watch Committee appointed Edward Purchase of Clun, a former constable of the Shropshire Constabulary, and Thomas Tompkins of Bridgnorth, as constables No. 3 and 4 of their borough police force. Tompkins was required to perform the duties of Inspector of Nuisances, slaughter-houses and water supply, which had formerly been attended to by Edward Webb, as Inspector of Nuisances.   Webb was now made redundant.

At Shrewsbury it was decided by the Watch Committee to close down the branch police stations situated at —Coleham, Castle-Foregate, and the Quarry Lodge.   Though the latter was still retained as a police-house.

The miles that the victorian constables covered on foot whilst tracing criminals, was to say the least, phenomenal.   An incident which illustrates this point ideally, was that of an aggravated felony, which was committed by a Thomas Jones, of Bromfield, on the 22 October 1871.

Information of the felony did not reach Sergeant Lear of the county constabulary until the following afternoon.   He at once proceeded to investigate the case.   At first no clue as to the perpetrator could be found.   House to house enquiries led him to believe that Thomas Jones could be the culprit.   Lear traced Jones to Whettleton Common (Stokesay), where he caught and charged him on the morning of the 27th.   It was estimated that Sergeant Lear must have walked upwards of one hundred miles during the investigation and chase, during the greater part of which it had rained heavily.   The stalwart sergeant was rewarded with the sum of three pounds from the Police Rate for his perseverence.

Such feats of walking were all part of the job.   Early in the following year yet another constable, this time in the north of the county, showed his mettle.   On March 30th a ham was stolen from William Overton of Higginswood, Moreton Say. Constable Richard Bradshaw of the Shropshire Constabulary, based on Market-Drayton, traced the culprit to Whitchurch. There he found that the ham had been sold for 10s. 6d. on the same day.   Still walking and making enquiries, Bradshaw followed the culprit to Wrexham, where he caught him, on the 1st of April.   The constable then marched his prisoner all the way back to Whitchurch.   It was there that one or the other of them, or perhaps both, being too tired to walk any further, the remainder of the journey — Whitchurch to Market-Drayton was completed by train.

Councillor McMichael speaking at a Bridgnorth Council Meeting, in September 1872, showed great concern as to the state of the Town Hall. He disapproved strongly of the habit of the borough police drilling within its walls. He pointed out that the vibration caused by these stalwart constables, during their drills, was causing the plaster to fall down. This brings to mind a mental picture which would surely be a gift to a contemporary cartoonist.

General Elections were always an excuse for rioting, which resulted in a great deal of damage being done to the public and their property. Colonel Edgell, as Chief Constable of Shropshire, decided to take a strong stand against such lawlessness. Edgell issued on the 7 November 1874, Order No. 187. This order dealt with the forthcoming election of a member of parliament to represent the Borough of Wenlock. It was a comprehensive document ordering the movement of the majority of the force from every police division in the county, to the Wenlock area. All sergeants and constables of the 'A' Division (not having cases at the Albrighton Petty Sessions) were to proceed by the 11.0 a.m. train to Ironbridge on the 12th instant, the remaining portion of the division, including Superintendent Caswell to follow on the 3.30 p.m. train on the same day. This division was to be stationed in reserve at the police station, Ironbridge, under the orders of Chief Superintendent Richardson.

Of 'B' Division, one sergeant and three constables were to remain on duty at Oswestry, and one constable in charge of the lock-up at Ellesmere. The rest of the division was to proceed by the 6.55 p.m. train on Wednesday the 11th, from Shrewsbury to Ironbridge, and thence to Broseley, where Superintendent Gough would take the polling duties on Thursday, with his division.

The orders for 'C' Division were — all sergeants and constables not having cases at Whitchurch Petty Sessions on the 13th, to proceed by the 11.0 a.m. train from Shrewsbury on the 12th. (Thursday) to Much Wenlock, and remain in reserve at the police station under the orders of Superintendent Ivins. One constable to be left in charge of Wem lock-up, and one in charge of the lock-up at Market-Drayton. 'D' Division were to take the polling duties at Coalbrookdale, Ironbridge and Madeley. Constables to be left in charge of the police stations at Newport, Shifnal and Wellington.

'E' Division were delegated to take the polling duties at Much Wenlock and Ditton Priors. One constable to be left in charge of Cleobury Mortimer lock-up. All sergeants and constables of 'F' Division were to proceed by the 9.0 a.m. and 11.25 a.m. trains on the Thursday, from Craven Arms to Much Wenlock, and remain in reserve at the police station. One constable to be left in charge of the lock-up at Bishops Castle, and one constable to remain with Superintendent Baxter at Church Stretton.

Needless to say, with all these military operations, swamping the area with manpower, the election passed off quite peacefully. Colonel Edgell had shown any would be rioters that he had the strength, and would use it, should they want to try anything. It was the first time that this type of order showing the movement of all the police divisions had been issued.

There passed away at Bridgnorth, on the 17 November 1873, Richard Evans, aged 77. He had been for a number of years landlord of the Bell and Talbot Inn. Although he would be better remembered as the Chief Constable of the Bridgnorth Borough Police Force, for the years 1841 to 1850. It was due to this man that the amalgamation between the Bridgnorth borough police force and the County Constabulary was delayed in 1850. It will be recalled that Bridgnorth corporation wanted the county to accept him into their force, but Mayne refused him, on the grounds that he could neither read nor write sufficiently.

The Shrewsbury Borough Police were having a rough time of it in 1875. It had become so bad in the suburb of Coleham, that Chief Constable Davies considered it too dangerous to send a single constable there, to walk the beat alone. It was necessary for their safety to walk the beat in pairs. Even then, on one occasion Constable Jesse Wilkinson had been knocked down, and kicked several times on the head. Assaults of a very brutal nature were made regularly upon the members of the local force. The press wrote strongly against this barbaric treatment meted out to those who stood for law and order. —

'It would seem as if the magistrates in some places did not become aware of the fact that a policeman is flesh and blood until an unfortunate policeman is kicked to death. They appear to be under the impression that he is helmet, buttons, blue-cloth, handcuffs and truncheon!

This is scarecely as things should be. We know that policemen have their weaknesses. Clothe them never so bluely like other sons of Adam they will do a surreptitious beer on their beats, but as a rule they do their work well, for very little pay, and they deserve protection from brutes who seem to think that kicking a policeman until he is nearly dead is legitimate sport. We are sorry to find from our police records, and the statement of the Chief Constable, that these assaults are so common in this town, and we are glad to hear that the magistrates are determined to protect the police. We do not, however, think that fines of 10s. 0d. or £1.0.0. will deter men who do such things. Ruffians deserve a lengthy acquaintance with the accelerated movements of the tread-mill'.[4]

Chief Superintendent John Richardson decided to retire in January 1876. A native of Pulford, Cheshire, he had served with the Shropshire Constabulary since 1842. His length of service included 23 years as superintendent of the Wellington Division, and 12 years as Deputy Chief-Constable. His total service amounted to 33 years 8 months. Colonel Edgell spoke very highly of his deputy, remarking that his division had been unsurpassed in intelligence, and readiness of action. This he put down to the ever watchful and untiring supervision of their superintendent. Credit was also given to Richardson for the way the police held the confidence of the public, in the populous and important part of the county, in which the division served.

Richardson was succeeded as Deputy Chief-Constable by Superintendent Joseph Ivins, a native of Chepstow, who had been with the force since 1859.

It had become necessary by 1877, to allot an additional constable to keep the peace at Oswestry. This called for a revision of the agreement of 1861, between the county and the Oswestry borough council. The new agreement, dated 30 October 1877, followed much the same lines as the previous one of 1861, but with a new clause to include the extra constable.

The years 1877 and 1878 saw many retirements from the county force. The hard life, out in all weathers, took its toll of the older members. Constable John Pierce retired after 33 years 7 months, he was in his 66th year. Constable William Martin was superannuated at the age of 56, having served 23 years one month, — 'incapacitated infirmity of mind and body'. Constable Arthur Passant whose illness was caused by jumping into the river in pursuit of a prisoner, died at Hodnet. Sergeant John Hayward was recommended for super-annuation, he was — 'incapacitated owing to attacks of rheumatic fever resulting from exposure in the performance of his duties'. Constable Andrew Moran recommended for super-annuation — 'by infirmity'. He had served eleven and a half years with the Revenue Police in Ireland previous to his twenty years with the Shropshire Constabulary.

Constable John Chase was given a temporary super-annuation 'because of Infirmity'. Chase had served six and threequarter years in the Wiltshire Constabulary before serving sixteen years in Salop. Sergeant William Collis — 'incapacitated', after ten months in the Flintshire Constabulary, one year in the Cheshire Force, and seventeen years in the Shropshire Constabulary. It was a very hard life, for very poor pay.

W.S. Gilbert did not exaggerate the truth about the Victorian policeman, when he wrote that much quoted refrain in the Pirates of Penzance —

'A policeman's lot is not a happy one'.

The policeman devoted himself to a way of life, that made great demands upon his health, unceasing hard work acquitted under conditions of rigid discipline. All this in exchange for a weekly pay packet that left him, and specifically the married constable with a family, near the bread line.

His wage at the level of an unskilled agricultural worker, a constable put in a seven day week. His average day's duty would be ten or twelve hours, generally performed in two shifts, the longer — up to seven hours — at night. It could be longer. His patrolling would be done on foot, men would tramp upwards of twenty miles a day for continuous weeks at a time. Apart from this arduous duty he was the target for all types of brutal attack, and abuse. Previous to 1887, he was not even allowed to vote in parliamentary elections. The Police Federation had yet to be formed. There was no one to protect his interests.

Keeping a close watch on public houses, and those drinking in them could be quite an exercise in itself. In 1879 the report of Colonel Cobbe, H.M. Inspector of Constabulary shows that the area policed by the Shropshire Constabulary contained 1,015 licensed houses, to control which, the county force had a total strength of 137 men. The Bridgnorth Borough Force of five men had to watch 59 licensed premises, whilst Ludlow was a little better off, with only 47 licensed houses for their five men to oversee. Shrewsbury as a larger town had a force of twenty-five men to control the 191 licensed houses scattered through its streets. It was from these numerous inns and beerhouses that the drunken brawls emanated, brawls that so often maimed the police officers trying, sometimes vainly, to keep the Queen's Peace.

A singular and daring escape was effected in 1879, from the Bridgnorth lock-up. A youth of 18 years of age, named William Jones alias Green, had been committed to the County Gaol, at Shrewsbury, for 14 days. At the end of his time, he had been released, only to find Constable Thomas Tompkins of the Bridgnorth Borough Police waiting for him. Tompkins apprehended Jones on a charge of stealing a suit of clothes from a Bridgnorth shop. The officer brought his prisoner back to Bridgnorth by train. Once there he was lodged, safely it was thought, in the lock-up. As it was daytime he was allowed the use of the yard. The lock-up keeper visiting the cells at 4.0 p.m. discovered, to his consternation that his young prisoner had escaped. From an examination of the premises, it would seem that Jones had, with great ingenuity, pulled out a large nail from the closet wall, which in turn he had used to take out one of the bars of a fire-grate in his cell.

With these crude tools the prisoner had made a hole through the 14 inch thick outer wall of the prison. He had carefully selected a place where the wall had been joined without the bricks being tied. After, no doubt, a considerable amount of labour, he had succeeded in pulling out sufficient bricks to make an aperture about 15 inches by 12 inches, through which he had squeezed his body. He had fully an hour's start before being missed, and succeeded in getting clear away. A reward was posted, of two pounds for his apprehension; and a description of his appearance and clothing given; but the police saw no more of him until the following night, when for reasons best known to himself, he gave himself up.

Chapter Six

1880 — 1889

It was at the Shrewsbury Race Meeting held in November 1880, that a truly incredible scene was witnessed by crowds of cheering punters. The story concerns Constable Richard Williams of the Shrewsbury Borough Police Force, and that jockey of immortal memory, Fred Archer. The latter, who was known as 'The Tinman' was noted for his wonderful record of 246 wins in one season. Here at Shrewsbury he was very nearly beaten by Richard Williams. On the first day of the race meeting, six constables (including Richard Williams) were chosen for mounted duty on the race course. A cavalcade of the six constables, led by the Chief Constable of Shrewsbury (John Davies) set out from the old market-place to the race course. Davies was mounted on a thoroughbred race-horse, which had been loaned to him by a sporting gentleman. To his embarrassment he had great difficulty in controlling his nervous mount, and on arriving at the race course exchanged horses with Richard Williams. The constable was ordered to take up a position near to the starting post. Fred Archer and the other three riders cantered up the course ready for the first race of the day, and Williams had the greatest difficulty in controlling his horse. He wanted to be off with them. The flag dropped for the start of the race, and as the riders galloped past Williams, his horse took control and dashed off amongst them. Soon two riders were left behind, and then a third was passed. Fred Archer and Williams were the only two riders in the race. Side by side they galloped together, passing the grandstand the crowd of

101

"Fred Archer & Constable Richard Williams Neck & Neck at the Shrewsbury Races, 1880"

more than a thousand, commenced shouting —

'10 to 1, 50 to 1, then 100 to 1 on the bobby.'

Neck and neck they passed the winning post, with Fred. Archer barely in front. When it is considered that Williams was wearing his heavy winter overcoat and leggings, helmet etc., as against Fred. Archer's light racing clothes, it was an incredible feat of racing. For many years after Richard Williams was known as the policeman jockey, and he remained on very friendly terms with Archer for several years. Richard Williams left the Shrewsbury Police Force in 1887, and joined the Burnley Borough Police, in which he served until 1913, retiring with the rank of chief inspector.

The tenders for clothing the Shropshire Constabulary in 1881 are most useful in bringing to life a picture of what the officers looked like.

The superintendents wore Frock-coats of rifle-green colour, with gold embossed crowns on the collars, strapped trousers of the same rifle-green colour; great coats of Oxford-grey, and silk top-hats. Constables and sergeants wore similar Frock-coats with breast-badges. Sergeants also wore three bar chevrons of gold lace. For sergeants and constables the head-gear consisted of cork helmets (Metropolitan shape) covered in rifle-green cloth. The whole conjures up a picture of neat smartness. The gold embossed crowns and gold lace chevrons would appear most effective on the dark background of the rifle-green cloth.

The Chief Constable of Shrewsbury, John Davies, tendered his resignation on the 7 May 1881. Which set the Watch Committee the task of choosing a successor. It had long been the custom of the county to choose a military man for their force, but it would seem that there was those of the inhabitants of Shrewsbury who did not approve of military men being offered the post of Chief Constable of the county town. A letter appeared on this subject in the Shropshire Journal.

'Sir, — I see by the newspaper reports that Shrewsbury is about to appoint a new Chief Constable, and it has been rumoured that some of the gentlemen who have the selection

P.C.29. George Williams. 1880
Shropshire Constabulary

of that officer are in favour of electing a military man, and that is my excuse for endeavouring to point out such an inconsistancy.

Whether a vacancy occurs in the governorship of a gaol or the chief constableship of a borough a host of Militia and half — pay officers (on the lookout for comfortable berths) offer themselves as candidates.

An impression seems to prevail among some persons that a military title is a proof of a sound and liberal education, and of administrative abilities of an exceptional order. I feel I do not err in saying that the idea is somewhat erroneous, and those gentlemen, when appointed, are occasionally found incapable of discharging the duties of their office.

It is unreasonable to expect from military officers the ability to perform duties of which they are perfectly ignorant, and such men, when once in office, are for years dependent upon one or two of their subordinates. I venture to ask can any army officer make a better Superintendent of Police than one who has had the advantage of a thorough practical training in the detection and prevention of crime?

Who ever heard of a soldier being sent to sea in command of a ship, or a sailor to take a battalion of soldiers into the field?

Even this would not be more absurd than some of the appointments which have been made of late years. Unfortunately for the military element it is generally admitted that old soldiers, even in the rank and file, seldom or never make good police officers, and there are military chief constables who will not employ, or recommend for employments, a discharged soldier. Apart from other considerations it is obvious that the highest commands and advantages in the police service should be given to officers who have displayed the greatest skill and energy in their profession, and other policy must and does destroy whatever laudable ambition exists in the ranks; it retards promotion and discourages those most deeply concerned. It is sometimes argued that soldiers are essential to maintain discipline and drill. A more erroneous impression could not get abroad, as their training specially unfits them for the police service. Soldiers are called upon to act collectively; policemen act individually. If it becomes a question of mere drill police sergeants are plentiful enough, at 30s. a week, who would drill the men as efficiently as any half-pay officer.

I hope, for the protection of the ratepayers and benefit of the police force, that these few remarks will have sound weight in the proper quarter, and that an experienced police officer will be appointed Chief Constable whose practical experience will enable him to cope satisfactorily with the law-breakers.

I am, Sir, your obedient servant, PRO BONO PUBLICO.'[1]

This letter, greatly to the point with its sound reasoning, would no doubt make the county chief constable (Colonel Cureton), himself a military man, raise his eyebrows. It certainly influenced the members of the Shrewsbury Watch Committee who were selecting the new borough chief of police.

The short list of three were all men of previous police experience. The appointment went to Joseph Harrop, Inspector and Chief Clerk of the Middlesborough Police Force.

Shropshire Chief Constable, Richard Edgell had a pleasant duty to perform in May 1882, when he promoted 2nd Class Constable Frederick Beckett to 1st Class Constable. This was not an everyday case of promotion, for Beckett had been upgraded with pay, as a reward for bravery and attention to duty. Beckett, in company with Constable Ledbury of the Staffordshire Constabulary, had followed up, and identified a gang of six armed poachers, despite the fact that they were constantly stoned and threatened with fire-arms. Bravery in this case had its reward.

A request was received, in May 1882, from the Chief Constable of Denbighshire, Major Leadbetter, for police assistance at Wrexham. A collier's strike had taken place, and great violence was feared. The Chief Constable of Shropshire quickly despatched Chief Superintendent Ivins with forty constables, to the trouble spot. The expected rioting did not take place, allowing the Shropshire contingent of police to return to their respective stations the following evening.

106

It was in the same year, 1882, that the Shrewsbury Corporation made the shrewd move of purchasing a piece of land to the rear of the 'Coach and Horses', on Swan Hill. The idea being to erect at some time in the future, a borough police station on the site. It was most appropriate that the land should have long borne the name of 'Scotland Yard'. However, it was not until 1900 that the new police station was built, and the move made from the old premises at the old Talbot Inn site.

The Shrewsbury Corps of the Salvation Army was inaugurated in the month of January 1884. The army was at first viewed with suspicion by the town council. The Watch Committee promptly instructing Chief Constable Harrop to issue a handbill giving notice —

'that for the future no crowd will be allowed to congregate in connection with this movement, and that all persons standing about and causing an obstruction will be summoned before the magistrates'[2].

This was no idle threat, as fifteen persons soon found out, when they were fined one shilling each and costs by the magistrates.

Constables of the Shrewsbury Borough Force were required to march with the Salvation Army whenever it held meetings, or marched about the town. Tensions relaxed somewhat in the following month, but the Chief Constable was still instructed 'to take all due precautions for the preservation of the public peace'. The order for constables to march with the Army was rescinded, although it was thought wise to keep a small reserve of men at the police station, in case of emergency.

The many changes of headgear of the Shrewsbury Police, must have mystified the inhabitants of Shrewsbury in the 1880's.

In 1883 sergeants were issued with helmets in lieu of hats, and stripes were ordered to be worn on the left arm of their coats instead of the double row of buttons as previously worn. The following year the sergeants had the metal on their

107

helmets laquered gold.   1885 the purchase of helmets was postponed until the Chief Constable obtained samples of helmets with chain and spike.   A new die was ordered for bulge buttons, which were to be silvered to match the metal-work of the helmets.

Another change of headgear came about in 1886 — caps were supplied instead of helmets.   Sergeant's caps to be trimmed with mohair.   Then in 1887 helmets were back in vogue, when they appeared with silver fittings, with a round knob substituted for the spike.

The Shropshire Constabulary were not to be outdone by the Shrewsbury police, and started to alter their image.   The superintendents lost their dignified silk top-hats in 1886, and green cloth caps were substituted.   The caps (when not in use) were kept in oilskin cases.   Serge jackets for summer wear, were supplied to the force in 1887.   It was late in 1887 when the whole appearance of the county force underwent a change. After forty years of wearing their distinctive rifle-green uniforms, it was decided to change the colour to blue, no doubt to comply with other forces.   The old style frock-coats now became a thing of the past, tunics being the modern style. The only familiar remnant of the old uniform was the Oxford-grey overcoat.   The superintendent's caps, now blue, and with peaks before and behind, had a badge in bronze of the county arms placed in front.

Bridgnorth's Chief Constable, John Cole resigned on the 6 October 1887, having held office since 1857.   His journal for the period 1860 — 1867 is a fascinating record.   He writes in it of the day that Bridgnorth celebrated the marriage of the Prince of Wales with the Princess Alexander of Denmark. Under the date 10 March 1863 he notes that he was on contin-ual duty from 7.0 a.m. in the morning to 3.0 a.m. the following morning.

'The Town was very gay with lights and all the men had a good dinner of Roast Beef and Plumb Pudding and a quart of Ale each.   The women had a good tea and Punch after.

It all passed off very quiet and orderly'.

Cole's successor was Sergeant Charles Childs of the Leominster Borough Police Force, with eighteen years experience of police work in five different forces.

Originally the Shropshire County Constabulary had been divided into six divisions, but later in 1858, an extra division had been created to include the territory surrounding Shrewsbury as a Headquarter Division. Now in 1887, a further division was established, making eight divisions in all. As from the 8 February 1887 the county force was divided as follows —

'A' Shrewsbury (Headquarters)
'B' Oswestry.
'C' Whitchurch.
'D' Wellington.
'E' Bridgnorth (excluding the borough)
'F' Church Stretton.
'G' Pontesbury.
'H' Burford. (excluding Ludlow borough)

This re-arrangement of the divisions called for two additional appointments of superintendents — Robert Straffen and John Simcox, who were put in charge of the divisions of Pontesbury and Burford.

In 1885, Superintendent George Gough had replaced Superintendent Joseph Ivins as deputy chief constable. In 1887, George Gough retired after serving 37 years with the county constabulary. A native of Shrewsbury, he had been appointed to the force in 1850, an ex-army man from the 14th Light Dragoons. In turn he was replaced by Superintendent William Galliers, who had joined the force in 1859.

It is interesting to note that for the period 1879 to 1888 inclusive, 144 recruits were enlisted into the county constabulary, all of whom, without exception, were single men. One wonders if it was the chief constable's policy at that time, not to employ married men.

A political meeting was held on the 27 November 1885, at the Corbet Arms Hotel, Market-Drayton. Prior to the meeting it was expected that a breach of the peace would take place.

It was therefore pointed out to the County Chief Constable that it would be well for him to recollect the composition of a Market-Drayton mob; and the serious disturbances that had taken place in that town some twenty years previously, which had only been quelled by bringing in the military.

Colonel Edgell appears to have ignored the warning, for no movement of extra police to the area is recorded.

The meeting took place in the evening, and from the moment it commenced, the yard at the back of the hotel, as well as the street, was filled by an unruly mob of people. The crowd kept up an uproar of noise for the whole duration of the meeting. When it came to a close, those inside were too frightened to emerge and face the fury of the mob. One farmer attempted to leave, but as soon as he opened the door leading into the yard, he received a stone full in the face, which broke several of his teeth. Lord Newport and Sir Robert Peel were warned not to leave the hotel, such was the fury of the mob, aggravated by the total absence of the police. Lord Newport managed to smuggle a messenger out, who promptly made his way to the police station, to request police assistance. But despite the fact that the police station was only five minutes walk from the hotel, the police did not put in an appearance until nearly and hour had passed.

What Sir Robert Peel, as son of the founder of the police system, thought of this sluggish reaction to a call for assistance, one shudders to think. Eventually Reginald Corbett, chairman of the Petty Sessional Division of Market-Drayton, and his son made a break for it, accompanied by a strong escort of friends. The party was hooted and pelted with mud and stones for nearly half a mile. The whole town by now was in an uproar.

A fly waiting for newspaper reporters was seriously damaged; and in fact would have been demolished, had not a sturdy helper from the hotel intervened. Two harmless farmers returning home in a gig, were waylaid and stoned, and their horse, a restive mare, struck with sticks, so that she bolted.

A strict enquiry was called for by the magistracy and townsfolk of Market-Drayton, who very rightly wanted to know why the police had held back, and had not come when called. They made known their desire that those culpable of so gross a dereliction of duty should be severely dealt with. The police files are oddly silent on this embarrassing point.

The superintendent of the Ludlow Borough Police Force, George Henry Brookes, resigned in 1885. He had been a member of the force since 1865. As its superintendent he had carried out the additional posts and duties of —

Inspector of Weights and Measures, at £10 per annum.

Inspector of Common Lodging Houses. No salary.

Billet Master. No salary.

Inspector of Contagious Diseases (Animals) No salary.

Superintendent of the Ludlow Fire Brigade at £8 per annum.

His successor was Sergeant James Cowmeadow Wheatstone, who had first joined the Ludlow Force in 1865, the same year as his predecessor. His wage was fixed at thirty-three shillings per week. Promotions then followed. Acting Sergeant George Higgins was promoted to full sergeant. Constable Thomas Higgins became acting sergeant. This left a vacancy for another constable. The man chosen was George Bluck, late a constable of the Herefordshire Constabulary, who was later to become a superintendent in the Shropshire Constabulary.

Bare-fist fighting was still a popular sport, although the police were bound by law to stop these illegal fights. Early in January 1886, information reached the police authorities at Shrewsbury and Wolverhampton, that a prize fight of a most determined character was taking place near Albrighton. At an early hour in the morning about 100 persons had reached that quiet Shropshire village. They selected a secluded place on the outskirts, where some of them proceeded to make a ring with ropes and stakes. The necessary preliminaries having been settled, two men named Perkins and Smith, both hailing from Oldbury, entered the

111

ring with their seconds, and soon got to work with 'nature's weapons'. At this point a number of police officers put in an appearance, with the result that the crowd including the principals, scattered, leaving the ropes and stakes in the hands of the guardians of the law, who thinking that the sporting fraternity would not dare to renew the fight, did not bother to follow them.

The pugilists and their fans, instead of leaving the district, proceeded to Beckbury, situated some four miles from Albrighton, and there the 'mill' was recommenced without ropes and stakes. Both men displayed extraordinary stamina and pluck. Altogether it is stated that forty-seven rounds were fought, the contest lasting nearly two hours.

At an early stage of the fight Perkins dealt his antagonist a terrific blow to the face, which fractured his jaw, but notwithstanding his injury, he continued with the fight, and in the sixteenth round completely disabled one of Perkin's arms, who carried on the battle to the end with only one hand. Both men were badly injured, the contest resulting in a draw. The punishment received by Smith would seem to have been of a serious character, as it was deemed unwise to remove him from the neighbourhood, but Perkins was able to proceed home. The news was flashed to Shrewsbury of the recommencement of the fight, and within the hour, a detachment of eight constables led by Sergeant Davies, proceeded to the spot. From there they spread out to the nearest railway stations, to which a message regarding their errand had been telegraphed. Too late, the sporting fraternity had moved quickly over the county border, and the constables failed to get a scent of the party. The constables returned to Shrewsbury empty handed. Most of these fights (being illegal) were highly organised, and the venues were chosen with great skill and secrecy. Places were chosen for their seclusion, generally near to a county border. It was a battle of wits, the organizers against the county constabulary.

It was to the great regret of the Mayor and the Watch Committee of Shrewsbury, that Joseph Harrop tendered his resignation as Chief Constable of the Borough, on the 25 May 1887. Harrop had successfully applied for the post of Chief Constable of the newly established Burnley Borough Police Force.

It speaks well of Harrop's popularity with the rank and file of the Shrewsbury Police Force, that three constables, including Richard Williams, of horse racing fame, all resigned to follow him to the new force.

His successor was Superintendent George William Whitfield, a police officer of great experience, who had come from the Monmouthsire Constabulary.

It was soon after his appointment that the Watch Committee decided that their chief constable should be dressed in uniform. Previous to this date the chief constables of Shrewsbury had not been issued with any distinguishing uniform.

The following year (1888) Whitfield made a successful application for the post of Chief Constable of the City of York. It had been a short stay.

For the third time in a decade, the Shrewsbury Corporation were faced with having to advertise for applicants for the post of Chief Constable of the Borough. The successful candidate was Henry Blackwell, who had been Chief Constable of the Borough of Newport, Isle of Wight. One of his first acts was to compile a new book of rules for the Shrewsbury Police Force, which by all accounts was badly needed.

Ludlow too, suffered a loss, when Superintendent Wheatstone retired in the October of 1888. His term of office had only lasted three years, his resignation having been forced through ill-health.

His retirement put the Ludlow Corporation in a quandry, for a new Local Government Act was at that time passing through parliament, wherein the borough police would be required to amalgamate with the county force. It was not worth appointing a new superintendent of their own for what promised to be a very short period of time. The only way out of their difficulty was to ask the county chief constable to

113

loan one of his superintendents until the evenutal amalgamation. The outcome was that Superintendent John Simcox, of the Burford Division of the county constabulary, took charge of the Ludlow Borough Police Force, whilst still his own division. The borough superintendent's salary being paid into the county police fund.

It was then found that Simcox would be counted on the strength of the county constabulary, and not on the strength of the borough force, which would leave it one below its authorised strength of five. In the event of an amalgamation, the county would only replace the number of men employed by the borough, at that time. So it was hurriedly proposed by the Ludlow corporation that they should appoint a further constable, to bring up the borough force to its authorised strength.

Herbert William Brookes, of Berkhamstead (the son of a previous borough superintendent) was appointed as constable.

The intention of eliminating the smaller borough police forces had continued to be an item of policy, which survived every change at the helm of the Home Office. Finally in 1888, the chance came with the decision to promote comprehensive legislation to reform local government in the counties, by establishing county councils.

A clause was inserted into the Local Government Act, 1888, abolishing police forces in boroughs with a population under 10,000. Parliament accepted the clause without protest, in fact an amendment was suggested that the population limit should be set at 20,000.

The effect of this bill was to reduce the number of separate forces by forty-eight — from 231 in 1881 to 183 in 1889.

Shropshire was doomed at this time, to lose two of its borough police forces, those of Bridgnorth and Ludlow. Which left Shrewsbury, the county town, the only borough in the county with its own police force.

The amalgamation of the two borough forces with the county constabulary took place on the 16 April 1889. At Bridgnorth, Chief Constable Charles Childs was taken into the

114

county constabulary, with the rank of inspector. He was given a salary of £120 per annum, (twenty pounds more than he had received as Chief Constable of Bridgnorth). Sergeant James Davies with constables John Partridge, Edward Purchase and William Stinton, were also absorbed into the county force.

The Ludlow policemen were also absorbed into the county force — Sergeant Thomas Higgins, who was reduced to constable; Constables George Higgins; Herbert William Brookes; George Bluck, and Thomas Watkins. The latter had been a coffee-house keeper in Ludlow when he joined the borough force in 1879, having then lately returned from Boston in America.

In 1889 the Shropshire Constabulary came under the control of a 'Standing Joint Committee'. Formerly they had been controlled by a 'Police Committee' composed of county magistrates. With the establishment of the county council, it was decided that they should be governed by a joint committee of county councillors and county magistrates, which were to be known as the 'Standing Joint Committee'. The committee's proceedings were not subject to debate by the county council, though it became a practice in Shropshire, for the committee to present formal reports for the county council's information.

Progress in the shape of the telephone came about in March 1889. The Shrewsbury police station was put in telephonic communication with the Turncock's house; by the Western and South Wales Telephone Company, who had set up in business in Shrewsbury some three years previously. It was important that the chief constable, as superintendent of the Borough Fire Brigade, should have a quick means of communication with the Turncock.

With the Shropshire Horticultural Show due to be held on the 21 and 22 August 1889, Henry Blackwell requested the Shrewsbury Watch Committee, to allow him to borrow twenty-five additional sergeants and constables (plus two detectives) from another force. The Watch Committee agreed to the additional strength for the two days of the show, 'but not from the County Constabulary'. The proviso is intriguing. Was there perhaps a rift between the Shrewsbury Watch Committee and the County Standing Joint Committee? or was there some simple reason to explain this unusual provision. At any rate the Chief Constable arranged for the extra men with the Chief Constables of Oldham and Rochdale, who brought a whiff of Lancashire dialect into the town for the two days.

The year 1889 was to finish on a sad note for the county constabulary. Colonel Richard Edgell, Chief Constable of Shropshire, died on 26 of November, of a heart attack. He had held office for twenty-three years. Edgell had been a most able and zealous officer, who had discharged his public dutires faithfully and with military exactitude.

The force under his supervision had always been maintained in a high state of efficiency, and throughout his long tenure as Chief Constable he had, despite the Market Drayton election meeting fiasco, enjoyed the entire confidence of the Police Committee and the county magistrates.

Deputy Chief Constable William Galliers took over command of the county police force, until such time as a new Chief Constable could be appointed.

Chapter Seven

1890 – 1899

The last decade of the nineteenth cenury witnessed a number of innovations within the Shropshire Constabulary. Their new Chief Constable, Captain George Charles Peere Williams-Freeman was an army officer with extensive military police experience. A keen disciplinarian he rapidly had the force running along military lines. Discipline and smartness became the watchword of the Shropshire Constabulary. There were several alterations to their uniforms, and the last link with the old style uniform went in 1890, when the 'Oxford-grey' greatcoats were exchanged for ones of waterproof, blue cloth. Capes were issued of similar cloth, and made to fasten at the collar, with a hook and chain of bronze, decorated with bronze shields, impressed with the county arms. Williams-Freeman decreed that 1st class constables should wear a chevron of yellow braid on their arms, to distinguish them from the second class constables. Within three months he had changed this order to chevrons of gold lace. Helmets were then issued instead of caps, which had formerly been in use.

Cattle rustling was not a crime confined to the Wild West of America. Shropshire farmer's had need to keep a close eye on their stock, as the following account will show.

Late one Sunday evening, in June 1891, David Pope, living at Tasker, was returning home from a visit to Lydham. On the way he met two men driving three heifers along the road, one heifer he identified as belonging to a man named Enock Ridge, of the Grit, and which he remembered seeing in a field near Apple-tree Hall, in the parish of Shelve. Suspecting that something was wrong, Pope made a point of calling on Enock Ridge, apprising him of his suspicions. Ridge went out at once to his field, only to find his three heifers missing. Constable Robert Brown, stationed in the Hope Valley, was informed.

The officer, after making local enquiries, obtained the loan of a horse and trap, and in company with Enock Ridge and a neighbour, started in search of the rustlers. At Craven Arms, the constable ascertained from enquiries, that two men driving three heifers had passed through on their way to Ludlow, where there was a fair in progress. The constable and his companions continued in hot pursuit. About one mile short of Ludlow they overtook the rustlers and the missing cattle. One of the men turned out to be a returned convict, named Thomas Whittal, alias Evans, a native of the Grit. This man put up a very stubborn resistance, but was at length secured by the constable.

The second culprit was discovered to be but a youth of nineteen, who gave his name as Joseph Ratcliffe, from Stoke-on-Trent. P.C. Brown conveyed his prisoners to Bishopscastle, where a magistrate committed them to the next Quarter Sessions. The Shrewsbury Chronicle were very fulsome in their compliments to P.C. Brown on the prompt measures he had taken to apprehend the men, and for the plucky manner in which he had tackled Whittal, who was a well-known thief.

His Chief Constable greatly impressed by his quick action, and successful results, promoted the constable.

Another of Williams-Freeman's innovations was the training of members of the County Constabulary in First Aid. By the July of 1891, he had been authorised to procure arm badges of St. John's Ambulance Association for members of the constabulary who had qualified. The following month a General Order gave instructions that all sergeants and constables who had obtained certificates from the St. John's Ambulance Association, should wear their badge.

'which will be placed on the right upper arm halfway

between the elbow and shoulder in a line with the joint of the cuff.'

The Chief Constable was most enthusiastic about the Ambulance training, and by 1906 every member (including himself), had gained his first aid certificate. With 167 officers trained to give first aid, in case of accidents, the force became in this respect, of inestimable value to the public.

In the October of 1891, Williams-Freeman went on to introduce merit badges, with extra pay, for special devotion to duty. The number to be awarded was limited to ten at any one time. The award carried an extra pay of twopence per day. The badge itself was worn on the arm, and was made of cloth, with the words 'FOR MERIT' embroidered in gold wire. This award was restricted to constables and sergeants. This was a popular idea, and a great incentive to attention to duty.

The Sabbath was strictly observed in Victorian times. Constables of the county force were ordered in 1892, to wear full dress uniform when attending 'Divine Service', on Sunday mornings.

The Bye-Laws of Shrewsbury forbade the movement of all wheeled traffic within the borough, during the Sabbath day. There had been an infringement of this bye-law in 1859 when Mrs Ann Wombell, proprietress of the famous menagerie, had been fined five pounds for allowing her carriages to be driven through the town on a Sunday morning. Later, Fossett's Circus fell foul of the same bye-law, when driving through during the time of divine service. It took a lone constable of the Shrewsbury Borough Police to uphold the bye-law in its fullest meaning.

The occasion happened at one o'clock on a Sunday morning, in October 1892. Lord John Sanger's Circus had packed up, after its last performance at Wellington. With waggons rolling, they set out for their next stop, Shrewsbury. They arrived at the outskirts of the town, but had not proceeded far along the London road, when they were halted by a constable of the borough force. The officer calmly informed the drivers that they could not proceed any further;

119

as it would be a breach of the bye-laws, for any of their waggons or cages to traverse any portion of the borough highways upon the Sabbath. The drivers argued and pleaded that they only had a quarter of a mile further to go. The location of the circus was to be in St. Julian's Friars. The lone constable was obdurate, flatly refusing to allow them to travel a wheel length further into the town. After several hours delay; during which time the air would no doubt turn a deeper blue than the constable's uniform, the drivers turned the cavalcade around, to retrace their steps and encamp for the day, in a field near Atcham. This was to be the first occasion that the borough authorities had exercised so fully their powers under the bye-laws to prevent a circus entering the town on the Sabbath. It is doubtful if any of the borough constabulary had free seats at that particular circus, then or ever again.

The latter end of 1893 witnessed the Derbyshire coalminers out on strike. From that county came a request for police assistance. A contingent of twenty-five men of the Shropshire Constabulary spent several weeks in the mining districts of Derbyshire. On their return they were inspected by Major Heber Percy, Chairman of the Salop Standing Joint Committee. Although the men had undergone many hardships during their tour of duty, they presented a very smart appearance. The Major in addressing the men said —

'it was a source of much pleasure to him to have heard such an excellent report of the character and general conduct of the men during their absence. They had brought credit to themselves and to the county to which they belonged. He knew they had had long hours of work, which had been efficiently and well done. At the same time he wished to take the opportunity of stating how well the work had been performed at home by the reduced force during their absence'.[1]

In 1894 Captain Williams-Freeman continued with his policy of tightening discipline within the county constabulary. In an order issued on the 14 May, he ordered superintendents of divisions to instruct sergeants and constables in the correct way to lay out a constable's accoutrements — Cutlass, staff, handcuffs, nightbelt and shield, valise, haversack and helmet in bag.

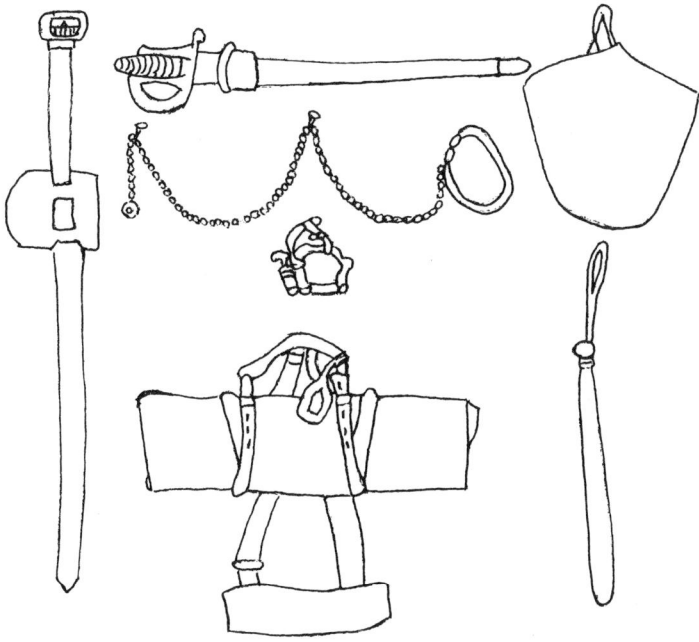

Accoutrements were to be hung arranged as in the above sketch.

The object of the exercise was to have the officer's accoutrements hung on some convenient wall at his station. There they would be readily available for inspection, should the chief constable or his superintendent visit his station. As all the layouts would be hung in matching order, they would be simple to check. Williams-Freeman was certainly running the force along military lines.

Another of the chief constable's ideas was to have the county force competing in annual exhibitions of drill. He presented a clock which went to the winning division. These drill competitions lasted from 1894 until 1904. The clock still exists in the museum at Divisional Headquarters, Shrewsbury.

The Shrewsbury Borough Force made a change in the Good Conduct badges worn by their sergeants. As from December 1895, sergeants wore a single star in lieu of a stripe, to represent five years service. Two stars represented ten years, while a silver crown denoted fifteen years service.

In 1895 the Shropshire Constabulary became partially mobile. The age of the bicycle had dawned, with constables pedalling furiously after startled criminals, who vainly attempted to outrun this new arm of the law. Both bicycles and tricycles were used, and appear to have been owned by the individual constables. The Shrewsbury Borough Force followed suit in the January of 1896, when the Chief Constable made enquiries about the price and makes of bicycles. The county constabulary resolved to purchase nine bicycles in July 1896. One bicycle to be supplied to each division.

It was decided in June 1898 to revive the rank of third class constable, which had been in abeyance since 1864. It would not be a popular move, for it would add another rung to the ladder of promotion, for the new recruits of the county force to climb.

A site on Swan Hill, Shrewsbury, was bought in 1899, by the county council for the sum of £830. It was earmarked for use as a proposed site for new police headquarters. A move being envisaged from the Shire Hall in the Square. A registered telegraphic address was also adapted. Someone with a penchant for Shakespeare, came up with — 'DOGBERRY SHREWSBURY'.

The Shrewsbury Borough Force extended their mobility in May 1899 to include mounted officers. Riding breeches and military boots were issued to the two horsemen. They appear on many photographs of ceremonial occasions.

A Merit Badge was awarded to P.C. Richard Tart in April 1899, in recognition of his endeavours rendered in the pursuit and final capture of the notorious ex-convict, Charles Henry

Phillips, alias Daniel Kinsey.

Thomas Cartwright, a wheelwright of Stanton-on-Hine-Heath, was also awarded a gratuity of one pound for his assistance in this arrest. Also involved in this pursuit were Sergeant Charles Wainwright and P.C. John Melhuish. The excitement of such a chase, and the capture of such a notorious character would be a highlight in the service of a constable, who only too often found his life of dull routine, to consist of long hours on his beat, which he had to suffer in all types of weather. Many of the county police were stationed in country areas far from the towns, and had to rely on their own resourcefulness, with only occasional visits from their sergeant or superintendent. For such constables the life was hard and lonely, and it is not difficult to see why so many resigned after a short period with the force.

Chapter Eight

1900 – 1909

The dawn of the twentieth century, a time to pause, to look back with an awareness of the spirit of change, that had been slowly converting the work of the police from a mere job into a vocation. No longer was the police constable a figure of fun, but a man to be reckoned with. The stolid Victorian policeman, the butt of Music Hall jokes; so often dismissed for drunkenness, was becoming a figure of the past. There was now emerging a smart, efficient officer of the law, respectable and respected. Not only did the officer himself have to be respectable, but even the future wife of an officer had to be vouched for. Officers wishing to get married had to put in an application to the Chief Constable, enclosing a testimonial from a magistrate or other reputable person, stating that his intended bride was not only respectable, but that she came from a background of good repute.

The Shrewsbury Borough Force decided in 1900, that in future there would be worn a white helmet during the hot summer months. Such helmets were generally made with a base of plaited straw, with a covering of white cloth, no helmet plates being worn. The result was an extremely light headgear.

It could be said that 1900 was the year of the bicycle. The Wellington Journal published a very fine illustration, in their issue dated 16 June 1900. The caption was 'Salop Police Cyclist Corps'. The event was a combined cycle ride of constables of the county constabulary with their Chief Constable. The ride is best described in the reporter's own

From "The Wellington Journal & Shrewsbury News" June 16th, 1900.

SALOP POLICE CYCLIST CORPS

Few Constabulary Forces can boast the possession of so efficient a cyclist corps as that belonging to the Shropshire County Police. A certain number of bicycles are provided by the County Council for the use of the men of each district, while in other cases, where constables find their own machines, an annual allowance is made for wear and tear. The value of such an adjunct to police duties in Shropshire has been fully recognised by the Chief Constable, Captain Williams-Freeman, who has left nothing undone to encourage and extend their use among the members of his force. Evidence of this was afforded on Thursday, when the whole of the cyclists, to the number of twenty-eight, assembled at Shrewsbury, and after being inspected, were photographed, the group also including Captain Williams-Freeman and Chief-Superintendent Edwards. Both the men and their machines looked very smart. The men were dressed in their summer serges and helmets, and wore light leather gaiters, while over the right shoulder was suspended a haversack, the capes being neatly folded and strapped on the front of the handles. Special instruction has been given in those parade movements pertaining to military cyclist corps, and the intelligent way the men drilled on Thursday, together with the smart turn-out, reflects the greatest credit on all concerned. In the afternoon the corps paraded at the head-quarters of the County Constabulary, and, under the command of Captain Williams-Freeman, had a run out as far as Wellington, advantage being taken to impart special instruction en route. Later in the afternoon the men were dismissed and returned independently to their different districts.

words —

'Few Constabulary Forces can boast the possession of so efficient a cyclist corps as that belonging to the Shropshire County Police. A certain number of bicycles are provided by the County Council for the use of the men of each district, while in other cases, where constables find their own machines, an annual allowance is made for wear and tear. The value of such an adjunct to police duties in Shropshire has been fully recognised by the Chief Constable, Captain Williams-Freeman, who has left nothing undone to encourage and extend their use among the members of his force.

Evidence of this was afforded on Thursday, when the whole of the cyclists, to the number of twenty-eight, assembled at Shrewsbury and after being inspected, were photographed, the group also including Captain Williams-Freeman and Chief-Superintendent Edwards. Both the men and their machines looked very smart. The men were dressed in their summer serges and helmets, and wore light leather gaitors, while over the right shoulder was suspended a haversack, the capes being neatly folded and strapped on the front of the handles. Special instruction had been given in those parade movements pertaining to military cyclist corps, and the intelligent way the men drilled on Thursday, together with the smart turnout, reflects the greatest credit on all concerned. In the afternoon the corps paraded at the headquarters of the County Constabulary, and under the command of Captain Williams-Freeman had a run out as far as Wellington, advantage being taken to impart special instructions en route. Later in the afternoon the men were dismissed and returned independently to their different districts.'[1]

Two thirds of the bicycles were provided by the men themselves, for which they received an allowance of six shillings per quarter. Six months later General Order No.755 laid down the rules to be followed by police cyclists when saluting.

'A cyclist standing with his cycle, will salute with the right hand, as laid down in infantry drill, returning the hand to the point of the saddle on the completion of the salute. A cyclist either mounted or leading his cycle will salute by coming to attention (if at ease) and turning his head slightly towards the Officer he salutes. A party of cyclists on the march will salute on the command 'Eyes Right' (or left) followed by 'Eyes Front', from the officer in command. The rules as to the distance at which the salute commences and ceases are the same as laid down in infantry drill.'

The influence of an ex-army chief-constable is very apparent.

The lease of the old Shrewsbury Borough Police Station (next to the Music Hall) ended the 15 March 1900. The force then moved with great pride, into their new purpose built home, on the site, known appropriately as 'Scotland Yard', which was situated on Swan Hill.

Queen Victoria died on the 22 January 1901. It was the end of a long and glorious reign. The Shropshire Constabulary, as was fitting, went into mourning. Arm-bands of black crepe were worn by superintendents and inspectors from the 24 January until the 17 April. Later in August, the Empress of Germany (Princess Royal of Great Britain) also died. The county force plunged into mourning for a further three weeks.

While the construction of the Birmingham Waterworks pipeline was taking place in 1901, it was found that many unlicenced ale-houses had come into being in the Ludlow area. There was a ready market of thirsty navvies working on the pipe-line. A large increase of drunkenness had been noted by the police since the work had started, helped not a little by this illegal traffic. To catch the offenders red-handed it became necessary for a couple of constables, of the county force to shed their uniforms, and don working clothes. Constables Steadman of Weston Rhyn, and Gough of Hope Valley were the ones chosen, as being unknown in the Ludlow area. The two constables soon obtained employment as navvies on the pipe-line. Finding a lodging at one of the suspected houses. That of Joseph Merry, of the Brick House, Bromfield, a ganger on the pipe-line. They soon found that ale was being plentifully sold, at threepence a pint, to all who

127

1900 Constable. Shropshire Constabulary

asked for it, and at all hours. Word was conveyed to Superintendent James Perry, who obtained a warrant to search the premises occupied by Merry. Early one morning, Perry with several officers closed in on the 'Brick House'. The amount of evidence found was of a damning character. In Merry's bedroom there was found a quart bottle of brandy, a similar amount of rum, a quantity of gin, a tundish, and nine pint cups; in another bedroom stood an 18 gallon cask of beer; in the wash-house another 18 gallon cask of beer. On the superintendent asking Merry how he accounted for such a large quantity of beer on his premises, he replied that he had bought it for his own consumption. Asked about the spirits, he replied that he had bought the brandy in case of an accident. Brought before the justices Merry was find £5 and 15s.0d costs, or a months hard labour. The police had a field day, altogether they issued 14 similar summonses. The penalties totalled £1,300 or six years imprisonment. It had been a large scale flaunting of the law, which had been sucessfully squashed.

A slate quarry workers strike in Caernarfonshire called for outside police help. Assistance was asked of the Shropshire Constabulary. On a cold morning in March, 1902, a contingent of the county force paraded at Shrewsbury, prior to setting out to help their Welsh colleagues. The contingent consisted of one superintendent, four sergeants and thirty-six constables. The emergency did not last long, and the Shropshire men were able to return to their normal duties. The Chief Constable of Caernarfonshire wrote to Williams-Freeman praising the men of his force.

'Your men will, I hope, return none the worse for their stay here. Their conduct has been all that could be wished and they were very willing and ready to do any duty that was required of them.'[2]

Co-operation with other police forces had become a tradition with the Shropshire Constabulary, dating back some forty years, when in 1862, they had assisted the Montgomeryshire Constabulary during the election riots at Llanidloes.

The Shropshire Constabulary moved into their new County Headquarters, also on Swan Hill, on the 2 November 1903. Here for the first time they found themselves on the phone. (Shrewsbury 53) All the divisional headquarters were connected up by the National Telephone Company. The Shrewsbury Borough Force were also put on the phone, in fact they had installed a private switchboard, which was manned by a police operator, who handled all the calls to, and between the various corporation offices.

General Orders were issued on a variety of subjects, some of which one would not think were the business of the police. Such a one was No. 895 issued on the 22 July 1903. It was concerned with recruitment for the Grenadier Guards. Any constable taking a recruit for this regiment to the local barracks, or to a recruiting sergeant, was on the recruits final approval, entitled to the sum of five shillings as a reward. In addition, the officers of the regiment were willing to give the constable an additional two shillings and sixpence for such a recruit. Many a bright eyed country boy must have wondered at the concern which his local bobbie was showing in his welfare.

The first petrol-driven motor cars had appeared on the roads of this country in the 1890's. At first, owing to their scarcity, it seems likely that the police did not bother to prosecute the odd drivers who exceeded the speed limit.

However, the increase in the numbers of cars on the roads by the beginning of the twentieth century made it clear that legislation would be necessary for their regulation. The speed limit, which had originally been four miles per hour, was gradually raised to twelve, then fourteen. In 1903 the limit had risen to twenty miles per hour, but the motorist found each small raise in the speed limit tedious enough to turn a blind eye to. Conflict between the police and the motorist had become inevitable. An order was issued by Williams-Freeman, in May 1905, directing constables to keep a record in their journals of the movements of motor-cars, showing the time seen, the direction travelling, and the number of the car. A

P.C.17. William Evans. 1903   Shrewsbury Borough Police

task which would not be conceivable in these days of heavy traffic, yet it illustrates how few cars there were at that time. In the July of the same year the County Chief Constable was authorised to purchase a 'Motor Car Speed Timing Apparatus'. The year 1905 witnessed the formation of the Automobile Association, bringing an active ally to help the harassed motorist. The patrols of the A.A. stopped motorists and warned them of police speed traps, this resulted in the patrols being prosecuted for obstructing the police in the execution of their duty.

The A.A. then adopted a more subtle policy. Members were advised to stop when a patrolman failed to salute them, the patrolman would then quietly advise them of any police activity in the area. Gradually, with the continued increase in numbers of cars upon the roads, the guerilla warfare diminished.

The death of Captain George Charles Peere Williams-Freeman took place on the 27 December, 1905. He had discharged the duties of the office of Chief Constable of Shropshire, for nearly 16 years; in a manner which had gained him the heartiest acknowledgements of the Salop Standing Joint Committee, and of the Justices of the county. The County Constabulary owed much to his leadership. The ambulance training which had been instituted by the late captain, had been extremely successful, so much so that in 1905, 159 members of the force could show 'First Aid' certificates. The constabulary sports inaugurated by Williams-Freeman in 1897, had, up to 1905, raised the sum of £2,031. 8s. 8d. which they gave to charities.

A sense of loss was also felt in Shrewsbury, when Henry Blackwell, their chief constable handed in his resignation, which was to take effect from the 21 January 1906. At a meeting of the Mayor's Court, he was presented with a cheque for seventy guineas, and an illuminated address. Mr. Blackwell responding to the many speeches, said that the seventeen years he had spent in Shrewsbury were the happiest in his official career. He retired to London, where his retirement was, sadly, very short. He died 19 April 1906.

Chief Inspector Arthur Baxter was appointed successor to Henry Blackwell, as Chief Constable of the Borough of Shrewsbury. A former member of the Shropshire Constabulary, he had transferred to the Shrewsbury Borough Police in 1896, as Chief Inspector.

It then became the turn of the Salop Standing Joint Committee to choose a successor to the late Captain Williams-Freeman.

Out of one hundred and sixty-four applications the choice fell upon Major Llewelyn William Atcherley, who entered upon his duties as Chief Constable of Shropshire the 1 March 1906.

Henry Blackwell's final report to the Watch Committee was mainly concerned with the General Election, held on the 16 January 1906. He was happy to inform them that there had not been a single case of serious disorder, or damage to property occurring in the borough during the period of the General Election. However with astute foresight he had asked for a sergeant and 14 constables of the county constabulary to be kept in reserve at Shrewsbury on the evening of the election. On the 20th of the same month the county chief constable asked for the assistance of the borough force. One sergeant and 14 constables were loaned for duty at Hadley, where a political meeting was being held. Another sergeant and seven constables proceeded to Oswestry for duty on the declaration of the poll. On the evening of the 24th one sergeant and 14 constables were — in answer to a telephone call — hurriedly despatched to Wellington. There they were kept in reserve, but were not required.

The hectic days of the middle of the previous century, when riot was just another name for elections, had gone. Quicker communications and travel enabled the police to move large forces of men rapidly to trouble spots, often with shrewd foresight before the trouble could start.

Science was coming to the aid of the police in many ways. In 1907 the National Telephone Company provided, and maintained six street alarms for the Shrewsbury borough

P.C. 117. Robert Steadman. 1908   Shropshire Constabulary

police, while at the headquarters of the county constabulary photographic apparatus had been installed. Criminals were finding that modern science was continually working against them. Photographs and fingerprints could now be sent to the Scotland Yard, Habitual Criminals Registry for checking.

Fingerprinting however was not a modern discovery. The system of using fingerprints for identification derives from China, where it has been in use for thousands of years. The system was introduced to Scotland Yard by Sir Edward Henry, a former Inspector-General of Bengal Police, who had perfected an earlier system developed by Sir William Hershel.

Major Atcherley accepted the Chief Constableship of the West Riding of Yorkshire in June 1908, his stay had been short, and he relinquished his duties as Chief Constable of Shropshire on the 5 July 1908. The Deputy Chief Constable, Chief-Superintendent George Edge taking temporary command of the county force. Captain Gerard Lysley Derriman was appointed the new chief constable of the Shropshire Constabulary on the 2 September 1908.

On assuming his duties, Captain Derriman lost no time in recording his appreciation of the great honour done to him, in appointing him to the command of so extremely efficient a body of men, as the Shropshire Constabulary. He made it very clear that it would be his earnest endeavour to maintain the high reputation which the corps enjoyed, and for that purpose he called upon all ranks to display the same fidelity, diligence and discipline that they had always shown.

His faith was justified, when the smartness of the constabulary, during the visit of their Royal Highnesses, The Prince and Princess of Wales, in November 1909, earned for Derriman, a letter of congratulations from the Lord Lieutenant of Shropshire.

Near the end of 1909 the Salop Standing Joint Committee assented, pursuant to section 25 of the Police Act 1890, to mutual aid agreements for police assistance being entered into with the counties of —

Cheshire, Derbyshire, Herefordshire, Staffordshire, Warwick

135

and Worcestershire.. Earlier, in 1904, a similar agreement had been made with Rádnorshire.

Chapter Nine

1910 — 1919

John Kempster had founded, in 1892, a journal entitled 'The Police Review'. To this man goes much of the credit for the fact that during 1906 and 1907 the Order Paper of the House of Commons contained so many questions urging the need for policemen to be allowed one day's leave in seven.

It was a campaign which after a lot of procrastination finally led to the appointment of a select committee on the subject in 1908, and the passing of the Police Forces (Weekly Rest-Day) Act two years later.

Winston Churchill in his role of Home Secretary, guided the Act through the House of Commons. There was some expected hostility towards the Act, mainly displayed by those responsible for the public purse. For it was understandable that rates would have to be increased, to cover the expence of taking on extra men (who would be needed in each force) to replace those on leave. Police authorities were required to implement the conditions of the Act by the 1 July 1914. This gave the police authorities plenty of time to work out all the details. And the poor constables (who it was to benefit), plenty of time to dream about it.

It was recorded at the Shrewsbury council meeting of the 15 July 1911 —

'that during the next three years the Police Force be gradually increased, so as to bring the Police (Weekly Rest-Day) Act, 1910, into operation in the Borough by the 1 July 1914, so the men have the full benefit of the Act by that date — being the date when the Act must be in full operation.'[1]

Shrewsbury Borough Police Pre-World War I

The Salop Standing Joint Committee noted the new Act at a meeting held on the 5 November 1910. Later, a letter dated 24 July 1913, from the Secretary of State was read, in which he expressed his approval of —

(1) the increase of the County Police Force by the addition of nine constables.

(2) the increase of Sergeants and 1st Class Constables to 23 and 65 respectively. The augmentation having been made to enable each member of the Police Force not being above the rank of Inspector to have one day's rest in every fourteen.

The Coronation of King George V and Queen Mary took place on 22 June 1911, all members of the county force receiving a gratuity of two day's pay, to mark the happy occasion.

Superintendents were brought up to date in 1913, when they were allowed to replace their outmoded horses and traps, for motor-cars. For which they were given an allowance of £52 per annum for running and maintenance costs.

The Royal Agricultural Show was held in Shrewsbury in 1914. An honour for the town, but what was even more exciting was the fact that H.M. King George V was to pay the show a visit on the third of July.

The Shrewsbury Watch Committee were soon busy organising traffic routes and issuing orders for the regulation of the expected heavy traffic. Assistance was given by a superintendent of the Metropolitan Police experienced in the regulation of such traffic.

It was realized that with the great influx of visitors, more police would be necessary to control the crowds. Ninety additional officers were thought to be required for the five days of the show, with at least an additional hundred officers on the day of the King's visit.

Fifty officers were borrowed from the Liverpool City Police Force, and another forty officers from the Shropshire Constabulary for the five days. The extra hundred officers for the day of the King's visit, were also borrowed from the Liverpool force.

From a police point of view, the Agricultural Show, and the Royal visit, passed off successfully, the Watch Committee reporting to the Shrewsbury corporation —

'It is with great satisfaction that your committee are able to report that the arrangements made for His Majesty's visit and for the Royal Show Week proved most effective, and were admirably carried out, much to the credit of all concerned. Your committee are pleased to be able to report that practically no untoward incident or accident occurred during the week, and that there was an entire absence of crime which could in anyway be attributed to the show.

The Borough may therefore be congratulated on the good order which prevailed.

Your committee desire to place on record their appreciation of the way in which the Chief Constable and the Police generally carried out the whole of their duties, and at the same time to thank the members of the Liverpool Police Force, the Shropshire Constabulary, and the Detectives engaged for the excellent services which they rendered to the Borough.

Your committee having considered the additional hours of duty and extra work performed by the Borough Police on the occasion of the visit of His Majesty the King, and of the Royal Agricultural Show have allowed the following sums as extra pay to the members of the force.

Thirty-Two constables at 15s. 0d. each.

Three acting-sergeants at 17s. 6d. each.

Five sergeants at 20s. 0d. each.

Two inspectors at 25s. 0d. each.'[2]

The Chief-Constable, Arthur Baxter, had the pleasure of being personally congratulated by His Majesty upon the police arrangements made on his visit.

Such pleasant occasions were soon to be memories of the past.

The following month war was declared on Germany. On the 24 August, Constable George Faulconbridge, still on his three months probation, became the first member of the Shrewsbury borough force to volunteer for the army.

140

Shrewsbury Borough Police Force. c.1915

141

The Chief-Constable of Shropshire, Captain Gerard Derriman, asked for leave to apply (as he was on the reserve of officers of the Grenadier Guards) to rejoin his old regiment. Consent was given. The Chief Constable left to join his regiment 31 December 1914.

Before he left Captain Derriman issued a General Order informing all ranks that he was going. He refers to his confidence that the superintendents would loyally carry on their work under the direction of the Deputy Chief Constable (Superintendent George Edge), and calling on all ranks to prove that his trust and confidence has not been displaced.

Captain Derriman had lacked the quality of leadership which his two predecessors — Williams-Freeman and Atcherley had given to the Force.

There had been a marked rise in the number of indictable offences committed in Shropshire during the early 1900's, but to combat this there had been a high detection rate for such crimes, this had been maintained by the Force under both Williams-Freeman and Atcherley. Thereafter the detection rate appears to have fallen, a state which continued throughout the war, when with so many men under military discipline, the amount of crime fell.

Many officers, both of the Shropshire Constabulary and of the Shrewsbury Borough Police Force, particularly the single men, resigned to join the armed forces. By the 26 July 1915, the Borough Police Force had sixteen of its forty-four men serving with the colours.

A letter of resignation was received by the Shrewsbury Watch Committee, from the Chief Constable, Arthur Baxter. His resignation took place as from 7 November 1915, on his completing twenty-five years service.

It was resolved that the office of Chief Constable be not filled in the usual way, but that, subject to the approval of the Home Office, the Chairman of the Watch Committee, Mr Herbert Frederick Harries be temporarily appointed Chief Constable of the Borough, until such time that a permanent appointment might be made. The temporary appointment was an honorary office, without remuneration, except for out of pocket expenses.

The Home Office suggested that for the duration of the war, the Borough Police Force might be supervised by the county — This suggestion struck at the independance of the borough. The Watch Committee indignantly refuted this suggestion. A strongly worded letter to the Home Secretary made this point more than clear, and a telegram from the Home Office then arrived, agreeing to the appointment of Councillor Harries as Honorary Chief Constable of Snrewsbury.

On the 7 August 1915, Captain Gerard Derriman died from wounds, received in action whilst serving with the Grenadier Guards in France.

Two day later, the Salop Standing Joint Committee decided, like Shrewsbury, to appoint an Honorary Chief Constable from amongst its own members.

The choice fell on its vice-chairman, Augustus Wood-Acton, a man in his seventies, but with a wide experience of the law, having been a Justice of the Peace for the counties of Hereford, Shropshire and Somerset.

Women's organizations first started a crusade for the employment of women, as police constables, in 1915. It became a miserable tale of apathy and predjudice. Few Chief Constables saw much value in the use of women as police constables. The Home Office in spite of the repeated pressure from women's movements, and high church officials, avoided encouraging their employment. During World War I there were two separate voluntary women's associations training and providing women police constables. The National Union of Women Workers (later to become the National Council of Women), and the Women's Police Service, each established voluntary patrols amongst the girls and women who frequented such likely places as the proximity of military camps, munition factories, and even local parks. They saw themselves in a preventative role with special emphasis on moral delinquency. By July 1915, pressure had been brought to bear on the Shrewsbury Watch Committee, by the Shropshire

Council of Social Workers, to employ women police. Letters flew back and forth, deputations waited on the Watch Committee, and articles appeared in the local press. But, to no avail. The Shrewsbury Watch Committee and its Chief Constable were firmly entrenched in a man's world, and more over, they intended that it should stay that way. Lady Magdalen Herbert, President of the Shropshire Council of Social Workers, offered the use of two, four, or even six ladies to act as police constables, salary paid, for a period of three months.

Even this munificent offer was turned down. The Watch Committee replied that —

'while in sympathy with the movement are of the opinion that the present time is unopportune to consider the question of appointing Women Police as the committee will shortly be appointing a new chief constable whose views on the matter should first be ascertained.'[3]

Another offer from the Shropshire Council of Social Workers came in January 1916, when they proposed to guarantee the salaries of two women police for six months.

It is true that the Watch Committee devoted considerable attention to the matter in all its indications, but still came unanimously to the conclusion —

'that there were technical difficulties that most of them held to be insuperable. Shrewsbury was not exactly the kind of place where an experiment of that kind could be tried effectively.'[4]

Their decision brought a quick letter in reply from Lady Herbert, who wanted to know what were 'the technical reasons.' She thought that the difficulties caused by the shortage of men police were so obvious that mere 'technical difficulties' could have been overcome.

Lady Herbert observed that the Chairman of the Watch Committee had said — 'that Shrewsbury was not a place in which to try experiments', and went on to say that even if such a charge against the town were true, it was worth pointing out that the movement for women police was not quite in an experimental stage. Women police were working with great success in such places as Hull, Grantham, and Southampton.

The Bishop of Lichfield wrote a letter to the Shrewsbury Chronicle in favour of women police, in March 1916. However, the Watch Committee remained totally unconverted by the Bishop. Their reply stated —

'the employment of women police is unnecessary and impracticable'.

And so it went on, a battle of the sexes. Throughout the 1920's letters were received from the Home Office (now in favour of women police), advocating the employment of women. No notice was taken. In fact it was not until the outbreak of World War II, the subject came up again.

In 1942 the Shrewsbury Watch Committee gave in under great pressure from the Home Office. For twenty-seven years the male bastion had held out against the inclusion of women police in the borough.

With the Shropshire Constabulary the story was very different, a letter to the Salop Standing Joint Committee from the Archdeacon of Salop, concerning the number of women and girls frequenting the vicinity of large army camps had the desired effect. Two women police were appointed forthwith, no argument at all.

On the 11th March 1918, Miss Emily Frances Stephings, with rank of woman sergeant, and Miss Isabella Charlotte Napier Hardy, a constable, commenced duty. They were stationed at Whitchurch, where they were given a daily patrol duty, consisting of two turns of four hours each.

They were required to patrol the vicinity of the Prees Heath military camp and the town of Whitchurch.

Towards the end of 1918, the Salop Standing Joint Committee received a deputation of the Shropshire Council of Social Workers, headed by Lady Herbert. They spoke highly of the work carried out by the women patrols at Whitchurch. Then strongly urged the committee to appoint women police as part of the established force.

W.P.C. Anna Westedick & W.P.C. Lilian Lenn. 1920.
Shropshire Constabulary.

After discussing the question, the committee resolved —

'(1) That subject to the approval of the Home Secretary the Chief Constable be authorised to make arrangements with the Women Police Service for the employment of Women Police in such numbers as this Committee may approve.

(2) That the present number be limited to four including the two women police stationed at Whitchurch.'

The Home Secretary approved the move, but with the proviso that these women should be regarded as an auxiliary part of the Police organization, he thought their uniform should indicate clearly that they were attached to the Salop Constabulary. It seemed to him of importance that there should be visable sign of their being in the service of the local police authority and responsible to the officers of the force.

The two additional police women now appointed were — Miss Anna Westerdick and Miss Lilian Lenn. The early uniforms of these police women were not such as would call for a wolf-whistle from any of the boys. High leather boots, a loose fitting blue mackintosh, jacket and long skirt, buttoned right down the front, which unbuttoned, enabled greater freedom of movement when giving chase to any offenders. The hats were round, with a round brim, bearing the Shropshire Constabulary badge at the front.

Sad to relate both Sergeant Stephings and Constable Hardy were dismissed as an economy measure in 1921.

Women Constables Lenn and Westerdick, who had been stationed at Oswestry, where they patrolled both the town, and the outskirts of the army camp at Park Hall, had become greatly endeared to the people of Oswestry.

Letters were sent in support of the retention of these two police women.

The Salop Standing Joint Committee first made sure that the Home Office would continue to contribute one half of their cost, then agreed to keep on the two women constables. Both ladies continued at Oswestry, as auxiliaries to the Shropshire Constabulary, (though unattested), up to, and into World War II.

With the great drain of officers from the police forces into the military services, a great strain was put on all police forces during the war. In October 1916, the Honorary Chief Constable of Shrewsbury suggested to his Watch Committee, that 50 special constables be appointed. Amongst the volunteers were two vicars, and two curates. The specials were asked to give four hours of their time, twice a week, mainly between the hours of six and ten P.M.

As far as possible their duties were arranged so as not to clash with the business arrangements of the special constables. A book of instructions compiled by Inspector Frank Davies gave the special constables an opportunity to digest its contents before being called upon to do duty. On the 12 February 1917 the Hon: Chief Constable was able to report that 67 special constables had been sworn in. At this time the Shrewsbury police force had been greatly depleted. Twenty-six of its regular members being in the armed forces. At the close of the war in 1918, there were 98 special constables in Shrewsbury, while 66% of the regular constables were still serving with the colours. It was in 1918 that special lapel badges, oval in shape, and of blue enamel, were issued to the Shrewsbury Specials.

The first war-time mention of the county constabulary recruiting specials, shows them commencing duty on the 20 February 1917. By the year 1919 the total number of special constables sworn into the county force, was one hundred and eight. Sterling work was done by the specials, relieving the small band of regular constables of a great deal of routine patrolling. The county specials also wore a lapel badge, which had been authorized in 1917. It was round in shape, surmounted by a crown. The centre bearing a shield of the county arms, with the inscription 'Shropshire Special Constabulary'. Brave acts were not unknown within their ranks. Two specials were responsible for averting a very serious conflagration, while another constable was instrumental in convicting a noted criminal, for shopbreaking. In the town of Oswestry they had rendered great assistance in regulating street traffic, which frequently increased in the evenings by the visit of as many as 16,000 troops from Park Hall Camp.

The Oswestry Special Constabulary entertained the regular police to dinner in 1919. Major Becke, the Chief Constable, speaking at the dinner, told his hosts that the Salop Standing Joint Committee had decided to issue to all its special constables, a certificate expressing the thanks of the county for their services. 'No where', he said, 'was the call for volunteers more readily and enthusiastically responded to than by the specials of the Oswestry Division, and no where was the work required of them done more efficiently. The greatest proof of this was the small number of arrests they had made, which showed they had grasped the main axiom of a policeman, the honoured tradition of the Shropshire Constabulary, that the prevention of crime was their first duty'.

Most police forces had at that time a very genuine grievance over pay, and its failure to rise with the cost of living, which had doubled during the war years. Here in Shropshire the county constabulary was also discontented about its rest day, granted under the 'Weekly Rest Day Act 1910'. The following three letters are very expressive of the feelings in the county constabulary in the early part of 1916, and paint a sad picture of the overworked, low paid officers. Published under the nom de plumes of 'Fed-Up', 'Sufferer', and 'Live and Let Live', their letters appeared in the Police Review. —

'I see in the last issue of "The Police Review" that the Southport Watch Committee have granted a day's pay to the police owing to the stoppage of the weekly rest days.

We in Shropshire have had one day's leave in fourteen since the 1st June 1914. On the outbreak of war this was stopped for a considerable period owing to additional work, which, of course, was willingly and cheerfully acceded to. After the rush we were again granted the fortnightly day's leave; but now we are told we can only have a day a month.

I do not know who is the instigator of this fresh arrangement. It may little effect the men in country stations, but a day a fortnight is eagerly looked forward to by those who only get a night in bed with twenty-four hours off; and now we shall have to wait a month without our day off, it seems selfish and altogether unnecessary. We have received no additional pay for all the days we sacrificed at the outbreak of the war, and nothing is said about it now, God speed the time when our rulers will have the interest of their subordinates more at heart.'[5]

'Sufferer' writes —

'I fully endorse "Live and Let Live's" letter in the Police Review 25th February, re Pay and Leave. It is high time something was done in Shropshire to relieve the sufferings of the poor P.C's for it is impossible to live on the low pay we receive and keep out of debt. Last April we were granted a War Bonus of the magnificent sum of 2s. 4d. per week, which does not even pay for the rise in bread and sugar, as foodstuffs have gone up 40 per cent, since the outbreak of war.

This force is seething with discontent, owing to the stoppage of our One Day's Rest in fourteen, and no mention of being paid for it. I do not know who is the instigator of this mean act. According to the Weekly Rest Day Act we should be having one day's rest in seven, which we have never had in this force. We are now told we can only have one Day's leave a month. We are worse paid than navvies, for there are many in this district now getting £2 a week. We sorely need a rise of pay of 3s or 4s a week, to meet the extra cost of living. We all like to be patriotic, but we cannot starve'.[6]

Two months later 'Fed-Up' states his views even more emphatically —

'Great discontent is seething throughout this Force (Shropshire Constabulary) because of the low pay and the price of foodstuffs still rising. May I impress upon the S.J.C. the urgent necessity of granting us a rise of 5s. a week.

At the present terrible prices the pay is insufficient for young married men to provide bare necessities, much less replace boots, clothing, etc. What can a married man with a family do on 24s. 6d. a week? WE ARE THE LOWEST PAID

FORCE IN ENGLAND. How would any member of our S.J.C. like to do the extra work we are now doing on our contemptable little wages? Have they no feeling for a poor P.C.? How can we keep our wives and families decent and keep out of debt?

Why cannot our pay equal Cheshire or Montgomeryshire adjoining counties? It is time the boot and bicycle allowances was altered, considering the extra work. A clean sweep is needed of the whole committee before we shall get justice.

Our C.C. must know we cannot maintain ourselves honourably and keep up a decent appearance.

We sincerely trust he will make the necessary appeal on our behalf.'[7]

Official records are silent on the subject, but an addition was made to the War Bonus on the 1 July 1916, of threepence a day, and later on the 1 October 1916 a further 1s. 6d. per week to all ranks. A help, but not anywhere near the sum that had been asked for. However, it would seem that the message had got through, for the very next year, a substantial addition to the War Bonus was agreed dating from the 15 April 1917. Superintendents were to receive an addition of 10s. 0d. per week. This, together with an allowance of 1s. 0d. per child (excluding the first) under 14 years of age. This was a partial understanding of the situation, and no doubt dissipated some of the discontent within the force.

While the seething discontent had been running through the ranks of the Shropshire Constabulary, the Shrewsbury Borough Police, perhaps a little better off in pay, put in for a raise. On the 9 November 1916, the Watch Committee, after careful consideration, adopted a scale which gave every man an increase of one shilling per week. On top of this the Boot Allowance was raised to tenpence per week; an addition to the War Bonus of 1s. 0d. per week. Later in 1917, they received another addition to the War Bonus of 2s. 0d. per week, with a further ninepence per week for every child under the age of 14.

At the beginning of 1918, Shrewsbury's Honorary Chief

151

Constable was advertising in the local press for 'Temporary Constables'. The applicants had to be at least five foot eight inches in height, and either discharged from army or navy, or men over military age. This was one of the last acts performed by Councillor Harries as Chief Constable, for a communication had been received from the Home Office (in common with other police authorities where Honorary Chief Constables were acting), requiring a permanent appointment of a Chief Constable.

Thus pressure from the Home Office to end the Honorary Chief Constableship resulted in promotion for, and appointment of Chief Inspector Frank Davies as Chief Constable of the Borough of Shrewsbury. To take effect from the 1 March 1918. Frank Davies was a native of Brecon, who had been appointed a probationary constable with the Shrewsbury Borough Police Force on the 12 January 1900.

He had risen through the various intermediary ranks to Chief Constable in 18 years, which showed great initiative, and knowledge of his duties.

The Honorary Chief Constable of Shropshire, Mr. Augustus Wood-Acton, was not relieved of his post, sadly he died on the 24 March 1918.

Chief Superintendent George Edge, once again took over temporary command of the Shropshire Constabulary. On the 1 July 1918, Major Jack Becke was appointed as Chief Constable of Shropshire.

The early years of Becke's command were to coincide with those troublesome times, which affected both civilian and police worlds, of the 1920 era.

The failure of police pay to rise with the cost of living, (which had doubled during the war years), had embittered the men of police forces all over the country. By 1918 many policemen with their families had sunk so low in poverty that they were actually under-nourished. There was considerable unrest amongst the Metropolitan Police, whose Commissioner, Sir Edward Henry, (nearing seventy years of age), was completely unable to understand. A policeman dismissed for union activities became the spark which finally brought out 6,000 of the Metropolitan Police on strike.

Sir Edward Henry was dismissed, and the strike resulted in a substantial pay rise for the Metropolitan Police.

The Police Union, so far unrecognised, claimed that they had been promised recognition at the cessation of hostilities, but the Home Office denied this statement. The seed of further contention was sown.

In March 1919 the 'Salop Constabulary Representative Board' was set up to represent the members of the force in matters concerning their conditions of service and general welfare, (other than questions of discipline). The board consisted of five sergeants; three acting sergeants and eight constables.

A similar board for the Metropolitan Police had been set up, but proved a failure, when extremists from the Police Union obtained control of the board, and clashed with the new Commissioner, Sir Nevil Macready. He regarded them as disloyal and subversive; while they regarded him as an autocratic tyrant. A stalemate of hatred led the way to a further strike.

In Shropshire the Standing Joint Committee, and the Chief Constable, with admirable foresight, issued several General Orders doing away with a number of minor annoyances. In March 1919 left hand salutes were abolished, all future salutes would be given with the right hand. Three days additional annual leave, to mark the occasion of officers returning from the war, would also help to relieve the strain. In the month of May, all constables with twelve months service were permitted to wear a single bar chevron on the right fore-arm. A decoration to uplift their pride. In the same month General Order 1328 was issued, which would be welcomed by every officer in the force. The Weekly Rest Day which they had been promised since the Act of 1910, was to be implemented from the 1 June 1919. This was to sweep away a lot of the discontent in the force.

On the 25 June 1919, Jack Becke issued a letter to all ranks conveying his appreciation for the loyalty of all ranks, the pains which everyone had taken to adopting new methods, and the willingness with which his wishes had been carried out. Five days later, the general unrest in the police world increasing, Major Becke found it necessary is issue another letter to the members of his force, expressing his confidence in their loyalty —

'The Chief Constable is aware that there is considerable unrest in the Police world at the present time.

The Chief Constable has implicit confidence in the common sense of the Shropshire Constabulary, and feels sure that they will not identify themselves with any extreme action which other Police Forces may be tempted to take. At the same time he realizes that efforts will be made to suborn members of the Force from the path of duty and loyalty.

He sincerely hopes that the older and more experienced Officers will exercise a steadying influence on any hotheads there may be, and that every member of the Force will studiously avoid in any way identifying himself with this retrograde movement.

The Chief Constable hopes that his actions have proved to all ranks that he has the best interests of the Force at heart, and that he can only assure all ranks that it is his privilege and his intention to see that the Shropshire Constabulary is second to none in conditions of service, efficiency, and contentment.

Shropshire Constabulary, remain loyal as you have been in the past, and allow no premature action on the part of a single Constable to place a blot on that fair fame which you have won for yourselves.

J. Becke, Major. Chief Constable.'[8]

In March 1919 the government appointed a committee under the chairmanship of Lord Desborough, to review the pay and the conditions of service of the police. The committee worked rapidly and efficiently. By the month of May, they were able to outline their main proposals — much higher pay, standardised for all forces, and machinery whereby the police and the police authorities could make representations to the Home Secretary. The Home Office accepted the Desborough Committees recommendation to raise the constable's weekly starting pay from £1.10s. to £3.10s. At the same time the Home Secretary obtained authorization to bring in legislation to prevent policemen from belonging to a trade union. A few days later when announcing his proposals to the House of Commons, he declared that any policeman who went on strike would be dismissed, without any hope of reinstatement. On July 8th the Police Bill was read to the House of Commons. It catered for the establishment of a Police Federation, and founded a Police Council as a consultative body. The Bill also included a ban on policemen belonging to a trade union. It passed successfully through parliament, and received the Royal Assent on August 17th.

The Police Union faced with extinction, called a second strike, not for more pay, but for the survival of the union. Thousands of policemen were in disagreement with the union's move, and tore up their union cards. Even so, a total of 2,364 men, from seven different forces, struck on the 31st July.

Metropolitan 1,056; City of London 57; Liverpool 954; Birmingham 119; Bootle 63; Birkenhead 114, and Wallasey 1. Bloody rioting broke out in Liverpool, and steel-helmeted troops and tanks moved into Merseyside, where bayonet charges were found necessary. The strike soon collapsed. All the strikers were dismissed as promised.

General Order 1345 issued by Major Becke on 1 August 1919 was to be the shortest ever written, consisting of just three words — 'I TRUST YOU'. It was understood and appreciated by the men of the Shropshire Constabulary who remained loyal, and unaffected by the strike.

Negotiations for a new scale of pay for the Shropshire Constabulary had been in progress, and in August it was announced that the new scale of pay would be backdated from the previous April. The new scale gave a constable £3.10s. 0d. per week, on appointment, as laid down in the Desborough report.   This in itself would be a great encouragement to recruits, while the standardisation of police pay would stop the shopping around by would be recruits, which had long been the case.

Looking back in time to the methods used in 1918 and 1919 in dealing with motorists who contravened the speed limit, is liable to make the modern constable think of the early motion picture series of the 'Keystone Cops'.   As with most things, only experience, and trial and error could reveal the best method of dealing with the offence.   A circular was issued to the Shropshire Constabulary in 1918 –

'I want it impressed on the men that the Telegraph poles are placed at a standard interval throughout the County, and therefore all they have to do is to remember the distance separating these poles and time a motor or other vehicle passing them to have an approximate idea of the pace the motor is travelling'.[9]

In 1919 another circular was issued, the ideas in the circular were quite logical, but the picture it brings to mind would have made excellent copy for a cartoonist of that period.

'The Chief Constable wishes all Constables who notice that motor cars are travelling along the road at an excessive speed to adopt the following procedure.

The Constable will hide in the hedge and take out his watch and note-book and give the impression that he is forming part of a police trap.   He should not be completely hidden, at the same time he should be partly hidden and give the motorist the impression of his trying to conceal himself completely.

Motorists have a habit of circulating information that a trap is in existance, and if this procedure is followed motorists generally will get the impression that there are numerous traps throughout the County, furthermore they will never be certain even if they got to know of the procedure whether the trap is a dummy or a real one.

The Chief Constable hopes by this means to lessen the number of motor accidents, and recommends that this practice be followed more particularly on Sundays, Bank Holidays and on other occasions when it is known that there will be an abnormal amount of motor traffic.

It will depend on the ingenuity of the individual Constable how effective this practice proves.

The Motor Scout if handled diplomatically can be as completely fooled by this scheme as the motorist, and Sergeants and other experienced officers should make it their business to arrange for the mystifying of these Motor Scouts, for the more motorists they warn the better for then there will be less accidents and lessen the number of reports that the motor season generally brings forth.'[10]

With the majority of the police officers returned from the war, the Chief Constable of the Shrewsbury Borough Police, Frank Davies, reported that he proposed to carry out the provisions of the Weekly Rest Day Act of 1910. Since April 1916 the borough police had only received one day in fourteen, although they had been paid one half day's pay in lieu, per week. An improvement on the county constabulary who had only received one day per month, and no pay in lieu. As from 27 April 1919, rest days were back to normal.

The war was finished, the forces were coming back to normal strength, pay was better, as was the conditions of work, the policeman was able to look forward to the 1920's with hope.

Chapter Ten

1920 – 1929

The year 1920 opened with the pleasant news that His Majesty King George the Fifth had approved the issue of a new medal. It was to be a mark of His Majesty's appreciation of the good services rendered by Special Constables during the late war. It was his desire to provide a means of recognising continued and efficient service in the future. It would be known as 'The Special Constabulary Medal'. The conditions required that the recipient must have at least nine years satisfactory service as a special constable.

The end of the old 'Bulls-Eye' oil-lamps came about in 1920. The Shrewsbury Borough Force had changed over to flashlights in 1916, but the county constabulary had kept on using the old oil-lamps until their stock became depleted. Most police forces had by this time disgarded the oil-lamps in favour of the more modern flashlights; in fact the majority of the county constables were now using their own flashlights, rather than bother with the messy filling of the official oil-lamps.

It had become increasingly evident that there was an intensification of the use of motor vehicles by criminals, and instructions were issued to the county police that the index number, type of vehicle, date, hour and place seen, plus the direction proceeding, should be recorded in respect of every motor vehicle seen after the hour of 10.0 p.m. No doubt in 1920 this would have been a feasible exercise.

Another step forward in keeping abreast of the mechanised criminal, was the approval in 1920, by the Salop Standing

Joint Committee, of divisional superintendents using motor cars. In the case of a new superintendent being appointed, he was granted fifty pounds towards the purchase of a car, and, if necessary, allowed to borrow a further hundred pounds (free of interest) from the county.

There was a solemn occasion at the Swan Hill headquarters, on the 4 August 1920. A memorial tablet was unveiled to those officers of the Shropshire Constabulary who had fallen in the 1914—1918 War. The tablet was inscribed with the following names. —

'Captain G.L. Derriman, Chief Constable.

P.C. 20. C. Richards.

P.C. 54. W.W. Jones.

P.C. 139. H.H. Stanley.

P.C. 153. J. Cadman.

P.C. 161. G. Broadhurst.

P.C. 162. T. Wynne.

P.C. 164. G. Meredith.

P.C. 168. J. Abbotts. '

General Order No. 1458 appears to be the origin of instructing schoolchildren in the matter of 'Road Safety'; issued in 1921, it directed that every school in the county should be visited by the police, and the children specially warned —

'1/ Of running across the road without first looking both ways; they should be cautioned not to play "Last Across" — a game much loved by the young.

2/ To be very careful when they pass in front of or behind a stationary vehicle on the road.

3/ Not to follow a rolling ball into the road, if there be any traffic on the road.

4/ Not to hang on to vehicles or clamber on to lorries.'[1]

And so was born the Road Safety lectures at schools, still carried on sixty years later.

The various police forces ran their own cricket and football teams, many of the officers being very keen sportsmen. Chief Constable Frank Davies, of the Shrewsbury Borough Force, took this a step further, by organizing charity football matches with other police forces. On the 24 February 1921 he arranged a match, to be played on the Gay Meadow ground at Shrewsbury, between his own force and the Wolverhampton Borough Police. Unfortunately Shrewsbury police team lost the match, but ultimately they won by handing over the gate-money of £326. 15s. to the Royal Salop Infirmary. The idea caught on. A return match was played at Wolverhampton, in aid of a charity of their choice. Later in the year the Shrewsbury police team played a game of cricket with the Kidderminster Borough Police, and proved that their cricket prowess was better than their football, by winning the match.

But, perhaps the most famous football game ever played by the Shrewsbury police, was the one played on the Gay Meadow, on the 15 December 1921. The match was the brain child of Chief Constable Davies. He had become aware of the many poor children in the town of Shrewsbury, whose parents were unable to provide them with boots and shoes. He decided that he would organize a football match, the proceeds of which would go to supplying these poor children with footwear. The match was the culmination of weeks of selling tickets. The whole force entered into the spirit of the movement with whole hearted enthusiasm, selling the red and yellow tickets almost as quickly as they were printed. Five hundred and ninety four pounds were raised. Even before the match had started Frank Davies had purchased three hundred and forty five pairs of boots, from local traders. The remainder of the money was banked, and the balance drawn upon as and when other cases of a deserving nature cropped up. As for the famous match itself, it was against their old opponents – the Wolverhampton Borough Police, who once again showed their superiority by winning the match. It was a splendid effort by the Shrewsbury Police, which was warmly praised by the local press. The charity had been inaugurated under the name of – 'The Borough Police Poor Children's Fund', but it was not long before it collected the popular name of – 'Boots For The Bairns'. It was to be the first of many such matches for this charity, which extended over many years.

The Salop Standing Joint Committee found it necessary in 1921 to dismiss two of the women police officers, as an economy measure. And so the two pioneers who had been taken on in 1918 — Sergeant E.F. Stephings and Constable I.C. Napier Hardy ended their short tour of duty with the Shropshire Constabluary.

At least they had shown the public that women police officers could be of use, as a letter to the local press points out —

'I see the County Council have decided to dispense with the services of two of the County Women Police. It is to be hoped that the remaining members of the force will be retained, for one cannot visit the various police courts in the county without noticing their tactfulness and helpfulness in dealing with women witnesses who for the first time in their lives find themselves taking a conspicuous part in police court proceedings. The work of the women police can be made of real value if the right women are secured, and it can be wholly spoiled by the wrong women. From what I have seen the right women have been chosen for the Shropshire W.P.'[2]

Early in 1922, an M.O. Department was created at County Headquarters. Great emphasis was laid not only on Modus Operandi, but on feature peculiarities of wanted persons. The new department was complimentary to the albums of photographs of criminals, which had been kept for some time. .

The substantial rise in pay, given in 1919, which had done so much good for the police, now took the opposite course, the Geddes Committee reported that owing to the 'Slump' reductions would have to made in pay, and later in allowances.

In April 1922, Shrewsbury Borough Police on traffic duty, became very noticeable. A departure being made from the familiar blue uniforms to white mackintosh coats, and in the summer months — white holland coats. Easy to see by the motorist, especially in the summer period, when the constable on point duty would also be wearing his white helmet.

Such changes, large and small, were continually taking place in the police forces. In the same year, all officers of the

"Shrewsbury Borough Police Armistice Day, 1922"

162

Shropshire Constabulary (below the rank of superintendent), ceased to carry sticks, except at night, for those on rural beats.

It was a day of pride, when in the month of September 1924, forty-four members of the Shrewsbury Special Constabulary were granted the Long Service Medal. They were the first men of this force to be eligible for the medal, which had been instituted in 1919.

The history of Special Constables can be traced back a long way in time. The first Act of Parliament authorising the appointment of special constables was passed in 1673. This was a tardy attempt to repair the havoc caused by the Civil War; but like many laws that found their way into the Statute Book during the seventeenth century, it might just as well have remained unprinted, for all the use that was made of it. In the nineteenth century the Reform Bill Riots had the government very concerned about the inadequacy of maintaining law and order.

The result was the passing of a Special Constable Act of 1831, which empowered justices of the peace to conscript men as Special Constables, on the occasion of a riot. This Act was usefully brought into force at the time of the Fenian Riots of 1868. At Shrewsbury alone, some 1,105 Special Constables were sworn in. During the Great War of 1914 — 1918 the Specials did sterling work in helping the depleted police forces keep law and order.

The year 1925, ended very pleasantly with the award of the King's Police Medal to Superintendent James Fulcher, the first officer to be so honoured in the Shropshire Constabulary. The medal had been instituted in 1909, to be awarded to 'those members of the force who have performed acts of exceptional courage and skill, or have exhibited conspicuous devotion to duty.'

The 'General Strike' greatly overshadowed the year 1926, and for ten days in May, paralyzed the whole of the country. The strike began as a stoppage of work by the coalminers, who were quickly joined in support, by railwaymen and other workers. Civil Commissioners were appointed in eleven districts in England and Wales to help local authorities to maintain essential supplies, and to preserve law and order. Once more the Special Constabulary stepped forward to assist the regular police. In addition masses of the public, estimated at 140,000 enrolled in a special whole-time, paid extention of the specials, known as the 'Civil Constabulary Reserve.' T.A. Critchley writes —

'So great was the demand for truncheons that Scotland Yard had to send to High Wycombe for a lorry-load of chair-legs, which were fitted up with lengths of rope and issued to those who were not lucky enough to have conventional truncheons.'[3]

Here in Shropshire the strikers were well behaved, and no trouble at all seems to have been reported. The impartiality and forbearance of the police in this time of national disaster, gained for them a greatly enhanced status. The confidence of the public was displayed by a flood of praise, at the ending of the strike. General Order No. 1553, dated 12 May 1926, warmly expressed Major Becke's appreciation to the Shropshire Constabulary —

'I wish to convey to all ranks my sincerest appreciation and thanks for the zeal, tact, cheerfulness and firmness shown by everyone. As Chief Constable my responsibilities must necessarily be heavy, but I can assure you my sense of responsibility was reduced to a minimum thanks to the grand response you gave to every call made on you.

My best thanks to you all.'[4]

Brigadier-General A.H.O. Lloyd, vice-chairman of the Salop Standing Joint Committee wrote congratulating Jack Becke and his officers, of all ranks, on the magnificent work carried out during the national crisis.

'The regular Force of Shropshire Police has given the lead to and set a fine example to, the whole County and its community.'[5]

At a Shrewsbury council meeting, Councillor L. Jackson, who described himself as — 'one of those terrible fellows who has been on strike,' thanked the Mayor, the members of the

Watch Committee, and the Borough Police for the tactful manner in which they had handled the situation. There had been no disorder, and nothing that was in anyway provocative had been done. He went on to say that the Chief Constable had been an 'absolute brick', and had helped the striker's leaders in every possible way in their efforts to provide amusement for the men who were on strike, and to keep them off the streets.

Nor were the people of Shropshire forgotten, a letter from Major Becke was published in the local press, praising the many volunteers who had come forward —

'From North, South, East and West of Shropshire her loyal citizens responded at once to His Majesty's Governments call for help. Thousands left their occupation and started work at once. Thousands registered or offered their assistance. I personally received dozens of letters cheery in tone, helpful in nature. We policemen probably realize more than anyone else how much this ready response towards law and order, and everyone must realize the important part the response played in carrying on the life of the county.

To one and all, we members of the Shropshire Constabulary tender our sincerest thanks.

I feel I must express to all strikers my appreciation of their good behaviour during the strike. I would only urge them in future to think for themselves; then their own common sense will guide them, I feel confident, into the right channels.'[6]

A story told and retold over the years, and which never failed to amuse the officers of the county force, was one which concerned the advent of a new Chief-Constable to the Shropshire Constabulary. A military man, he was at first inclined to look down his nose, at the rural police force, which he was now to command. Determined to show these slow country bobbies just how efficient and alert he was going to be, he decided to make lightning visits to out of the way districts of his new command. His idea being to trap unwary constables into indiscretions before they were aware of who he was. With this in mind, and sure that he would not be recognised, he walked one hot summer afternoon through a small village in the south of the county. Casually meeting the village constable; which he had hoped for, he greeted him with great affability, remarking on the warmth of the day. He soon steered the conversation around to the subject of alcoholic drink, and wondered where he might obtain one. The constable informed him that it was outside licensing hours, the village pub was shut. The Chief Constable persisted saying — 'but you of course will know how to get one.'

Eventually the local bobbie took the would be stranger to the back of the local hostelry, and knocked on the door. The landlord greeted the constable with — 'your usual constable, and what will your friend have?'

With a drink in his hand the Chief Constable, all set to close his trap, asked the constable — 'what would you say to your sergeant if he was to appear now?' The constable slowly smiled, and replied 'I would say sir, that I was having a drink at the invitation of the Chief Constable.'

History has not recorded the re-action of the Chief Constable, his trap so neatly foiled, by one whom he thought was a slow thinking country constable, but no doubt his first impressions of the men of the Shropshire Constabulary underwent a rapid change at this example of resourcefulness.

Mechanization of the Shrewsbury Borough Police appears to have started in March 1927, when the watch committee authorised the purchase of a 'Motor Utility Van' at a cost of £430. The make was a 'Bean', which perhaps gave the Watch Committee the idea of painting it a dark green. It had the Borough arms painted on each side. In the June of the same year, a register of criminals was first inaugurated by the Shrewsbury force.

The resignation of Constable Harry Garnet Hay from the Borough Force, is recorded on the 16 January 1928, after completing twenty-five years service. He was one of the two mounted constables. These mounted police officers had been a colourful feature of the Borough Police since their establishment in 1899. One of the early officers had been constable (later sergeant) Robert (Bob) Roberts, who, when in his teens, had served in the Boer War, with the 17th Lancers. His exciting tales of exploits with the 'Death or Glory Boys' were always in demand by the younger constables.

Chapter Eleven

1930 – 1939

Motor traffic was becoming more and more of a responsibility to police forces all over the country. In 1930, the Shropshire Constabulary established a 'Traffic Department' to deal with this ever increasing activity, and it was in this year that the general speed limit of twenty miles an hour was abolished.

The Chief Constable spoke to the Salop Standing Joint Committee, about his concern over the number of accidents, in which motor vehicles had been involved over the previous few years. He suggested that it might prove a deterrent to dangerous driving, if he were allowed to have a fast light motor car in charge of a uniformed officer, to patrol the roads of the county. He pointed out that the majority of cases did not come to the notice of the police until after an accident had occurred. He was of the opinion that if it was known that a police car was on patrol, this fact might cause motorists to exercise more care in their driving. Major Becke recommended that a 'Wolsey Hornet' 'six cylinder, fabric saloon be purchased as a police car, at a price of £175. However the car chosen by the committee was a 'Standard Ensign Six', costing £247. 10s. The first motor patrol in Shropshire started operating on the 1 December 1930.

In Shrewsbury the great innovation of 1930, was the erection of four street police boxes. The boxes were erected at – Monkmoor Road Railway Bridge; The Mount; St. Michael's Street Recreation Ground, and at the Column.

An interesting suggestion that the County of Montgomeryshire might amalgamate with the County of Shropshire for police purposes, was made in 1931. It would appear that the Standing Joint Committee of Montgomeryshire had made the same offer to Radnorshire. Later however Montgomeryshire decided against amalgamation with either county, and stayed in control of their own police force.

On 21 July 1931, a house in Llandrindod Wells was broken into, and £800 of jewellery stolen. The thief's fingerprints were found by the Radnorshire police, and sent to Scotland Yard who identified them as those of a man named Owain Glyndwr Evans, a dangerous criminal who usually carried firearms. The following month Evans broke into a house in Shrewsbury and shot at a policeman who attempted to arrest him as he left the premises. Luckily the constable was unhurt. Posters were printed offering a reward for information leading to Evan's arrest. Freely distributed in the London area, they brought results. Information was received on the 14 September 1931, that Evans was at a house in Tachbrook Street, S.W.1. Here the Metropolitan Police found Evans, armed with a revolver, hiding in a cupboard. He was handed over to the Shrewsbury Police to be dealt with on the serious charge of shooting at a policeman. Sentenced to seven years penal servitude, the charge of stealing the jewellery was taken into consideration. This was a good example of fingerprint evidence identifying a criminal.

At the beginning of 1931, the Shrewsbury Watch Committee made a report to the Borough Council, that they had under consideration the installation of automatic traffic control signals, at various points within the town. Relieving for patrol duties, officers now engaged in traffic control. The suggestion was approved by the council, and an application was made to the Ministry of Transport for approval, and a grant. Application granted, the traffic lights were put up in two instalments. The first batch in late 1931, at the junction of Cross Street and Castle-Foregate; New Street corner, Frankwell; Coleham Head and the English Bridge, with the final one of this instalment being erected at Post Office corner (Pride-Hill and St. Mary's Street).

The second instalment of traffic lights were erected at — bottom of Wyle-Cop; Mardol Head; Lloyd's Bank corner (Pride Hill and High Street), and Castle Gates (Railway Station).

As with all new and revolutionary ideas, there were people who took time to understand them. In the December of 1931, the first accident was reported, when a car and a cycle were in collision at the English Bridge lights. The Chief Constable, Frank Davies, decided that it was time he took a strong line, and published his warning —

'The Chief Constable said there were several people who were not obeying the traffic signals as they should do, and he would like it known that the police had been instructed to take proceedings against all persons who disobeyed the signals.

They had been set up for two months, and it was time people got to know what they were there for. It was now his intention to take proceedings against people who did not obey those signals, and there was no excuse for anyone not seeing them.'

From 1931 onwards, traffic signals became accepted into our way of life, an added frustration to some, but a mechanical robot which released constables to carry on with their more important duties of keeping the peace.

The merging of borough forces with the county constabularies had received considerable prominance for many years. The report of the Desborough Committee (January 1920) expressed views in favour of such mergers. In 1922 the government included a clause on the same subject (Clause 19) in the Economy (Misc: Provisions) Bill, which was not proceeded with . During the course of the inquiry by a Royal Commission on Local Government in 1928, suggestions were made of the abolition of police forces in boroughs, with populations below 75,000.

On all the above occasions the Shrewsbury Corporation had expressed strong disagreement with the proposals. In 1931 a Select Committee of the House of Commons was appointed to consider the amalgamations of the smaller police forces of

England and Wales with the larger units of police administration. Shrewsbury once more opposed the idea. The Watch Committee reported that they were convinced that the amalgamation of the borough police with that of the county, would be a most retrogade step. It would not effect any appreciable economy in the cost of the service, and would throw a heavy financial burden on the ratepayers. In their opinion the proposal would be detrimental to the efficient policing of the town. With regard to the Fire Fighting service now run by the police, the result of the amalgamation of police forces would be that less wealthy towns, such as Shrewsbury, would be debarred from operating economic police fire brigades, whereas larger towns with their own police forces would be allowed to continue to do so under the Act of 1893. However, once again the borough police forces were reprieved, and the fears of towns in a similar case to Shrewsbury were allayed.

Police Constable Humphreys of the Shropshire Constabulary retired in 1932. He had been stationed for twenty-five years at Hadley. It was at that time a record stay on one beat, so far as the Shropshire force was concerned. In fact his record was not beaten for some forty years or more, not until Constable 156. Eric Ellis retired in 1976, after being stationed at Cressage for 28 years. With the amalgamation of 1967, he became P.C. 1010 of the new West Mercia Constabulary, but still stayed on at Cressage until his retirement, after twenty-nine years service.

The visit of the Prince of Wales to Shrewsbury in 1932, called for extra police precautions. The Chief Constable of Shrewsbury was authorised to call in additional officers from outside the borough. Four detectives were loaned from the city forces of Birmingham, Liverpool, Manchester and Wolverhampton. While seventy officers of the Shropshire Constabulary were drafted into the town. The strength of the police being such as to deter anyone with criminal leanings. The royal visit passed off peaceably.

The Shrewsbury Borough Police officers were noted for

"Shrewsbury Police Fire Engine" c. 1930

172

being very careful with uniform issues. In 1933 it was found necessary to purchase forty-one summer and forty-one winter helmets for a new issue to the force. It was noted at the time that the white (summer) helmets which were being replaced, were the ones bought in 1900, thirty-three years before. Considering that these helmets were only constructed of plaited straw, it spoke well of the care that had been taken of them.

A long link with the county police was broken at the end of 1933, when Chief Superintendent James Fulcher retired. He had joined the Shropshire Constabulary in 1885, at the age of twenty. In 1919 he had been appointed Deputy Chief Constable, a position that he had held for fourteen years. Now he had become the longest serving member of the force, having completed forty-eight years and two hundred and nine days approved service. At the age of sixty-nine his retirement was well earned.

In January 1934, Chief Constable Frank Davies, appeared in the New Year's Honours List, when he was awarded the King's Police Medal for distinguished service. It was a very popular award at Shrewsbury, for under Mr. Davies's command the borough force had won a high reputation. Relations between police and public were excellent, and the fair and impartial manner in which Mr. Davies and his men carried out their duties commanded the respect of the townspeople.

The Silver Jubilee of the reign of King George V was celebrated nationally in 1935. It was the first time that country wide festivities had taken place to celebrate the Silver Jubilee of a British monarch. There had not been a celebration in 1785, when George III attained the twenty-fifth year of his reign, illness of the principal figure, ruled out any such festivities. Likewise Queen Victoria, who had lost her consort, Prince Albert in 1861, was still in mourning in 1862, so did not wish her Silver Jubilee to be marked by any festivities.

Jubilee medals were presented by the Mayor of Shrewsbury to three members of the borough police force — Chief

"Frank Davies, K.P.M. Chief Constable, Shrewsbury
1918–1940. Caricature by Sabine."

174

Constable Frank Davies; Inspector George Henry Faulconbridge, and Police Constable Walter Henry Jones.

A similar presentation was made by the Earl of Powis to
members of the Shropshire Constabulary. Recipients were —
Major Jack Becke, Chief Constable; Superintendents — C.H.
Roberts; R.W. Barber; R. Evans; T.E. Barnwell; W.T. Hayes
and A. Smith. Inspector A.J. Ridgway. Sergeants — J.H.
Machin and T.E. Harris. Constables — R.W. Brunt; T.H.
Hopley; J. Penney; C.W. Penney, and E. Tonkinson.

Amongst the many events of 1935, was a National Police
Parade, held in Hyde Park, on the 20 July, before King George
V. Officers representing every police force in the country
attended the parade. Contingents from both the Shropshire
constabulary and the Shrewsbury Borough Police proudly
represented their county and borough.

On the extention of the Shrewsbury borough boundaries,
on the 1 April 1934, the strength of the Borough Police force
was enlarged by the addition of three more constables. The
authorised establishment now being fifty officers.

The force now consisted of — One Chief Constable; three
inspectors; five sergeants; two acting-sergeants and thirty-
nine constables.

His Majesty King George V awarded, in the 1935 New
Year's Honours List, the King's Police Medal to Police Constable 131. J. Evason, of the Shropshire Constabulary, for
gallantry. This brave officer had made an heroic attempt to
save the life of a child, trapped in a burning cottage at
Rowton, Halfway House, on the 2 June 1934. Braving the
flames he had managed to find the child, and brought it out
of the burning cottage, unfortunately too late to save its life.
The Chief Constable, to signify his appreciation of the act, and
of the honour won by Constable Evason, promoted him to the
rank of Acting-Sergeant.

Superintendent Edward Morris retired in the February of
1935. A noted athlete in his younger days, he had been an
international footballer. He ranked amongst the few who had
played for his country (Wales) against each of the other three

175

countries which made up the British Isles, for two years in succession. He had been capped six times for Wales. After playing for Wales against England in 1892, he was signed on for Accrington Stanley, then a power in English football. He left Accrington in the following year to join the Shropshire Constabulary. Although a centre-half, Morris was also a sprinter, and won many trophies in both the Midlands and the North. At the Shropshire Police Sports, he had won the hundred yards title, six years running. He was replaced as Deputy Chief Constable by Superintendent Henry Roberts.

The death was reported in January 1935, of ex-superintendent Alfred Edmund Taylor, M.B.E., J.P. A native of Hull, he had joined the Shropshire Constabulary in 1893. The superintendent founded the 'Oswestry Boy's Club', reputed to be only the second of its kind, when it was established in 1920. He had been invested with the M.B.E. in 1928, the year before his retirement.

At the end of September 1935, Major Jack Becke, O.B.E., resigned his post as Chief Constable of Shropshire, to take up a similar post in the neighbouring county of Cheshire.

Of the hundred candidates who came forward to apply for the now vacant post of chief constable, the Salop Standing Joint Committee chose Captain Harold Arthur Golden, an instructor at the Royal Military Academy, Woolwich, as the tenth chief constable of the Shropshire Constabulary.

It was in 1935 that the lone patrol car of the Shropshire Constabulary was joined by two more patrol cars — twelve horse-power Humbers. One was based at Bridgnorth, and the other at Whitchurch.

A former inspector of the Shropshire Constabulary made headlines in the national press during the 1930's. Anthony William Hall claimed the throne of England. He had joined the Shropshire Constabulary after World War I, as Police Constable 168. He was spoken of in general orders as a first class photographer, shorthand -writer, and typist, with a good working knowledge on the subject of fingerprints. At the age of twenty-eight, he had risen to be one of the youngest police inspectors in the country. His meteoric police career came to an abrupt end in the mid-twenties, after a disagreement with his chief constable.

On leaving the force, he went to North America, returning to this country some time in late 1930, when he went to live at Hereford.

It was from Hereford that he posted a letter addressed to — 'George Frederick Ernest Albert Windsor (alias Guelph) Buckingham Palace, St. James' Park. S.W.1.' It was a lengthy epistle of eleven foolscap pages, and required King George V — 'in the name of the law to relinquish the Imperial Crown of this realm.' A mass of genealogical details followed to prove his claim to the throne. He based his claim on being a descendent of a male child born to Henry VIII and Anne Boleyn, prior to their marriage. The boy's name was John, and he had been brought up by a farmer, named Hall. Anthony Hall addressed meetings all over the country. One such meeting at Ludlow in 1931, was held in Castle Square, where he spoke at length on being the rightful heir to the throne. He elaborated a scheme for the rebuilding of Britain, which, he claimed would result in the extinction of the National Debt and the abolition of income tax. His remarks were generally received with amused tolerance by his listeners. It is said that in a six year period he addressed 1,000 meetings.

There were unruly scenes at some of these, and Hall was fined on a number of occasions for obstruction or breaches of the peace. This happened at Hereford in 1936. Hall had made an attempt to hold a public meeting in St. Peter's Square, on a Saturday evening. He was charged with obstructing the free passage of the square. Causing a crowd to collect. Assaulting Inspector Brommage while in the execution of his duty, and conducting himself in a manner likely to cause a breach of the peace. He informed the magistrates of the Hereford City Court, that he would make Hereford his capital and that he would establish royal mints in every city in the country. When fined twenty pounds by the magistrates he at first protested that as their lawful king they could not demand

177

it, but then quietly paid up. One of his more popular pledges was to increase the strength of beer. He left Hereford to live in London, which he pledged to rebuild — to accommodate 100,000,000 inhabitants. He continued to serve King George V with notices to quit the throne, and even had printed his own currency, which he signed with a flourish — Anthony I. He was known jocularly in the Shropshire Constabulary as King Antonio. He died in 1947, at Little Dewhurst, Hereford.

The only crown that he ever wore, was the one depicted on the badge of the Shropshire Constabulary, which he wore whilst serving with the force.

Major Golden, Chief Constable of Shropshire endeared himself to his officers, by joining in their sports. In a football match played against the 'Whitchurch — Amateurs' the 25 March 1936, the Chief Constable took to the field in the position of centre-forward. Fifty pounds were raised by this match for charity. Charity matches had always been a strong point of the police teams. A few months later, a cricket match was played at St. George's, between the Shropshire Constabulary and the St. George's team. This was an annual event, which had begun in 1924, and had been the means of raising over five hundred pounds for local hospital and nursing associations.

Nazi Germany was by now casting a cloud over Europe. Thoughts of war, and preparations for it, were beginning to be thought of. A draft scheme for air raid precautions was adopted in Shropshire in October 1936. The County Chief Constable was appointed 'County Controller.'

A report given in February 1937, by Frank Davies, Chief Constable of Shrewsbury, to the Watch Committee, lists all the items (live and otherwise) which had been found in the streets of Shrewsbury, during the year 1936. Taken to the borough police-station for safe custody were — twenty-six motor-cars; two motor-cycles, and two hundred and seventy-four bicycles, which had been found unattended in the streets. In addition one hundred and eighteen dogs were seized, of which ninety-one were claimed, and twenty-seven painlessly destroyed. All of the fifteen horses; thirty-three cattle; eight pigs and two hundred and eighty five sheep found straying, and taken by the police, were later claimed by their owners. It paints a very rural picture of the town's streets, and makes one wonder if the duties of shepherd and cattle-drover, were included in a constable's curriculum. There was also mentioned in the same report that there had been one hundred and twenty-five street accidents involving personal injuries, three persons killed and one hundred and twenty-seven injured.

A great sigh of relief must have gone up from the officers of police forces in 1936, when a change-over was made from brass buttons, cap, and helmet badges to chromium regalia. The old order of spit and polish before breakfast every day, had become a chore of the past.

Major Golden had by now, overhauled and streamlined the force administration and filing systems; including a new filing system at each beat station. The constabulary sports were also revived in 1936, and were held on the Gay Meadow.

Not all offenders brought before the magistrates by the police were hardened criminals, many were merely of a nuisance value. Such a one was Henry Jones, better known by his nickname as 'Spaniel'. Of no fixed abode, Henry was very averse to being out of doors on a cold night. One of his regular habits was that of breaking shop-windows, not I may add with the criminal intent of stealing the contents, but for the purpose of having a constable arrest him. A night in a warm cell, out of the rain and cold, was all that 'Spaniel' asked.

One very cold night in January 1936, 'Spaniel' approached Police Constable Tuttle of the Shrewsbury Borough Police, and asked him to come and look at a window. The constable accompanied him to Groves, jeweller's shop on Castle Gates, where he admitted to breaking the window. He told Tuttle, most plaintively, 'I'm not staying out on a night like this'.

Next morning he was brought before the Shrewsbury magistrates, when the Chief Constable himself, had a word or two about him. Mr. Davies remarked — 'When this man gets in the mood he was in last night he will do anything.' 'If he is refused admittance to the police station he will go out and break a window to make us lock him up.' He went on to say that he was one of the worst characters that he had struck during his thirty-six years police experience.' Spaniel had 103 previous convictions for stealing, fighting, bad-language and being drunk. It was the third time that he had broken this particular jeweller's window. 'Spaniel' told the court that it had not been fit for a dog to be out that particular night.

His 104th conviction decided the magistrates to get rid of this nuisance to the police for more than a night, and he was given a sentence of three months hard labour. Little Spaniel would not be under the policemen's feet again until the weather was warm enough for him to stay outside.

The Coronation of King George VI was held in 1937, and presentations of the Coronation Medals were much in the news. The Mayor of Shrewsbury presented medals to the Borough Police. Firstly to Alderman H.O. Ashton (Chairman of the Watch Committee) and a special constable since 1916. Medals were also awarded to Chief Constable Frank Davies, Inspector J. Lunt, and Sergeant G.H. Macdivitt. One day's leave with pay was awarded to all members of the county constabulary who had served on the day of the Coronation. While the following members of the county constabulary were awarded the Coronation Medal — Major H.A. Golden, Chief Constable; Deputy Chief Constable C.H. Roberts; Superintendents — R. Evans; T.E. Barnwell; W.T. Hayes; A. Smith and A.J. Ridgway; Sergeant C.A.T. Vale; Constables — H. Dodd; P.E. Ewels; G. Lewis and A. Ogilvie.

In August 1937, three boys escaped from the Saltersford Training School in Cheshire, making their way towards Shrewsbury. The Borough Police after a long hard chase had them cornered against a bend of the river Severn, when one of them dived in, attempting to escape to the opposite bank. Constable Henry Speake, himself only twenty-one, dived in after him. The result was disaster, three quarters of the way

180

across Speake disappeared. It was eight hours before his body was recovered. In the opinion of the police surgeon he had died of heart failure, supervening on acute congestion of the lungs, which was caused by the shock of having entered the water whilst in a breathless condition.

The three boys were caught and sent back to Saltersford. But the price had been far too high.

Detective training courses first started in 1936, at Wakefield, Yorkshire. In the following year, four constables of the Shropshire Constabulary set a very high standard, when out of a total of twenty students on each course, a Shropshire officer occupied either a first, second or third place in the finals.

The annual report submitted to the Watch Committee by Frank Davies, Chief Constable of Shrewsbury, in 1938, made mention of the state of the Air Raid Precautions within the town. Volunteers had not been slow to step forward — one hundred and eighty-nine special constables; fifty-one auxiliary firemen; one hundred air-raid wardens; eight motor-drivers; one hundred and twenty-eight first aid volunteers and three messengers had enrolled for duty.

In the wider area of the county, instruction in air-raid precaution work was well on its way. A scheme for the rural areas was issued by the County Controller, Major H.A. Golden, which divided the county into forty-two districts, each district coinciding with one or more beat areas of the county constabulary. In a General Order issued in May 1938, all ranks of the Shropshire Constabulary, and particularly the sergeants, were reminded that responsibility for the success of the organization must in the end depend on the police, and that whatever the situation may be in peace-time, the police would undoubtedly be in executive control in time of war. A considerable amount of police time was spent in recruiting, instruction and the issuing of equipment in connection with the Air Raid Precaution Scheme.

At the beginning of April 1938, Police-woman Lilian Lenn retired. Miss Lenn had spent the whole of her twenty years service at Oswestry. A historic figure, she had been one of the first policewomen to join the Shropshire Constabulary in 1918.

Of the four appointed in 1918, two had been made redundant in 1921, leaving just Miss Lenn and Miss Westerdick, still at Oswestry. Now only Miss Westerdick was left. The sole policewoman in the Shropshire Constabulary.

The death of ex-superintendent Peter Harrison of the Shropshire Constabulary was recorded on the 24 July 1938, aged seventy-seven. He had retired in 1921, after serving for forty years with the force. He had followed in his father's footsteps, the late Inspector Henry Harrison, who had joined the Shropshire Constabulary in 1858, serving over thirty years. Peter Harrison's uncle had also been a member of the county force, whilst his son, Constable Frank Harrison served for many years with the Cheshire Constabulary. Thus three generations of the Harrison family, between them, completed over a century of service in the Shropshire Constabulary, becoming an excellent example of how the police service has become a traditional way of life in some families.

Eagerness to make the Shrewsbury Fire Service a more efficient body, cost Inspector George Henry Faulconbridge his life. A senior inspector of the Shrewsbury Borough Police, and second in command of the town's fire-brigade, he was fatally injured at a drill held on the 24 August 1938, when he fell about twenty feet, whilst demonstrating how two people could be lowered to the ground with a fire-escape. A very popular officer, he had been with the Shrewsbury Borough Police since 1914, and a member of the Police Fire Brigade since its formation in 1918. His death was a great loss to both the police and fire brigade of the borough.

Superintendent Richard Evans retired in March 1939, after forty-one year's service. Once again we witness an outstanding example of a family tradition of service in the Shropshire Constabulary. His brother, Superintendent Alfred Evans had retired in 1925, served nearly thirty-four years, whilst a third brother, Constable George Evans had retired on reaching twenty-six years service. Inspector John George Evans, a son of Superintendent Alfred Evans, served over twenty-seven years. The total service of one hundred and twenty-eight years given by the Evans family must stand as an all time record within the Shropshire Constabulary.

With war clouds looming nearer, plans were made to augment the police forces. A First Police Reserve had been constituted, which consisted of ex-policemen, who had volunteered to return to full-time duty when called upon. In return for which they had been paid a retaining fee. The Shropshire Constabulary had sixty-one members in this reserve, all ready to return should an emergency call for them. Also there were seven hundred and sixty special constables willing to serve. These men were available for part-time duties, though a number in the event were able to offer full-time service.

Another category of reserves were the newly formed (1939) Police War Reserve, consisting of men recruited solely for war service. Recruitment was from men over the age of thirty, who would wear uniform similar to that of the regular police and whose full range of duties they would eventually carry out.

With regard to the Shrewsbury Borough Police, it was decided by the watch committee that ten men should be recruited from their First Police Reserve, and provided with uniforms and equipment. In respect of the Police War Reserve (general part-time and unpaid) the Chief Constable had been authorised to enroll up to fifty-two (the establishment of the regular borough police), whom it would be necessary to train and provide with uniform and equipment in advance.

War was declared on the 3 September 1939. Park Hall Military Camp, near Oswestry, was soon bursting at the seams with army recruits in training. Concern over relations between the men, and the local young girls of Oswestry, caused representations to be made to the Salop Standing Joint Committee, for further policewomen. Application was then made to the Secretary of State for augmentation of the women police constables to bring the establishment up to

183

"Shropshire Constabulary Women's Auxiliary Police Corps 1944"

184

four.   Approval was obtained, and three more policewomen were appointed.

Two policewomen were then stationed at Cosford, to keep an eye on the morals around that camp, and one went to join Policewoman Westerdick at Oswestry, to assist her in patrolling Oswestry and the outskirts of Park Hall Camp.

A Women's Auxiliary Police Corps was instituted in August 1939, for women between the ages of eighteen and fifty-five. The first batch of uniforms were well cut, having been made locally, and to measure, at Messrs. Major's of Shrewsbury. Later the uniforms became issue from a central depot, and were supplied in a similar way to those of the men.

In the early days of the war these auxiliary policewomen were only allowed to carry out a rather restricted range of police duties, mainly consisting of indoor duties – clerical; telephone operators; radio and canteen work.   In some cases the driving of police cars and their maintenance came within their scope.   Later many of these women were attested as police constables, enabling them to extend their duties to include the whole range of law enforcement.

The day after war was declared on Germany, four patriotic young ladies turned up at the 'Porch House', (headquarters of the County Air Raid Precautions) as volunteers.   The first two – Miss Evelyn Anne (Toni) Norton and Mrs. Carol Doulton (an American lady) were immediately sent next door, to the headquarters of the Shropshire Constabulary, where they became the first two members of the Women's Auxiliary Police Corps in Shropshire.   The second two – Miss Margaret Carswell and Miss Patricia Duggan were at first accepted into the Air Raid Precaution service, but were later transferred into the Women's Auxiliary Police Corps, with the county constabulary.   The older members of the police force did not approve of the young ladies, who were to them, trespassers into what had always been a male preserve.

But, nothing daunted, the ladies soon proved their worth.

Towards the end of 1939, Shropshire police officers who belonged to the army reserve were recalled to the colours.

185

November saw thirty-eight of them rejoining their old regiments. Five constables of the Shrewsbury Borough Police took off their blue uniforms to don khaki.

In no case did the recalls necessitate promotions or transfers amongst the remaining officers. Some of the vacancies were filled by calling upon members of the First Police Reserve, many of whom were retired police constables.

To offset the losses in manpower to both the police and fire services, the Police and Firemen (War Service) Act 1939, suspended the right to retire on pension without a medical certificate, except with the consent of a Chief Constable or the Police Authority. The auxiliary policemen were prevented from resigning by the Defence Regulations.

The early days of the war found the police forces of the country increased in numbers by at least 50%, by the added strength of the various reserves and special constables, despite the loss of reservists to the armed services.

A considerable burden of extra work was now imposed on both regular police and specials alike. When on duty, all officers had to carry a service respirator and a steel helmet, painted either blue or white, according to rank, and bearing the legend 'POLICE'.

Chapter Twelve

1940 — 1949

The centenary of the Shropshire Constabulary occurred in March 1940, it passed by very quietly. Wartime put a check on celebrations even of the most historic kind.

After forty years in the Shrewsbury Borough Police, of which for twenty-one years he had been Chief Constable, Mr. Frank Davies resigned on 31 March 1940. During Mr. Frank Davies's term of office, the borough force had been maintained at a very high level of efficiency, and the same could be said of the police fire brigade, of which he had been superintendent. During his period of office there had been many changes in police work and techniques. New legislation, particularly enactments concerning road traffic, had greatly added to the duties of the police, and the greater mobility of the criminal had made crime detection more difficult, hence the need for an ever-increasing level of co-operation between the forces which still remained in England and Wales. Many presentations were made to the retiring Chief Constable, including a certificate of appreciation from the Watch Committee, chronicling details of his career and services with the Shrewsbury Borough Police.

In his speech of thanks the ex-Chief Constable spoke of the qualifications necessary to be a good policeman —

'the strength of a lion, the eye-sight of an eagle, the tact of an ambassador, the worldly knowledge of an undergraduate, the patience of a husband and the memory of a wronged woman.'[1]

His successor was Chief Inspector George Harold Macdivitt,

who was appointed Chief Constable of the Borough of Shrewsbury on the 1 April 1940.

Macdivitt was also appointed chief officer of the Shrewsbury Fire Brigade on the same terms as his predecessor, namely, £25 per annum, plus fees for attendances at fires and £25 per annum in lieu of uniform. The latter appointment was subject to termination on three months notice, in view of the possible reorganization of the Shrewsbury Fire Brigade under the act of 1938. The first day of office for the new Chief Constable was one for him to remember, for it was also the day on which the Princess Royal visited Shrewsbury. Macdivitt had the pleasure of having the princess wish him every success in his new office.

A number of German pamphlets were dropped on Shropshire in mid 1940, which were confiscated by the county constabulary. Major Golden decided that he would make Herr Hitler's words work to the benefit of the Red Cross, and had the pamphlets sold at all the county police stations at sixpence each. This raised a total amount of £116. 2s. 3d for the Red Cross, well done Adolf.

At long last the special constables were to be put into uniform. The Shrewsbury Watch Committee decided in September 1940 to issue their specials with — Cap, greatcoat, tunic and trousers.

Two months later the Salop Standing Joint Committee decided to supply full uniforms to the 364 county special constables who had signed a guarantee as to service, but — a raincoat only to the remaining 398 who had not signed such a guarantee.

In the same month, the committee informed the Secretary of State that in their opinion the present establishment of women police in Shropshire should not be increased. This is in variance with their statement made four months later, in February 1941, when they record that the establishment of women police in Shropshire had been increased from four to six, the additional appointments had been made to complete the establishment.

The Shrewsbury Watch Committee were still adamant in refusing to employ women police officers. A Home Office circular, dated 8 August 1940 was received by the Chief Constable – it stated that the Police Authority should consider the desirability of the employment of Women Police or Women Police Auxiliaries during the present war.

The reply went back from Shrewsbury to the Home Office – 'that no such appointments were contemplated at present.'

A new service was established towards the end of 1940, that of Police Auxiliary Messengers. A Home Office circular had authorised the engagement of messengers up to the strength of the force. The messengers were to be youths of the age of 16 years and upwards. They would be paid 21s. 6d per week up to and including 17 years of age, and 26s. 6d over 17 years. The whole cost of the messengers would be borne by the Government. The messengers were intended to assist in police work generally, and would be especially useful in the event of any dislocation of telephone services.

The Chief Constable recommended that six auxiliary messengers be appointed to the Shrewsbury Force. In February 1941 the purchase of 60 badges for the use of the police messengers shows that the numbers had risen steeply.

The sight of policemen on duty in gas-masks, was a great source of surprise at first. The local press sought to allay any cause of alarm by assuring everyone that it was to become part of the Shropshire scene, and that in time it would become as familiar as the blackout and rationing.

The wearing of gas-masks was due to a decision of the Chief Constable that all members of the Shropshire Constabulary should wear their masks on duty, for at least half-an-hour each week.

Wartime was a period when mutual aid was a compelling necessity. One sergeant with nine constables of the Shrewsbury Borough Police left on 15 November 1940 to assist the Coventry City Police, following one of the many severe air-raids which that city suffered.

Under the wartime reinforcement scheme every police force

189

with an establishment of over fifty men had a quota of officers fixed by the Home Office, who were made available for reinforcing police colleagues in other areas, as the need arose. The City of Coventry with its many severe air-raids received assistance from a total of 941 police officers, who came from thirteen different forces.

The Shrewsbury Watch Committee with its borough police, had fought successfully all attempts to appoint women police officers for 27 years. In 1942, at long last, the male bastion was successfully stormed. The Chief Constable, George Macdivitt, reported that the Acting Inspector of Constabulary had, at a recent interview, impressed upon him the urgent necessity for the recruitment of members of the Women's Auxiliary Police Corps, to assist in police work. The employment of women would release for outside work, men now employed on clerical and telephone duties. The Home Office recommended that three women should be engaged to perform duties now carried out by two men. The Chief Constable went on to say that women engaged as full-time members of the Women's Auxiliary Police Corps would be paid a weekly wage of 47s. 0d. and would be provided with uniform, or if engaged on indoor work, with overalls. The advice of the Home Office also provided for the enlistment of part-time, unpaid members of the W.A.P.C. to perform duty on weekday evenings and at weekends. These volunteers would also be provided with uniform. The wages of the W.A.P.C. full-time personnel would be borne by the Exchequer, and their uniforms would attract a 50% police grant.

The Chief Constable then recommended that four paid, full-time, and twenty unpaid part-time members of the W.A.P.C. be appointed. The Watch Committee agreeing to his recommendations.

The following month Macdivitt reported that he had appointed three of the four full-time W.A.P.C. The three ladies making history were —

Miss Vera E. Bezant. 7 February 1942.

Mrs. E. Oulton-Dorrofield. 16 February 1942.

Miss W. Bettina Blandford. 28 February 1942.

In July 1942, the Salop Standing Joint Committee reported that the call-up of Shropshire Constabulary officers under the age of 25, would result in the loss of twenty-three men. To counterbalance this loss, the Home Secretary had approved the appointment of eight additional Police War Reservists and six Women's Auxiliary Police Corps.

The authorised strength of the Shrewsbury Borough Police force now stood at fifty-two. viz:- Chief Constable; Chief Inspector; two Inspectors; seven sergeants; one Acting Sergeant, and forty constables. One sergeant employed whole time on A.R.P. duties was additional to the authorised strength.

The authorised establishment of police auxiliaries was three First Police Reserves, and eleven Police War Reserves. All of whom had been employed full-time. In addition to the regular police and full-time auxiliaries, there were 140 special constables performing part-time duties.

Major H.A. Golden, the Chief Constable of Shropshire appeared in the New Year's Honours List for 1943, on being awarded the Order of the British Empire, in recognition of his war work.

Stopping runaway horses, or even bolting cattle on the way to the Smithfield, was not an unusual undertaking for a constable of the Shrewsbury force, but there is on record one outstanding example. On the 27 March 1943, Constable 77R J. Turner of the Police War Reserve was commended for devotion to duty when he valiantly stopped two heavy draught horses which had bolted on the English Bridge. An act of bravery in itself, but without which there could have been disaster in the town. At that precise moment there was a 'Wings for Victory' procession progressing through the streets of Shrewsbury, had the horses carried on into the town, there would have been a serious dislocation of traffic, chaotic confusion in the procession, and possibly injuries to the many people both bystanders and those involved in the procession.

Constable Turner was awarded the Certificate of the

Carnegie Hero Trust Fund together with a cheque for ten pounds, in recognition of his gallant action. This was the first occasion that an award of this kind had been made to a member of the Shrewsbury Borough Police Force.

The Shrewsbury Borough Police found themselves becoming concerned in matters international, brushes with the American armed forces were taking place in the town. Macdivitt reported the receipt of a letter from the official shorthand writer commending Sergeants R. Lambert and F.J. Evans with Constable I.R. Jones for the manner in which they had given evidence at a U.S.A. Court Martial on the 18 May 1943. Later in the year, commendations were once more in the news, this time for Sergeant E.J. Talbot. It would appear that the sergeant accompanied by a constable, saw at 4.55 a.m. on the morning of 9 October 1943, four armed American soldiers, under the control of a U.S. Colonel, about to break into a private house in Shrewsbury. The sergeant ascertained that the colonel had ordered the men to force an entry into the house. Talbot regardless of his personal safety, and in the face of threats of violence, prevented the Americans from carrying out their intention. Colonel Vince of the Home Office, stated that Sergeant Talbot had dealt with the situation in a very praiseworthy manner.

Commendations were the order of the day for Sergeant H.R. Maule, and Constables R.E. Chidley; C.J. Jones; J. Stone, and Police War Reserve Constable Lewis.

The Chief Constable in reporting their bravery, spoke of the day — 31 May 1943 when the above officers of the Shrewsbury Borough Police, at great risk to their personal safety, made a brave attempt to rescue the crew of a Mosquito aircraft, which had crashed at Berwick Road. The Mosquito had collided with a Spitfire which had crashed in flames a short distance away. The officers had hurried to the scene of the crashed Mosquito, immediately following the accident, and regardless of the danger of explosion, which might well have occurred, (the plane containing live ammunition, and with large quantities of petrol issuing from the wrecked aircraft), at once proceeded to recover the bodies of the dead airmen.

Major H.A. Golden relinquished his post as Chief Constable of Shropshire on 1 November 1943, to return to the army. It was decided by the Salop Standing Joint Committee that during his absence, the present deputy, Superintendent Thomas Edward Barnwell, would as from that date, be appointed Acting Chief Constable of Shropshire, and County A.R.P. Controller.

Superintendent John Edward Martin then moved up to be Acting Deputy Chief Constable.

During 1943 the Shrewsbury Watch Committee were under great pressure to appoint regular policewomen. The Home Office gave approval to the appointment of two women police. It was not until the following April 1944 that a suitable applicant appeared. Miss Emily May Porter, who had been employed as a Welfare Officer at Brown's Aircraft Factory at Bedford, and previous to which she had been a woman constable with the Metropolitan Police Force, was sworn in on the 1 May 1944. The first regular woman police officer in the Shrewsbury Borough Police force.

The Salop Standing Joint Committee received a communication from the Home Office about the same time, with regard to the appointment of women police to the county force. The committee expressed their opinion that the number of policewomen in the county should be not less than twelve. Brig:General A.H.O. Lloyd remarked that the Home Office had now sanctioned 'A baker's dozen' for Shropshire — one sergeant and twelve policewomen, which he thought was satisfactory.

From the 1 January 1944 the Shropshire Constabulary was reduced in strength from 232 to 205, to conserve manpower.

The following month, Macdivitt made his report on the strength of the Borough Police. The strength of the regular police was given as thirty-two (authorised strength being fifty-four) with the addition of eighteen whole-time police auxiliaries, together with 130 special constables and twenty auxiliary police messengers performing part-time duties.

In November 1944, an expert committee was appointed by

the Home Secretary to consider the improvement of the police service after the war. It is of interest to note that three of its members had connections with Shropshire — Major-General Sir Llewelyn Atcherley, a former Chief Constable of Shropshire; Major Sir Jack Becke, Chief Constable of Cheshire, and former Chief Constable of Shropshire, and Major L.H. Morris, Chief Constable of Devon, and a member of a well-known Shrewsbury family.

The Shrewsbury Chronicle, dated 1 December 1944, included an appeal for policewomen —

'POLICEWOMEN NEEDED.

An appeal is published in this issue for volunteers for the W.A.P.C. in the Shrewsbury area. The job is responsible, and certain qualifications are necessary. Women must be aged between 22 and 35, five feet four inches or more in height, of good physique and of sensible character. Anyone with these qualifications, who has a desire for social service, should find the job extremely interesting. In Shrewsbury area, Auxiliary Policewomen are needed mainly for patrol duties.

Girls who are interested, or are changing their jobs, should enquire at the Shrewsbury Employment Exchange.'[2]

Policewoman E.M. Porter, who had been appointed to the Shrewsbury Police in May 1944, was sent by the Chief Constable on a six weeks course of training at Birmingham, starting on the 1 January 1945. At the end of the course Miss Porter returned proudly to Shrewsbury, having obtained first place, with an average of 90.75% marks for the four examinations taken. This highly creditable performance must have left the old male diehards at a loss for words.

From the 1 April 1945, the pay and general conditions of service members of the Police War Reserve and full time special constables, were aligned with those of the regular police. That is to say, as from that date they would receive the pay and allowances of regular constables of the same service. They also became eligible for pensions under the Police Pensions Act, but only if they were injured on duty. The cost would be re-imbursed in full by the Exchequer until the cessation of hostilities in Europe. When that stage was reached the cost of providing an efficient police force would revert to the normal basis, and the cost of such auxiliaries as were then still needed would fall upon local police funds. Subject to the normal Exchequer grant.

On Monday, 13 August 1945, the regular and special constables of the county constabulary, stationed at Ellesmere, entertained the children of Ellesmere, to a mammoth garden party. The men in blue excelled themselves by putting on a show, that was said at the time, to have been one of the finest parties that Ellesmere had ever witnessed. There was music, racing events, sideshows, pony-riding, tea and buns (to keep up the youngsters strength), and ending with a magnificent firework display. Excellent weather helped to make the day a grand success. It also created a very cordial relationship between the inhabitants of Ellesmere, (particularly the children), and the guardians of the law.

Lieut. Colonel H.A. Golden, Chief Constable of Shropshire since 1935, was appointed Chief Constable of Wiltshire, taking up his new office on the 1 January 1946. The Salop Standing Joint Committee made the choice of Inspector A.M. Tew, of Lincoln, as their new chief constable. Unfortunately Tew failed to pass his medical examination, and had to withdraw. The second choice was Inspector Douglas Osmond, of the Metropolitan Police.

The Government introduced on the 18 October 1945, 'The Police Bill', the first clause of which, was to have great effect on the Borough of Shrewsbury. It provided that, as from 1 April 1947, all separate Non-County Borough Police Forces would cease to exist, and for police purposes Non-County Boroughs would then in all respects form part of the county in which they were situated. Forty-seven Non-County Boroughs possessing separate police forces would be effected. There were many more clauses effecting County Boroughs etc., but Clause one was the one of most importance here in Shropshire, for it signed the death warrant of the Shrewsbury Borough Police force. The last of the Borough Police Forces in the county. Of course as with all previous moves to amalgamate borough forces with their counties, there was considerable opposition, this time it was to be of no avail. The Police Act became law on 15 April 1946. Forty-five non-county borough forces were abolished on 1 April 1947. It was the end of some very find old police forces, including that of Shrewsbury.

The W.A.P.C. was formally disbanded on 31 March 1946, after playing a most important part in keeping the peace during the course of the war. In the Borough Force, seven ladies had resigned by 1945, while another three resigned in January and February 1946.

It was recommended that Miss Vera Bezant should be retained in a civilian capacity to be employed on clerical duties. Two other civilian women clerks were also appointed. A former member of the W.A.P.C. Miss Marjorie Hookham had been appointed Woman Police-Constable No. 2 on the 2 July 1945, resigning for health reasons on 31 January 1946. Later, on the 2 June 1946, Miss Emily Porter, W.P.C.1. also resigned.

At a meeting of the Shrewsbury Borough Council in June 1946, the Chairman of the Watch Committee reported that (with the approval of the Home Office) it was proposed to extend the police communication system within the Borough of Shrewsbury. Provision was suggested of twenty-two new street police posts throughout the district. The existing system operated through six police boxes and six street pillars, in various parts of the borough. The new system, covering existing and new posts, would be operated on the G.P.O. system. It would be so arranged that calls from the public side of the pillars could be switched to the various departments at police headquarters. The initial cost would be £214. 14s. 0d. and the annual rental to the G.P.O. of £725. 5s. 0d. In answer to criticism regarding the expence, at a time when the police force of the borough was to be shortly turned over to the county, the chairman pointed out that the posts would be for the benefit of the borough, whilst the rental would be borne by the county.

In July 1946, Detective-Sergeant Lewis Samuel Evans, a member of the county constabulary, stationed at Oswestry, was seconded to the Allied Control Commission in Germany, as a police staff officer. After a period of one year at this duty, he returned to this country, to become the first Shropshire police officer to attend the new Police College at Ryton-on-Dunsmore.

There was no ceremonial to mark the absorption of the Shrewsbury Borough Police into the county constabulary, which took place at midnight, 31 March 1947. None the less the occasion was one of local historic importance, which should not be overlooked.

It marked the end of the last separate borough police force in Shropshire. One which had existed since regular police were first established under the authority of the Municipal Corporations Act of 1835. The Shrewsbury Borough Police Force had preserved its independence longer than was at one time expected. The Shrewsbury Chronicle recorded the passing of the force in these words —

'This is an appropriate time to say that the townspeople have the highest regard for the members of the Borough Police Force and feel that although the change is inevitable, it is in no way due to lack of efficiency or to unwillingness to co-operate with neighbouring forces. The Shrewsbury Police have done good work for many years and they will do equally good work as members of the County Force'.[3]

With the passing of the Borough Police Force, its Chief Constable, George Macdivitt, decided to retire, which he did on the 1 April. Exactly seven years to the day from when he had taken over as Chief Constable from his predecessor, Frank Davies.

Apart from his duties as Chief Constable, Macdivitt had been required to supervise the town's air raid precautions, and act as chief officer of the Shrewsbury Fire Brigade. Outside his official duties, he found time to organise in 1942, the 'Police Concert Party', which raised over £2,000 for local charities. When the merger took place, Superintendent T.E.

197

Sir Douglas Osmond C.B.E., Q.P.M.
Chief Constable of Shropshire 1946–1962

Barnwell (Shropshire's Deputy Chief Constable) took charge of all arrangements. Chief Inspector Leonard Trentham and Inspector Bryn Jones becoming responsible for supervising the policing of the borough and adjacent rural areas.

Perhaps the only visible change that the public would notice in the amalgamation, would be in the change in helmet and cap-badges of constables patrolling the streets of Shrewsbury. Changes in the police divisions of the Shropshire Constabulary had to be made to accommodate the town of Shrewsbury, and the country area south of the town (at the time of amalgamation in the Pontesbury Division) which now became incorporated into the new Shrewsbury Division. One Superintendent overseeing both areas.

The Chief Constable of Shropshire, Douglas Osmond, announced plans in July 1947, for establishing a police radio station in Shropshire. The site chosen was the highest spot in the county, Abdon Burf on the Brown Clee, 1,806 feet above sea level. The radio station would provide two way communication, by radio telephone between the Shrewsbury headquarters of the force, and police cars and vehicles, and also divisional police stations.

Perhaps one of the biggest headaches facing the Chief Constable in 1948, was the long standing shortage of housing for the men of his force.

It has always been a well known fact that the efficiency of a police force is based on its officers being content, and they cannot be content if they have not proper accommodation for themselves and their families.

A lengthy report on police housing was made by the Chief Constable, Douglas Osmond, to his Standing Joint Committee, in March 1948. It was a highly detailed account, running to 44 pages, which clearly and concisely depicts the serious lack of police housing within the county. Nearly 10% of the strength of the force were without proper accommodation, which made for discontent. As Douglas Osmond wrote – 'Discontent is infectious'. The discontent was likely to spread to those who were housed, for many of them were in very

199

poor accommodation, with a complete lack of modern amenities.

A typical example being the police house at Longden, a rented property, where the water had to be carried from the conduit, some 100 yards distant. The lighting was by oil-lamp, and the lavatory consisted of a bucket. A bathroom was a luxury unheard of. Constables occupying such properties could justifiably look for improvements to be made to their homes, or modern accommodation provided. Failing which they could easily fall victims to the germ of discontent, which is liable to be spread by those that were homeless, thereby increasing further the percentage of discontent and unrest within the force. It was the Chief Constable's opinion, that the men would accept their position with good grace, were they assured that the Police Authority had in hand, a constructive and far-sighted plan for a general improvement of housing conditions. The Chief Constable then proceeded to outline the housing situation as it stood at that time. Then in conclusion his recommendations for a programme of building and improvements needed.

The future increase in the establishment of the force being taken into consideration. The report is an amazing eye-opener into the social conditions of the Shropshire Constabulary in the year 1948. Douglas Osmond quotes an example of what some of the police wives had to tolerate —

'the wife of one serving officer who is also the daughter of an ex-Police Officer of this Force, who has spent the 30 years of her life living in Police Houses. During that time she has never been fortunate enough to live in a house provided with gas or electricity, mains water, bathroom, or other than bucket sanitation.'[4]

He finishes his excellent report with this paragraph —

'It is now asked that the Committee consider the recommendations contained in this memorandum and that it should adopt them as its policy. By so doing a considerable step forward will have been taken towards remedying the very unsatisfactory position with regard to housing that exists at present, and a substantial contribution will have been made to the future efficiency of the Force.'

The following year saw the culmination of nearly two years work, and the official opening on the 28 January 1949, of Shropshire's first police hostel. The house chosen was Lindisfarne, Kennedy Road, Shrewsbury. Alterations were made so that it would house seventeen single police officers, nearly all probationers. The reason for the hostel was the difficulty in obtaining suitable lodgings for the many single police recruits in Shrewsbury, which was the chief training ground for the force. The men's welfare was in the hands of a resident cook-housekeeper and two non-resident maids. The main point about the hostel was that there were no rules. Each man was on his honour to treat the place as his home.

The Royal Show was held at Shrewsbury in July 1949. The great event being honoured by a visit of H.R.H. The Princess Elizabeth and H.R.H. The Prince Philip. The final touches had been given to the new and elaborate police radio system. Twelve police cars and a police van, five fire service cars and a number of ambulances had receivers and transmitters fitted. In addition to the cars a number of 'Walkie talkie' sets were to be brought into use.

The police coverage for the Royal Show was very carefully planned out. Extra police were drafted in from out of county sources, all of whom had to be housed and fed. As part. of their contribution to the Royal Show, pupils of the Shropshire College of Domestic Science and Dairywork, at Radbrooke, catered for one hundred and thirty police reinforcements, who were housed at the A.F.V. depot at Harlescott for the duration of the Show.

Over the four days of the Show there were 250 police officers on duty.

On the Wednesday, the day of the Royal Visit, there were 300 additional police. The extra contingents were drawn from Cheshire, Herefordshire, Mid-Wales and Staffordshire, and included sixty Special Constables and fifty Military Police.

Despite all the well-thought out plans to control the

immense volume of traffic, nature stepped in to cause an unexpected hold-up — something that the traffic planners could not forsee. Royal Show traffic and local buses travelling through Harlescott on the Tuesday were held up for some time on the Whitchurch Road, by two swans and five cygnets, who, one behind the other, did a stately walk along the white line for about half a mile.

Efforts were made to divert them, but to no avail. Eventually the R.S.P.C.A. were summoned, and Mr. and Mrs. Swan and family were gently guided towards the river, and the greatly frustrated drivers allowed to proceed on their way.

A campaign to arouse public interest in the various methods of obtaining help from the police in an emergency was launched in December 1949, by Douglas Osmond, the Chief Constable. It commenced with an exhibition in the shop of Messrs R. Maddox & Co.Ltd; at Shrewsbury, where there was a distribution of pamphlets describing the various methods of getting in touch with the police in an emergency. The Chief Constable speaking at a press conference on the 8 December said —

'The whole of our present communication system depends entirely on having public support and public interest. We have now added wireless to our means of communication, and this has been working on an organised basis for the past two months.

Police cars are now in constant touch with the control room, and we are able to divert police assistance speedily to any part of the county. We have already seen striking advantages from this.'[6]

Chapter Thirteen

1950 — 1959

The year 1950 was a year of precedents for the Shropshire Constabulary. Mrs. Evelyn Anne Evans was a great believer in being first on the spot. Under her maiden name of (Toni) Norton, she had been the first member of the Women's Auxiliary Police Corps in Shropshire, joining the day after war was declared in 1939. Now on the 5 January 1950, she became the first Woman Special Constable in the county's history. In the following May, her husband, Detective/ Inspector L. S. Evans set yet another precedent in the county, by being promoted to a new rank in the Shropshire Constabulary, that of Det/Chief Inspector, and in the following year Det/Superintendent. In 1947 he had been the first officer of the Shropshire Force to attend the new Police College at Ryton-on-Dunsmore.

The world of sport produced the next precedents. The first annual cricket match between senior officers and constables of the Shropshire Constabulary took place on the county ground at Shrewsbury. It was a fine July day, and ended with both sides content with a draw.

The Constabulary were also represented in the mile relay, at the annual Athletic Association races at Leeds. The runners — P.C. Fielder, P.C.'s Blyth, McVittie and Peach ran for the first time in the county colours of blue and gold. In November 1950, the Police Probationers Cup was presented for the first time. It was won by P.C. Trickett of the Shrewsbury 'G' Division. Trickett was chosen as the probationer who had made the most progress during his service. This was thereafter to be an annual event.

Douglas Osmond presenting his Annual Report in April 1950, spoke of the considerable shortage of manpower. The total authorised establishment of the force was 382. However, the actual strength at the end of 1949, had been 297, a deficiency of 85 men.

The main concern of the Chief Constable's report in the following year, was still recruitment. The deficiency had been brought down to 50, but out of 220 candidates for the force, 142 had to be rejected. The chief reason being their inability to achieve the necessary minimum elementary educational standard, even though — 'any man who had had the usual elementary education — as it used to be called — should be in a position to pass into the force'.

The test papers showed, that generally speaking, their spelling was shocking, and only a few could write a coherent essay.

The Chief Constable ended his report on a more cheerful note —

'Thanks to the considerable welfare measures which have been undertaken by the Committee during the past few years morale is very good, and, I am certain could not be bettered in any police force in the country.'[1]

The Bridgnorth and Ludlow police divisions were amalgamated in June 1951. Superintendent Joseph Taylor was appointed to command the new amalgamated division. A native of Sheffield, Taylor had been promoted superintendent at the age of 35, and at that time was the youngest man to hold that rank in the British Isles. Now he found himself in charge of the largest single police area in the county. To gain some idea of the immense area of the new division, it was said to be half again as large as the county of Bedfordshire.

The Post Office Telephone's '999' system was inaugurated (for Shropshire) at the Shrewsbury Telephone Exchange on the 30 December 1946, when the then Chief Constable of Shrewsbury, George Macdivitt, visited the exchange to give the new service his blessing. However, it would seem that this excellent new facility only operated at that time in larger towns such as Shrewsbury. It was not until 1 October 1951, that the system was extended to include the smaller village exchanges in the Shrewsbury area.

Not before time, long and faithful service in the police forces of the country became recognised. A medal was, in 1951, issued in recognition of long service and good conduct. In October 1951, fifty-four officers of the Shropshire Constabulary attended a parade to receive their medals.

No doubt after the parade, there would be many tales recounted, of what had happened to them and fellow officers, spanning the years that it had taken them to gain the new medal. It was a step in the right direction, recognition of their faithful service had been long overdue.

The end of the nineteenth century had seen the first attempt to mechanize the Shropshire Constabulary, when a number of the country or rural officers were equipped with bicycles. For many years mechanization of the police progressed very slowly. Opinion on the subject differed greatly, some for mechanization, some against. In 1952, Mr. Douglas Osmond, as Chief Constable of Shropshire, submitting his Annual Report to the Salop Standing Joint Committee, said –

'that there is a limit to which mechanization can be carried and that it is not possible to provide any effective substitute in towns for the foot policeman on his beat or the policeman on a bicycle in the country areas.'[2]

This was a view which was condemned as old fashioned by many of the police officers of that time, but he goes on to say –

'Nevertheless, the provision of an adequate number of motor and motor cycle patrols as support for the beat policeman must be regarded as one of the most important features of present day policing.'[3]

Thirty years later, the Chief Constable of the West Mercia Constabulary, Mr. Robert Cozens, Q.P.M. supported this view, when he stressed that a primary task of a police force

205

was to establish and maintain relationships with the public. 'These could be best achieved by officers working on the beat.' He then went on to refer to beat policemen as 'one of the most important assets we have got.'[4]

The position of the county force in 1952 showed that 80% of the men available for routine duties, were those with under five years service, this being widely regarded as the minimum time it takes to make an experienced constable. Many of the pre-war men were moving towards retirement, or were being promoted. To hasten the training of the young recruits, a programme of great intensity was devised. The effect of this was to tie up twenty-four officers on permanent training, but the long term results, it was hoped, would be fruitful. Later, Shropshire's outstanding results in promotion exams proved its success.

Team policing was a new system, first tried out in Aberdeen. It was one of several attempts to compensate for shortages of manpower, by squeezing a quart out of a pint pot. It was doomed to eventual failure. A number of forces scattered about the country tried out the system. A few finding it successful. Of these Salford was the town in which it was an unqualified success. As a compactly built-up industrialized city, it was best adapted to the system. Team policing as it was carried out was no different in principle from the older method of policing by the beat system, but was really a modernized adaptation of it. The man on the beat had not disappeared from Salford, but covered a much wider and more varied area, and was more likely to appear when not expected. He was conveyed to his beat by a radio-equipped car in company with four or five other officers, and a sergeant, who was in charge of the patrol.

The patrol worked as a team, and the sergeant was entirely responsible for the disposition of his men. The time at which a constable would be covering any one beat was not disclosed until he was taken there, and the route of the beat was deliberately varied so that no intending offender could rely on a policeman being (or not being) at any given point at any given time.　The element of surprise was a valuable feature in team policing.

But all towns were not of the compact nature of Salford, and many forces trying the system found that for various reasons their old beat method was better.　In Shropshire, Douglas Osmond examined in detail what was then, the modern trend towards Team Policing, but came to the conclusion that it was not suitable for the town of Shrewsbury, 'where experiments of this method have been carried out.　For one thing, under the team system a man's pride and sense of responsibility in his own beat was lost.'

The Shropshire National Farmer's Union presented in its journal for December 1953, a pointed message from the new Shropshire Crime Prevention Squad.　It was directed at the farmers of the area.　Warning them to be on guard against Christmas poultry thieves.　Posters were also issued bearing the same message.　These posters were headed 'Nursery Crimes' below which they were decorated with the emergency '999' comically drawn with helmets, feet and small arms holding truncheons.　The main part of the poster consisted of a topical verse —

'Christmas is coming
The geese are getting fat
Don't you think the Wide Boys
Are well aware of that?
In Liverpool and Manchester,
Birmingham and Crewe
They find a ready market
For your cock-a-doodle-do!'

The local press were not allowed to know who the mystery police poet was.　A number of posters each bearing a different poetical message were put up about the county.　The Christmas one was followed by one warning motorists.　The short snappy verses with their topical contents became very popular.　In actual fact it can now be revealed that the mysterious police poet was the Chief Constable himself, Mr. Douglas Osmond.

The following year, 1954, brought a problem of an unusual nature, that of the transfer of trained officers to Colonial police forces.

The Chief Constable mentions this drift away in his annual report —

'Generally speaking the man accepted for the Colonial Service is one who is just reaching a stage in his life as a British policeman where he really becomes useful.

When we bear in mind that it takes at least two years before a man becomes of any value, and during that time a considerable sum of money is spent on his pay, his equipment and his training, only to have overseas forces reap the benefit of this expenditure and work, it is regrettable that the Police Authority or the Chief Constable should not be able to set a limit to the number of men that are lost in this way.'[5]

At this time, five officers had already transferred from the Shropshire Constabulary in this way. One such constable was William Lucas, who had served from 1947 until 1953. He became a Detective-Inspector with the Kenya Police. It was not a peaceful post that he transferred to, for he found himself posted to an area where the Mau Mau troubles were rife at that time. In a period of just over six months he had led fifteen murder hunts, which is more than most British Chief Constables expect to deal with in a lifetime.

Although the German police had extensively used dogs for police work since the beginning of the century, the British police forces were slow to realize their value. Experiments were carried out with dogs in the latter half of the 1930's, but these came to a halt with the outbreak of war. Several chief constables then carried on with the experiment after the War, and with encouraging results. The number of police forces using dogs began to increase. By 1954 some twenty-eight of the hundred and twenty-six police forces (including Shropshire) were using dogs. In July 1954, two dogs were purchased by the Shropshire Constabulary. An Alsation named 'Sultan', and a Dobermann Pinscher named 'Taxel'. Police constables Bob Roberts of Shifnal, and Roy Duncalfe of Wrockwardine were chosen as the first dog-handlers in the Shropshire Constabulary. Both officers attended (with their dogs), a course on elementary dog-handling at the Surrey Constabulary headquarters. This was to be the beginning of a long tradition in using police dogs in this county.

Brilliant spring-like sunshine favoured the opening of the new divisional police headquarters in Glebe Street, Wellington, on the 10 October 1955. It had been built at a cost of £69,000, and occupied the site of an old orchard. The Home Secretary, Major Gwilym Lloyd-George officially opening the new building said —

'it was a matter of the highest importance that the police should be provided with the most efficient means of carrying out their heavy duties. For many years Wellington police had served the public in inadequate premises. He was glad the standing joint committee took early steps to remove that state of affairs.'[6]

He went on to say —

'that he heard with great interest of an experiment recently begun in the county entailing the appointment of an officer specially to deal with crime prevention.

He had been told that very good results have already been achieved, and further progress of the experiment would be watched with a great deal of interest.'[7]

After twenty-five year's service with the Shropshire Constabulary, the county's C.I.D. chief, Detective-Superintendent Leonard Samuel Evans retired on 2 January 1956. Not content to sit back in retirement he took up a police appointment with the Government of Quatar, an independent Arab sheikdom, situated on the Persian Gulf. His successor as chief of the Shropshire C.I.D. was Detective-Inspector Geoffrey Woolham, who had started his police career in 1926, as a boy clerk with the Shrewsbury Borough Police. It was in that year, that his father, Frank Woolham, a constable with the borough force, was killed in a road accident whilst on traffic duty.

During the year 1957, no less than four of the police

women resigned from the force, which was a serious depletion from an establishment of eleven.

The trend followed through into the following year, when a further three resignations made matters really serious. Then in May 1958, a call came for volunteers to form a United Kingdom Police Unit in Cyprus. Amongst those who answered the call was Policewoman Audrey Foster of the Shropshire Constabulary. This was to create a hopeless situation. Apart from Policewoman Sergeant H.M. Hazlehurst, there were only two experienced policewomen in the force; the remaining five (at that time) were all young probationers. The Chief Constable was left with no possibility of making available to each division an experienced policewoman, and at the same time attaching a probationer to the experienced officer for training. The overriding problem was that it was imperative that there should be available throughout the county at all times, the services of an experienced woman police officer. As a temporary expedient, all policewomen were concentrated in 1958 at police headquarters in Shrewsbury. The experienced ones being made available for call to other parts of the county, on short notice, whenever they were required.

Another volunteer for service in Cyprus, was Constable Leonard Morris who was seconded for a short term attachment of three months. All told there were 300 police volunteers from all over the British Isles.

Barney's Pool, Madeley, became the scene of a rescue drama, in January 1959. Nine year old Billy Anson in attempting to retrieve one of his school books, which one of his school friends had thrown on the ice in the middle of the pool, fell through the ice. An extending ladder was laid across the ice by Hubert Carter and William Rowlands who had seen the boy's plight. Constable Maurice Servantie, who had been called to the scene, took off his helmet, tunic and boots, and managed to crawl two thirds of the way across the ice to the boy. Then the ice breaking under his weight, he too was in the icy water. Undismayed he made his way to the boy, and holding him, pushed him to the end of the ladder, where with William Rowlands he dragged him to safety. For this brave act both men were awarded the Royal Humane Societies' Testimonial on vellum. But sometimes fishing things out of water can be a joy, as it was with Constable Peter Hyde, who in the following February 'Arrested' the first salmon of the season at Shrewsbury. With a home-made bait he landed a twenty pound salmon.

Chapter Fourteen

1960 – 1967

December 1960 was a disastrous month, with a great part of Britain hit with floods. Shropshire suffered badly. Aerial photographs of Shrewsbury taken at that time, show it virtually as an island, in what appears to be a large lake. Such disasters always brought extra work to the police. In this case they laboured day and night to rescue people from their flooded homes. Diversions of traffic had to be arranged, and food supplies taken by boat, to those who were cut off. Animals on farms needed rescuing, and like the humans, they needed food taking to them.

The duties of the police were infinite, but although tired and often wet through to the skin, they carried on without a grumble, the efficiency of the force never being in question.

Teleprinter communication was installed in the control room at the Shrewsbury headquarters in 1960. It was to prove of immense value, though at the time the busy control room staff, looked upon it as an additional burden.

Robert Boynton, using a sawn-off shotgun, shot and permanently blinded Constable Arthur Rowlands of the Gwynedd Constabulary, on the 2 August 1961. The result was an immediate and extensive manhunt which took place in the wild mountainous country of Mid-Wales. Dog-handlers with their dogs were sent from the neighbouring forces. Constable Robert William Roberts of the Shropshire Constabulary, with his dog, Taxel, being one. Robert Boynton eluded capture for several days, with the police tirelessly searching for him. At last contact was made by Constable (Bob) Roberts, who found himself literally staring down the muzzle of the menacing shotgun. Roberts giving evidence said — 'He fired at me when he was about three yards from me. I ducked, and I heard the shots going through the leaves of the bushes over my head.' Roberts then called off his dog, Taxel because it looked as if Boynton would shoot it. In fact, Boynton did shoot another police dog later on.

The day before Boynton was captured, Superintendent John Du Rose of Scotland Yard, who was in charge of the manhunt, made an urgent telephone call to the War Department. He informed them that if Robert Boynton remained at large for another twenty-four hours he would require 1,000 troops to assist in the search. The very next day, Boynton was captured some eight miles from Machynlleth, when Constable Thomas Davies of the Mid-Wales Constabulary brought him down with a rugby tackle. At the trial, the judge had this to say about the police service —

'The police force as a whole show fearlessness and conspicuous courage in the course of their difficult duties. Both Roberts and Carswell knew full well that the armed man had previously injured one of their colleagues. Certain insignificant and contemptuous sections of the public seek to belittle the courage and skill of the police whenever the opportunity presents itself. But responsible citizens realise and are proud of the way in which they carry out their duties.'

Constables Arthur Rowlands (Gwynedd Constabulary); Robert Roberts (Shropshire Constabulary); Robert Carswell (Liverpool City Police) and Thomas Davies (Mid-Wales Constabulary) were all awarded the George Medal for their bravery.

These four awards in respect of the same incident are a striking example of the co-operation of police forces (in this case four forces) in helping each other in the investigation of serious crimes.

The value of police dogs in the above case was clearly demonstrated. Two dogs had been acquired on an experimental basis in Shropshire, in 1954, now in 1961 a third had come to join the team. 'Charbonnie' an Alsation bitch, was the daughter of 'Sultan', which made her the second generation to serve as a police dog in Shropshire. The two original dogs, 'Sultan' and 'Taxel' were instrumental in making many arrests. Their deterrent value against hooliganism when used on patrol, was undoubted.

Chief Constable, Douglas Osmond relinquished his command of the Shropshire Constabulary 14 May 1962. In his last annual report to the Salop Standing Joint Committee, before taking over his new post, as Chief Constable of the Hampshire and Isle of Wight Constabulary, Douglas Osmond paid a warm tribute to the officers who had served under his command since 1946 —

'Every year in this report I have paid a sincere tribute to the help given by the Police Authority to me personally and to all the Force as a whole, and to the loyalty and devotion to duty of all members of the Force. On leaving Shropshire I must again express my gratitude for the way in which the Authority and the Force have made my work easy and rewarding.

In 1946 when I took up my appointment, the Force was in serious difficulties through a shortage of manpower, the inadequacy of housing, communications and equipment and the lack of training facilities, all of which were due to the abnormal conditions created by the war. I found a Police Authority that was sympathetic towards those difficulties and a body of men who were working long hours without thought of self, with the very finest sense of discipline and tradition.

The work of a police force cannot stand still and undoubtedly there is scope for a great deal of development.

I take my leave of the Police Authority with very real regret at parting from so many friends and at the severance of my connection with a Force with which I shall always be proud to have been associated.'[1]

The appointment of Chief Constable of Shropshire went to Mr. Robert George Fenwick, who had been Assistant Chief

Constable of Gloucestershire since 1960. His first week in his new post, turned out to be a busy one, with a Royal Visit to deal with. Princess Margaret was paying an official visit to the town of Market Drayton. The new Chief Constable was presented to Her Royal Highness, an auspicious start to his term of office.

The system of police cadets (under various names), had existed in Shropshire since the 1920's, when it was the custom to employ 'boy clerks' in police offices. Many of the boys would receive a little instruction in physical training, law and police duties, in the hope that they might, on attaining the right age, join the force as constables.

During the second world war, a Police Auxiliary Messenger Service had been established for youths between the ages of 16 and 18, these youths were mainly employed on clerical, telephone and similar duties. Post-war development of such cadet schemes were left to local initiative. In 1962 an establishment of sixteen for a Police Cadet Force was agreed by the Salop Standing Joint Committee. This was to form a nucleus of high quality youths who would have served an apprenticeship for the Force providing an additional source of recruitment. Considerable interest in the Police Cadet Scheme was shown throughout the county, and indications showed no shortage of suitable applicants. It was hoped to recruit the first half of the Cadet establishment in July 1963, which was the end of the school year, and the remainder in 1964.

On 31 January 1963, Superintendent John W. McKiernan (Deputy Chief Constable) retired from the force, after 37 years service. He was to be the last Deputy Chief Constable of the county, for on his retirement a new appointment was to come into being, that of Assistant Chief Constable.

His successor, and first Assistant Chief Constable of Shropshire, was Alexander Rennie, a Superintendent of the Durham County Constabulary.

In August 1963, Superintendent Victor Henry Roberts and Constable John Durnell published in typescript, 'The First

215

Hundred Years', an outline of the history of the Shropshire Constabulary for the period 1840 — 1940. This useful publication, based on the General Orders of the force, was perhaps one of the last jobs of the superintendent, for at the end of the same month, he retired. His colleague, Constable John Durnell no doubt amazed his fellow constables, when he resigned in 1964, to train for holy orders. It must be confessed that it was an unusual step from police to church, and a first time that it had happened in the Shropshire Constabulary. However, on reflection, twelve years as a constable was a good training ground for meeting people of all walks of life, of listening to their many troubles, and most of all, of being of help. He was ordained in 1966 at Lichfield Cathedral, to become Curate of St. Nicholas's Church, Newport, Shropshire.

One policewoman who really made a career in the Shropshire Constabulary was Mrs. Hilda Mary (Pat) Hazlehurst, who joined the force in January 1948. She was the first Shropshire policewoman to attend a C.I.D. course. Again first to be appointed as a Det/Constable in 1951. First Woman Sergeant in 1953, and in 1964, first again to be appointed Woman Police Inspector. Later after the amalgamation in 1967, she was promoted to Superintendent in charge of policewomen in the newly formed West Mercia Constabulary. Retiring in 1973, she received the Queen's Police Medal.

One of the innovations of 1964 in Shropshire, were Radar Meters for detecting speeding motorists. The equipment proved very effective as a means of reducing accidents caused by excessive speed.

The establishment of police cadets was increased in 1964, to sixteen. The new intake were given a five week course at the Police Headquarters at Shrewsbury. The cadets attended the Shrewsbury Technical College for one day each week, and were encouraged to attend other classes in their own time. Three cadets were awarded silver medals under the Duke of Edinburgh's Scheme. One gained a Judo Blue Belt.

During 1964, eight cadets attended the Birmingham City

HER MAJESTY'S ASSISTANT INSPECTOR OF CONSTABULARY MISS J.S. LAW
INSPECTING POLICEWOMEN OF SHROPSHIRE CONSTABULARY
AT COUNTY POLICE HEADQUARTERS SHREWSBURY ON WEDNESDAY 13th JULY 1966

WPC 7 WILLIAMS SHREWSBURY • WPC 8 DAVIES WELLINGTON • WPC 4 DAVIES SHREWSBURY • WPC 15 LORD WELLINGTON
WPC 10 SALTER WELLINGTON • WPC 16 JAMES SHREWSBURY • WPC 6 WERNON OSWESTRY • WPC 3 VERNON MARKET DRAYTON
WPC 9 SNOW SHELLINGTON • WPC 14 HALL WELLINGTON
MISS CAMPON BREWSTER ACC • WPC 11 INSPECTOR 11-MS. SHACKLEHURST • SUPT. 9 ATKORS (ADMINISTRATION)
PW 11 JONES • PW 5 PLATT • PW 12 CRAWFORD (INSPECTED AT BRIDGNORTH)

217

Police Training Camp in the Elan Valley, Mid-Wales, on a course designed to stimulate leadership, initiative and manly qualities. Every cadet was expected to spend one month assisting in the Casualty Department of a local hospital. The training programme for police cadets in Shropshire was designed to prepare them not only for their chosen career, but to widen their experience of life generally. Four cadets became regular officers during 1964, and nine more were expected to be attested in 1965.

Many police officers had another side to their careers. Such a one was Superintendent John Brynmor Jones, a native of Caersws. A keen sportsman he had represented Wales in two amateur football internationals, and played cricket for Montgomeryshire. While superintendent of the Ludlow Division he had interested himself in the local Boy Scout movement, firstly as secretary, then as chairman, and ending as Assistant District Commissioner.

Standing Joint Committees were replaced in 1965 by Police Committees, on which county council representation was increased to two-thirds. The proceedings of this committee were for the first time subject to some county council inspection. This change was brought about by the Police Act of 1964.

The main functions of the Police Authority was defined as —

'the maintenance of an adequate and efficient force, properly housed and equipped, and the appointment, and if necessary removal, of the chief constable.'

One of the county's top police dogs retired in January 1966. 'Charbonnie' with forty-five arrests in her five and a half years service, was considered the top dog in the Shropshire Constabulary. Her record of arrests beat by five, those of her father, 'Sultan'. Perhaps her most outstanding effort was an eight mile track in four and a half hours, ending in the arrest of two men.

A volunteer force of twelve police cadets was formed at Ellesmere College, in 1966. Each cadet was issued with a uniform and received instruction on police history and organization. They were attached to various departments of the county constabulary, in a similar way to the regular cadets.

It was in this year that Cadet Ronald George Hemmings became the second cadet of the Shropshire Constabulary to win the coveted gold award of the Duke of Edinburgh Scheme.

Valuable experience was gained by seven Shropshire police officers, who were attached to a Mobile Police Column for training purposes. In October 1966 they moved with the column to the Aberfan Disaster area, where they assisted the Merthyr Tydfil Borough Police.

The provision of a new county headquarters for the Shropshire Constabulary, was first considered by the Salop Standing Joint Committee in 1944.

Meanwhile over the years alterations, improvements and additions were made to the old 1903 headquarters on Swan Hill, in an attempt to meet the more urgent needs of the force.

It was finally decided in 1962, that new premises should be built on the outskirts of Shrewsbury, and that a Section Station would be provided within the area of the bridges, to cater for the immediate needs of the town centre. A decision was taken to establish the headquarters building on the column site, at the top of Abbey Foregate.

In May 1966, the Home Secretary informed the Salop Police Committee, that he considered the amalgamation of the Shropshire, Worcestershire, Worcester City and Herefordshire police forces to be necessary in the interests of efficiency.

'During the course of his statement in the House of Commons on the 18th May, the Home Secretary said that with the expert advice of Her Majesty's Inspectors of Constabulary and having taken full account of the recommendations made in 1962 by the Royal Commission on the Police he was satisfied that the continuing increase in crime and its changing pattern, as well as growing traffic problems, justified a more far-reaching re-organisation than was contemplated by

219

the Commission. He had not thought it sensible to adopt any rigid formula for determining the right size of police forces but having examined each area he had sought to establish police forces of a size most likely to achieve full efficiency in the prevention and detection of crime and the control of traffic.

He expressed the hope that local authorities concerned would recognise the need for his proposals and enter into voluntary schemes, but if they did not he must use his powers under the Police Act 1964, to promote compulsory amalgamations because he was satisfied that these amalgamations were essential to a determined attack on crime.'[2]

In the Home Office letter formally notifying the Home Secretary's decision on Shropshire, the police authorities concerned were given until the 27 June to indicate whether they would be prepared to enter into a voluntary amalgamation scheme, and it was made quite clear that if not, the Home Secretary would think it necessary to promote a compulsory scheme for the areas concerned.

The Home Secretary's letter came as a bombshell. It ran contrary to what the Salop Police Committee had previously been told.

During recent discussions with the Home Office and H.M. Inspector of Constabulary, with particular reference to the proposed erection of the new headquarters for the police force, no doubts had been expressed by either parties, as to the continuance of the Shropshire Constabulary as a separate force. In fact only a month previous, H.M. Inspector of Constabulary, J.T. Manuel, when asked by a member of the County Council whether there was any misapprehension regarding the future of the force, Mr. Manuel had stated quite categorically,

'that no change was envisaged in the foreseeable future, so that there was no risk of the buildings being wasted.'[3]

This statement of course related to the envisaged new police headquarters. Work on the planning of the new buildings was immediately cancelled. The Chairman of the Police Committee instantly sought an interview with the Home

Office, where he was assured that there was no reflection whatever on the efficiency of the Shropshire Constabulary, they readily agreed that Shropshire had a particularly fine record.

It was recognised that the Shropshire Force had initiated the development of crime prevention work which had become a national feature. The standard of training, reflected in national examination results, was amongst the highest, and the force had a crime detection rate well above the national average.

The Police Committee gave, as their opinion, that the amalgamation could only be detrimental to the progress and efficiency of the police service in Shropshire, at least for several years.

What appears to have changed the Home Secretary's mind, was outside influences — for when the admittedly weak police forces had been dealt with, and the borough forces absorbed by their surrounding counties, Shropshire began to show up as small in comparison, and had at the eleventh hour, despite the Home Secretary's statement to the contrary, been made the victim of statistics.

The geography of the amalgamated area shows it to be mainly rural in character, but apart from that they had little in common. There was no town which could be called a convenient centre for a headquarters, and the only long common boundary was in South Shropshire — which was a hilly, sparsely populated area, with no pressing police problems, and with poor lines of communication. Most of Shropshire's crime and traffic problems were in the area from Shrewsbury north and east, isolated from the amalgamated area.

The Police Committee after a full discussion affirmed as their opinion —

'that Shropshire in view of its geographical situation is most effectively administered as a single unit for police purposes.'[4]

But, with no other option the Police Committee finally agreed to a voluntary amalgamation scheme. The new force

221

came into being on the 1 October 1967, and bore the name 'WEST MERCIA CONSTABULARY', with its headquarters at Hindlip Hall, Worcester. Shropshire was reduced from five operational divisions to two, with divisional headquarters at Shrewsbury and Wellington.

Shropshire's Chief Constable, Mr. R.G. Fenwick, in his last annual report, said —

'For almost five years I have had the privilege of commanding a very fine body of men & women with an esprit de corps & dedication to public service second to none.

The Force will join with the larger organisation in good heart & determined to make a success of the new venture. The improved facilities & equipment which a much larger force can provide will ensure that the progress made in recent years continues.

There is no lack of goodwill on the part of all concerned and I am confident the future holds bright prospects for police & public alike.[5]

Meanwhile in the hiatus caused by the statement of the amalgamation and the actual change-over date, police work was carried on as usual by the Shropshire Constabulary. Superintendent Ernest Smith retired at the end of 1966, after thirty years with the force. As with most officers he found himself involved in many curious situations and cases. At one time he had been commended for descending more than thirty feet down a well to recover the body of a suicide. On another occasion whilst investigating the theft of a quantity of silver from Shrewsbury, his enquiries led him to a ship at Birkenhead. Whilst he was making a search of the vessel it sailed, and he had to be taken off by the pilot boat at the mouth of the Mersey — but not before he had found the stolen silver. This was a story which took a lot of living down — the policeman who was nearly shanghaid.

Visits of police officers from other countries had by now, become commonplace. Two senior police officers of the Bahrein Police Force spent a month with the Shropshire Constabulary, in February 1967, while two officers of the

Kuwait Police Force spent two weeks in the county in the following July. All seeking methods which would improve their own forces.

A great deal of publicity appeared in the press when the first breathalysers appeared in September 1967. This deterrent to drinking and driving was taken very seriously by the motoring public. The manager of the 'White Horse Inn' at Castle Pulverbatch actually provided a taxi service for those of his clients who felt that they were not capable of driving home.

Another newcomer on the scene, in September, was the 'Panda Car'. These were motor car patrols (which quickly and affectionately, became known as 'Panda Cars' because of their blue and white colouring) and were used in a form of unit beat policing. This was the latest in a series of attempts to make the most of an inadequate number of police officers and was largely responsible for worsening police/public relations by distancing the patrolling constable from his public.

Mr. Robert Fenwick who had been designated Deputy Chief Constable elect of the new West Mercia Constabulary, was now appointed by the Home Secretary as one of Her Majesty's Inspectors of Constabulary, in the place of Mr. J. T. Manuel who retired. As Sir Eric St Johnston (H.M. Chief Inspector of Constabulary) wrote in his book —

'This was a happy choice for Bob, who is a barrister of Gray's Inn, is lucid of expression and applies his mind objectively and with sound judgement to any problems put to him. We became good friends and close colleagues.'[6]

One of Robert Fenwick's last acts as Chief Constable of Shropshire, was to deposit a large number of old records of the Shropshire Constabulary with the Salop County Record Office, that they might be preserved in the county of their origin, for the interest of future generations of Salopians.

Farewell parties were much to the fore in the final month of the force. Shrewsbury based policewomen held their last get-together, when past and serving members gathered at the

Swan Hill headquarters to eat, drink and no doubt to reminisce. The Chief Constable and Mrs. Fenwick joined in the happy occasion. In their turn they were guests at a party at the Prince Rupert Hotel, Shrewsbury, in the same month, when they were presented with a silver candelabra to mark Mr. Fenwick's retirement from the Shropshire Constabulary. The final party was a Farewell Dinner and Dance which took place at the Longmynd Hotel, Church Stretton, on Saturday, 30 September 1967.

As the clock struck midnight, the dancing ceased, glasses were raised, and a toast was solemnly drunk to the memory of the **SHROPSHIRE CONSTABULARY**, whilst officers unlucky enough to be on duty in their patrol cars, could be heard singing 'Auld Lang Syne' over their car radios.

From that hour the Shropshire, Herefordshire, Worcestershire and Worcester City Police Forces ceased to exist as separate entities, whilst the officers of those forces, working now as one body, took on the new title of the —

'WEST MERCIA CONSTABULARY'

'Paddy Mayne's Grasshoppers' had come a long way through time, with an ever growing efficiency. Shropshire has every reason to be proud of them.

Now they were to take their place in the new larger force where they could continue their proud record.

AGREEMENT BETWEEN THE COUNTY AUTHORITIES & THE BOROUGH OF WENLOCK. 1841.

'It is agreed this fourth day of January One thousand eight hundred and forty one BETWEEN Her Majesty's Justices of the Peace of and for the county of Salop in General Quarter Sessions assembled on the one hand and The Mayor aldermen and Burgesses of the Borough of Wenlock in the said County by their Council on the other hand as follows (that is to say) That the said County and Borough Police Establishments shall from and after the date hereof be consolidated into one Police Establishment pursuant to an Act passed in the third and fourth years of her present Majesty's reign C: 88.

That the Chief Constable shall appoint all Constables to be employed in the said Borough in the same way as he appoints Constables for the said county.

That the said Chief Constable shall from time to time furnish the name or names of any Constable or Constables which he proposes to send into the said Borough to the Mayor of the said Borough and if such Constable or Constables shall be objected to by the said Mayor he or they shall be changed by the said Chief Constable. That two Constables at the least shall be sent into the said Borough by the said Chief Constable immediately after the execution of this agreement by both parties and the County Magistrates will if requisite apply to the Secretary of State to enable them to add to the number of the present force. That the said Chief Constable shall pay due attention to any communications which he may from time to time receive from the Mayor of the said Borough as to the best places in which to station the Constables who shall be sent into the said Borough.

And lastly it is agreed by and between both the said parties that the Justices of the said county of Salop shall from time to time for the purpose of derfraying the expences of the said Act and the Act passed in the second and third years of her said Majesty's reign cap. 93 within the said county and Borough assess and tax the said Borough of Wenlock at the same sum in the pound according to the value of the rateable property therein as shall be rated by the said Justices upon the other parts of the said county for the same purpose.

That such rates shall from time to time be duly paid by the said Borough to such person or persons and at such time or times as the said County Justices shall by their Warrant direct and the said County Justices shall have all the powers for the recovery thereof within the said Borough as they now have or may hereafter have for recovering the same in any other part of the said County. IN WITNESS whereof the Mayor of the said Borough by the direction of the Council hath hereunto affixed the common seal of the said Borough the day and year above written.

Witness to the affixing hereto of the common seal of the said Borough by John Davis Esquire the Mayor thereof

R.d Hinton.'

RULES AND REGULATIONS FOR THE BRIDGNORTH
BOROUGH POLICE FORCE. 1841.

' 1st. That both police officers shall give up the whole of
their time to the duties of their office.

2nd. That the Borough be divided into two police districts
to be called the East Division and the West Division.
The East Division to comprise the Bridge, Underhill
Street to the New Road Gate the River side both
below and above the Bridge the whole of the lower
Town, and the Rural part of the Borough on the East
side of the Severn. The West Division to consist of the
other part of the Town and Borough.

3rd. The Rural parts of the Borough to be visited at least
three times a week.

4th. Whenever either Officer is going on duty out of the
Town he shall previous to his leaving inform the other
Officer who shall take charge and visit the whole of the
Town during such absence.

5th. Each Officer to make a daily written report to the
Mayor according to the Form furnished for that
purpose.

6th. Both Officers to attend the General Quarter Sessions
of the Borough and to employ at such Sessions (if
necessary) two special constables to assist in keeping
order.

7th. One of the police Officers to be in attendance at each
petty and Special Sessions.

8th. All Warrants Summons and other process issued by the Recorder and all precepts warrants summons and other process issued by the Borough Magistrates, including Notices of Licencing days to Victuallers shall be executed by the Police Officers for which a fee of one shilling each shall be received by the Justice's Clerk to be paid over by him to the account of the Borough Fund with the Fines.

9th. Each Police Officer to have the perquisite of all process executed by them out of the Borough at the rate of sixpence per mile together with the moiety of any penalties to which they may become entitled .... as informers under any statute.

10th. In all cases of emergency each Officer is with the Authority of a Borough Magistrate to call out one or more of the Special Constables to aid and assist as circumstances may require.

11th. That each Officer shall visit every Public House and Beer Shop within his District (except Quatford and that place occasionally) on Sundays Good Friday and Christmas Day during the hours of divine Service but neither Officer to be allowed to eat or drink in any Public House or Beer Shop within the Borough nor to remain therein longer than his duty may require on pain of immediate dismissal.

12th. That neither Officer shall receive any compliment gift or reward from any licensed Victualler Beer House keeper or other person except rewards given for the apprehension of any Felon nor any share profit or benefit arising from the Sale of any Tickets or from the receipt of any monies for admission into the Theatre.

13th. That the Officers shall see that the Bye Laws of the Borough be duly observed and report any offences against the same from time to time to the Mayor.

14th. The Officer acting for the West Division to see that all standing and stalls in the Streets and under the Town

Hall on Market and Fair days be properly arranged so as not to obstruct the public thoroughfare.

15th. One of the Officers to be appointed and sworn High Constable at the next General Borough Sessions who shall execute all precepts issued by the Clerk of the Peace and Borough Coroner for summoning Juries and who is not to communicate directly or indirectly to any person the name of any Juror so summoned to Act at any General Quarter Sessions.

16th. In cases of dismissal or resignation all Clothes, Hat and shoes furnished by the Borough within the six months preceding the dismissal or resignation to be given up to the Watch Committee together with the Greatcoat then in possession of such police officer at the cost of the Borough Fund.

17th. That the Officer shall serve alternately in each police District and change Districts once a fortnight.

18th. That the hours of regular attendance of the police on Duty in their respective districts shall commence not later than seven o'clock in the morning Summer and Winter every day in the Week except Sunday and not later than eight on the morning of that day, and nine o'clock and Eleven at night alternate nights one police officer being always on duty until Eleven at night except Saturday night and then both police to remain on duty until half-past twelve at night and on any special occasion to be under the order and direction of the Mayor for the time being.'

THE CHIEF CONSTABLES OF THE COUNTY OF
SHROPSHIRE AND OF THE BOROUGHS OF
BRIDGNORTH, OSWESTRY, LUDLOW AND
SHREWSBURY *   *   *   *

Captain Dawson Mayne. R.N. 1840–1859

Born 24 December 1799, in the City of Dublin. Son of Justice Edward Mayne, of the Court of Queen's Bench, Ireland. Younger brother of Sir Richard Mayne, Commissioner of the Metropolitan Police. Dawson Mayne entered the Royal Navy in 1812, within four months he had sailed with H.M.S. Doris, escorting a large convoy to the East Indies and China. While in that frigate he took part in blockading several American merchantmen in the harbour of Whampoa. He was rated Midshipman in 1814. Mayne was present at the bombardment of Algiers in 1816, where a slight wound in the foot and a severe one in the thigh, procured him a grant from the Patriotic Fund, and a pension which lasted until his promotion to Lieutenant in 1821. In 1817 he proceeded to the North American station. Appointed to H.M.S. Druid in 1825, a vessel which formed part of the escort of General Bolivar from La Guiara to Carthagena. Promoted in 1829 to the command of H.M.S. Icarus, and later in 1830 to H.M.S. Sparrowhawk. He was nominated in 1831, Acting-Captain of H.M.S. Magnificent, a receiving ship at Port Royal, Jamaica. Returning home to England, he was employed as an Inspecting Commander in the Coastguard Service, 1834–1840.

On the 6 February 1840 he became the first Chief Constable of the Shropshire Constabulary, a post which he held until his resignation, some 19 years later, in 1859. He married 14 May 1840, Elizabeth Mary, daughter of William Hewitt of Jamaica, a cousin of Rowland Hill, 2nd Viscount Hill.

Dawson Mayne died 25 September 1872, at Killaloe, Ireland.

Captain Philip Henry Crampton. 1859–1864

Born c. 1818 in the county of Wicklow, Ireland. Son of Philip Henry Crampton. Served in the 20th Regiment of Foot

(East Devonshires) with the rank of captain. Appointed as 1st Class Superintendent of the Somerset County Constabulary, September 1856. In the December of the same year, he was posted as Superintendent of Police & Inspector of Weights & Measures for the Glastonbury Division. On the 6 January 1857, now Chief Superintendent, he was appointed Deputy Chief Constable of Somerset.

On the 7 March 1859, he was chosen out of 100 applicants, as Chief Constable of Shropshire. A widower, with one young son, he married for the second time, in 1861, at Wilton near Taunton — Blanche Constantia, eldest daughter of the late Rev. William Walter Quartley, rector of Washfield, Devon.

He resigned from the post of Chief Constable of Shropshire in a letter dated 30 July 1864.

Lieutenant-Colonel Edward Burgoyne Cureton. 1864—1866

Twenty-five years in the army. Served in India from March 1840 until January 1847. Present at the actions of Maharajpoor 1843, for which he received the Maharajpoor Star, and Moodkee 1845, at which battle he was wounded, receiving the Sutlej Medal, of Sobraon, for which he added a clasp to the latter medal.

He also served in the Crimean War, and was present at the battle of the Tchernaya 1855. Cureton took part in the Kaffir War of 1851 — 1853 adding the appropriate medal to those he already had. In 1862 he was appointed Assistant-Quatermaster General of the Dublin Division.

On the 17 October 1864 he was appointed Chief Constable of Shropshire. Two years later, in the January of 1866, he resigned the office.

Colonel Richard John Edgell. 1866—1889

Served twenty-three years in Her Majesty's Bengal Army. Joined the 53rd Regiment of Native Infantry 28 December 1841, serving with this force under Major-General Sir. G.

232

Pollock, G.C.B., in Afganistan the following year, for which he was awarded the Cabul Medal 1842. Served with the army of the Punjab 1848–49 (Punjab Medal 1849). Appointed Adjutant G.O.C.C. 1845–1851. Appointed Captain of Punjab Police 8 January 1851; raised, organized, and equipped four troops of Horse, and one Battalion of Infantry Police for service in the Jhelum Division, held this post until 1853. Rejoined 53rd Regiment 1856, served through the siege of the Lucknow Residency 1857, in action at Chinhut. Appointed Military Secretary to Sir Henry Lawrence 1857. Indian Mutiny Medal with clasp for Lucknow.

Appointed to officiate as Deputy/Judge-Advocate, Benares Circle, G.O.C.C. until 1860. Appointed Brigade Major 1861 at Barrackpoor, continuing until returning to England 10 June 1864.

Applied unsuccessfully for post of Chief Constable of Shropshire in 1864. Studied the workings of the Essex County Constabulary during 1865. Appointed Chief Constable of Shropshire January 1866.

Died in office 26 November 1889.

Captain George Charles Peere Williams-Freeman, F.R.G.S.
1890–1905

A native of Bitterne, Hants. Born 1856. Son of Frederick Peere Williams-Freeman, of Greatham Manor, Sussex. Educated at Haileybury and Sandhurst. Entered the army 1875, served with the Royal Sussex Regiment in the West Indies, Malta, Cyprus, and took part in the suppression of the riots in Barbados 1876. Acted as Commandant of Police and Governor of Gaol, Famagusta district, Cyprus in 1881. Served as Adjutant of half battalion Royal Sussex Regiment throughout the Egyptian Campaign of 1882. (Medal and Khedive's Star). June 1883, appointed Provost Marshal and Commandant of Military Police in Egypt, relinquishing same on completion of staff employment in June 1888. Received thanks of Commander in Chief for services rendered during cholera epidemic, 1883.

Served as Provost Marshal on Sir G. Graham's staff during expedition to Eastern Soudan in 1884, and was present at the battle of El Teb, relief of Tokar, and reconnaisance to Tamanieb (mentioned in despatches; two clasps, and 4th class of Medjidieh), and commanded a company of mounted infantry during Suakim Expedition of 1885, including battle of Hasheen and destruction of Tamai (clasp).

Was for three years Governor of Military Prison, Cairo. Passed Army Veterinary School at Aldershot.

Appointed Chief Constable of Shropshire 1890.

Married 17 October 1883, Lavinia, daughter of General Sir Arthur Cunynghame.

Died 27 December 1905, while still holding office as Chief Constable.

Major-General Sir Llewellyn William Atcherley, C.M.G.,C.V.O.
1906—1908

Youngest son of the late Lieut-Colonel Francis Topping Atcherley, 30th Regiment, of Marton Hall, Shropshire; born 1890. Educated at Oundle. Entered the East Lancashire Regiment 1890, promoted Captain. A.S.C. 1898; Brevet-Major 1900, Major 1905 (retired 1906).

Chief Constable of Shropshire 1906—1908, and Chief Constable of the West Riding of Yorkshire 1908 to 1919.

Took part in the Ashanti Expedition 1895—6 (mentioned in despatches, star); South Africa 1899—1902, as D.A.A.G. (despatches, Queen's medal with six clasps, King's medal with two clasps), European War 1914—1918 (despatches, C.M.G.); Sometime Adjutant and Assistant Instructor, Army Service Corps.

Schools of Instruction, Aldershot; King's Police Medal; appointed A.Q.M.S. Administrative Staff 1914, D.A. and Q.M.G. 1915, and controller of Salvage at the War Office 1917.

Appointed one of His Majesty's Inspectors of Constabulary

1919–1936, and re-employed in the same post 1940–1945.
Married 1897, Eleanor Frances, daughter of the late Richard
Micklewaite, J.P., D.L., of Ardsley House, Barnley.
Father of the R.A.F's famous flying twins — Air Vice-
Marshall R.L.R. Atcherley and Air Vice Marshall D.F.W.
Atcherley.
Created M.V.O. (4th class) 1912; C.M.G. 1916; C.V.O.
1918; Knighted 1925.
Died 17 February 1954, at Fulford, York.

Captain Gerald Lysley Derriman. 1908–1915

Eldest son of Admiral Samuel Hoskins Derriman, C.B.,
Educated at Eton.   Joined the Grenadier Guards in 1889.
Served during the whole of the South African War, as Staff-
Captain for the Imperial Yeomanry at the base depot at Cape-
town.   He received both the Queen's and the King's South
African War Medals with five clasps.
Gazetted captain in 1904, when he went into the reserve.
Before coming to Shropshire, he was Chief Secretary of the
Royal Society for the Prevention of Cruelty to Animals.
Appointed Chief Constable of Shropshire 11 August 1908.
He was recalled to military service on the 1 January 1915,
rejoining his old regiment.
He died in France, 7 August 1915, from wounds received in
action.

Augustus Wood-Acton, D.L., J.P. 1915–1918

A native of London.   Born 1842.   Son of John Wood, J.P.,
of Martock, Somerset, by Mary, niece of Thomas Pendarves
Stackhouse Acton, of Acton Scott Hall, Church Stretton.
Educated at Harrow and Trinity College, Cambridge. B.A.,
1864.   Justice for the Peace for the counties of Salop, Here-
ford and Somerset, and Deputy-Lieutenant for Herefordshire.
County councillor for the Church Stretton district, and
Chairman of the Church Stretton Board of Guardians for nine

235

years.   Held a commission in the West Somersetshire Yeomanry for eight years.   Married in 1880.   Laura Charlotte, daughter of the Rev. Richard Surtees, Vicar of Holby, Yorkshire.

Assumed the additional name of Acton by Royal License 1874.

Appointed 19 October 1915 (then in his seventies) to the Honorary office of Chief Constable of Shropshire, for the duration of the war, at the request of the Salop Standing Joint Committee, of which he was Vice-Chairman.

Died, whilst still in office, 24 March 1918, at his home at Acton Scott.

Major Sir Jack Becke, C.B.E., K.P.M. 1918—1935

Son of Captain John Becke of the Bombay Sappers and Miners;   born 1878.   Educated at Cheltenham College; called to the bar 1918; Prizewinner of Grays Inn.   Served in the South African War 1899—1902, firstly as a trooper in the Ceylon Mounted Infantry, and later commissioned as a Lieutenant in the Imperial Yeomanry.

Major Becke received some experience in police work, serving in the Leeward Islands 1906—1907.   He was second in command of the 2nd Battalion South Lancashire Regiment in Flanders, at the start of World War I, where he was seriously wounded at Ypres.   In 1916 he was appointed to M.I.5, for contra-espionage work; from which he retired in 1918.

Appointed Chief Constable of Shropshire 1918.   Resigned after seventeen years in 1935, becoming Chief Constable of Cheshire.   An authority on traffic questions and an expert on criminal investigation.

Major Becke received the O.B.E. 1931;   Silver Jubilee Medal George V. 1935; Coronation Medal George VI. 1937; King's Police Medal 1937; C.B.E. 1941, Knighted 1943.

Major Sir Jack Becke retired September 1946 after eleven years as Chief Constable of Cheshire.

He died 2 March 1962, in the Northwich Infirmary, Cheshire.

Lieut. Colonel Harold Arthur Golden. 1935–1946

Born 14 January 1896. Educated St. John's College, Cambridge, B.A. with honours in the mechanical sciences tripos. Barrister at Law, of Gray's Inn. Served for 19 years as an officer in the Royal Engineers, with four years war service in India, Egypt and Palestine.

After the war he was seconded to the Egyptian Army. Later he served for four years as Staff Officer. R.E. in both the Northern and Southern Commands. Prior to coming to Shropshire he was an instructor at the Royal Military Academy, Woolwich.

Appointed Chief Constable of Shropshire 3 October 1935.

Relinquished his post as Chief Constable and County A.R.P. Controller 1 November 1943, to return to the army.

Appointed Chief Constable of Wiltshire 1 January 1946.

Awarded Coronation Medal of George VI. 1937.

O.B.E. (New Year's Honours) 1943.

Police Long Service and Good Conduct Medal. 1958.

C.B.E. 1960.

Retired as Chief Constable of Wiltshire 2 October 1963.

Died in Norfolk, early in 1976.

Sir Douglas Osmond, C.B.E., Q.P.M. 1946–1962

Educated at Bournemouth and University College, London. B.Sc. in Mathematics. Entered the Metropolitan Police College, Hendon in 1935. Rose to the rank of Inspector with the Metropolitan Police Force. Called up December 1943 for service with the Royal Navy. Released October 1944, when he joined the Control Commission for Germany, taking part in the re-organization of the German Police and the building up of the British police organization in Germany. Appointed Chief Constable of Shropshire in 1946, a post which he held until 1962, in which year he was appointed Chief Constable of the Hampshire and Isle of Wight Police Force. Sir Douglas Osmond has chaired many police committees, both regional and national, including The Police Council for the United Kingdom, 1972 and 1974. He was President of the Association of Chief Police Officers of England and Wales, 1967—69; Provincial Police Representative, Interpol, 1968—70; Regional Police Commander (designate), No. 6 Region, 1962—77. He also served on innumerable committees, sat on the Board of Governors, Police College, 1968—72, and on the Advisory Committee of the same college, 1959—77. Home Secretary's special representative to investigate conditions in Northern Ireland, 1969; Police Advisor to the Association of County Councils, 1963—75; Association of Chief Police Officers representative to give evidence to the Royal Commission on the Police, 1959—62. Member of the Royal Commission on Criminal Procedure from 1977.

Awarded O.B.E. 1958; Queen's Police Medal 1962; C.B.E. 1968; Order of St. John 1971, and was knighted 1971.

Retired as Chief Constable of Hampshire in 1979.

Robert George Fenwick, C.B.E., Q.P.M. 1962—1967

Educated at Dame Allen's School - Barrister at Law, Gray's Inn 1951; son of George R.F. Fenwick of Horton Grange, Northumberland.

Joined the Metropolitan Police in 1934, where the greater part of his service was spent in the various branches of the C.I.D., at New Scotland Yard. From 1955 to 1957 he was attached to the Metropolitan Police Detective Training School at Hendon.

Seconded to the Foreign Office, he went to Brazil as Advisor to the State of Sao Paulo 1957—1958. He later acted as liaison officer to a Brazilian Police Mission visiting this country.

Mr. Fenwick became a member of the Directing Staff of the National Police College in Hampshire - 1950—1960.

Appointed Assistant Chief Constable of Gloucestershire
1960–1962. Became Chief Constable of Shropshire 1962–
1967.

Appointed one of Her Majesty's Regional Inspectors of
Constabulary 1967–77.

Adviser to the Qatar Police 1972–1977.

Awarded the Queen's Police Medal 1969; Created
Commander of the Order of the British Empire 1975.

CHIEF CONSTABLES OF THE BOROUGH OF BRIDGNORTH

Edward Goodall

Appointed Chief Constable of Bridgnorth 1.1.1836.
Appointed Inspector of Weights & Measures. 19.2.1836.
Buried at Bridgnorth, aged 45. 19.5.1836.

George Evans

A native of Bridgnorth, born 1798.
Succeeded his father, John Evans, as Town Crier. c. 1834.
Joined Bridgnorth Police Force. 18.1.1836.
Appointed Sergeant for the execution of process in the Bridgnorth Court of Record. 20.5. 1836.
Appointed Chief Constable of Bridgnorth. 7.10.1836.
Succeeded by his son, Thomas Evans, as Town Crier. August 1859.
Buried at Bridgnorth, aged 61. 19.1.1859.

Luke Edwards

Joined Bridgnorth Police Force. 1.12.1837.
Appointed Chief Constable of Bridgnorth. 3.2.1840.
Resigned his office. 6.8.1841.
Joined Shropshire Constabulary, age 31. 8.9.1841.
Resigned as 1st Class Constable. 29.4.1848.

Richard Evans

Appointed Chief Constable of Bridgnorth. 6. 8.1841.
Gave up post on amalgamation of Bridgnorth Borough Police Force with the Shropshire Constabulary July 1850.
Became landlord of the Bell & Talbot Inn, Bridgnorth.
Died at Bridgnorth, aged 77, 17.11.1873.

George Ross

Joined Shropshire Constabulary. 25.7.1846.
Resigned 30. 6. 1855.
Appointed Chief Constable of the re-formed Bridgnorth Borough Police Force. 8.6.1855.
Joined Devon Constabulary, with the rank of Inspector 30.1.1857.
Promoted 2nd Class Superintendent 11.1.1859.
Promoted 1st Class Superintendent 3.7 1860.
Retired on pension 18.10.1870.
Died 27.3.1887.

John Cole

A native of Hanbury, Worcestershire.
Joined the Staffordshire County Constabulary 26.2.1853.
Resigned 14.7.1854.
Joined Stafford Borough Police Force with rank of Sergeant 11.7.1854.
Appointed Chief Constable of Bridgnorth 13.2.1857.
Retired 10.10.1887.

Charles Childs

A native of Bitterley, near Ludlow.
Joined Leominster Borough Police Force 1869.
Resigned 1870.
Joined Hereford County Constabulary 1870.
Resigned 1871.
Joined Newport (Monmouthsire) Borough Police Force 25.10.1871.
Reputed to have served for a short period in the Metropolitan Police Force.
Rejoined Leominster Borough Police Force c.1876.
Promoted to rank of Sergeant c. 1880.
Appointed Chief Constable of Bridgnorth 11.10.1887.

Transferred to Shropshire Constabulary with rank of Inspector, on amalgamation of forces. 1.4.1889. Superannuated 8.10.1892.

SUPERINTENDENTS OF THE LUDLOW BOROUGH POLICE FORCE.

William Davies

Sergeant at Mace and gaoler to the Borough of Ludlow discontinued as superintendent of the Borough Police Force 10 August 1837.

Robert Jones

A native of Stafford. Son of Robert Jones, Head Constable of the Borough of Stafford for some thirty years.
Joined the Shropshire Constabulary 19 July 1841.
Promoted superintendent 2nd class 8 April 1850.
Resigned 1 February 1851.
Appointed superintendent of Ludlow Borough Police Force 1851.
Appointed Inspector of Lodging-houses 26 October 1853.
Resigned 1855.

Henry Biggs

A native of English Bicknor, Gloucestershire. Born c.1817.
Joined Gloucestershire Constabulary 1 March 1843.
Promoted 1st Class Constable 1 August 1844.
Still in this rank 1 September 1849.
Dismissed for being under the influence of liquor.
Appointed Superintendent of the Ludlow Borough Police Force July 1855.
Appointed Inspector of Nuisances November 1855.
Died in office. 27 February 1865.

Geogre Henry Brookes

A native of Birmingham.   Formerly of the Birmingham

243

Police Force, in which he rose to the rank of sergeant.
Joined Leominster Borough Police Force 1862.
Resigned March 1865.
Appointed Superintendent of the Ludlow Borough Police Force 23 March 1865.
Resigned through ill-health 31 July 1885.
Died at Ludlow 1886.

James Cowmeadow Wheatstone

A native of East Dean, Gloucestershire.   Born c. 1837.
Joined Ludlow Borough Police Force as a constable 19.4.1865.
Promoted to rank of sergeant by 1869.
Appointed Superintendent of the Ludlow Borough Force 6.8.1885.
Also Superintendent of the Ludlow Fire Brigade.
Resigned through ill-health 4.10.1888.

John Simcox

A native of Morville, Shropshire.
Joined Shropshire Constabulary 6.1.1866.
Promoted 2nd Class Sergeant 4.5.1872.
Promoted 1st Class Sergeant 1883.
Promoted Superintendent in charge of Burford Division 1887.
Put in temporary charge of the Ludlow Borough Police Force 11.10.1888 until its amalgamation with the Shropshire Constabulary 16.4.1889.
Superannuated from the Shropshire Constabulary 9.4.1892.

HEAD POLICE OFFICERS OF THE BOROUGH OF OSWESTRY.

Jacob Smith

A native of Leicestershire. Ex-soldier.
Senior Sergeant at Mace, Oswestry. 1831—1851.
Head Police Officer, variously entitled - Chief Constable, Superintendent & Inspector of the Borough Police.
Resigned 1 October 1851.
Died at Oswestry, aged 71, on the 21 January 1854.

John Donald

A native of Disington, near Whitehaven, Cumberland.
Served for a time in the Liverpool Police Force.
Appointed Head Police Officer of Oswestry 1 October 1851.
Stabbed by a drunken prisoner, William Baverstock 12 February 1855. Resigned his post the following year.
Appointed Superintendent of the Cumberland & Westmorland County Constabulary 3 December 1856.
Died on the 23 April 1861, while on a visit to Oswestry. Age 43.

William Sykes

Appointed Superintendent of the Oswestry Borough Police Force September 1857. Appointed Superintendent of the Markets; Inspector of Common Lodging Houses, and Senior Sergeant - at Mace Oswestry 9 November 1857.
Made redundant by the amalgamation of the Oswestry Borough Police Force with the Shropshire Constabulary 1 April 1861.

CHIEF CONSTABLES OF THE BOROUGH OF SHREWSBURY.

Samuel Farlow

Born 1799, a native of Shrewsbury. Enrolled as a Burgess of the town 1820. Appointed Marshall of Shrewsbury 1826—1844. Appointed Sergeant at Mace 1834—1846. Chief Officer of Police 1840. Died aged 57, 6 April 1857.

Edward John Blake

Saw service in the Royal Navy from the age of 14, when as a midshipman he was present at the battle of Copenhagen. Two years later he took part in the capture of Martinique from the French, for which action he was awarded a medal and clasp. In the same year he was attached to the Walcheron Expedition, at the mouth of the Scheldt in Holland. He transferred to the Royal Marines Light Infantry in 1812. Served in the Adriatic, being present at the siege and reduction of Trieste, at the blockade of Venice, and the taking of some forts at the mouth of the River Po.

He ably defended the fort of Magna Vacce with only eighteen men, against a very superior force of the French Army. At this time he was severely wounded. He also served in ships of the Royal Navy off the coast of America. Blake was rewarded by the Patriotic Fund, and mentioned in despatches. He retired on half-pay, at the extremely early age of nineteen.

Appointed Chief Constable of the Borough of Shrewsbury November 1844. Dismissed November 1845.

Died at Birkenhead, 1 February 1867, aged 70.

William Harper

A native of Shrewsbury. Appointed a Police Office for the Borough of Shrewsbury 15 August 1839. Appointed Superintendent of Night and Day Constables 9 November 1839. Became Superintendent in charge of the Shrewsbury Borough Police Force 10 November 1845. Noted as Chief Constable 1846–1851.

Died (late Chief Constable) 19 February 1855.

Joseph Shackell

Appointed as sergeant to the newly formed Metropolitan Police Force 21 September 1829. Promoted to the rank of Inspector 25 December 1839. Retired on pension 22 November 1848.

Six years elapsed between his retirement and his appointment at Shrewsbury, during this time he is reputed to have gained further experience with other forces.

Appointed Chief Constable of Shrewsbury 24 March 1854.

A widower, he married Sarah, widow of the late Richard Jones, baker and confectioner, of Milk Street, Shrewsbury 3 July 1854.

Resignation tendered to the Shrewsbury Watch Committee on the 22 February 1856.

John Hughes

A native of Shrewsbury. Joined the Shrewsbury Borough Police Force 1845. Appointed Sergeant at Mace 1851, while holding the rank of Inspector of the Borough Police.

Elected Chief Constable of Shrewsbury 29 February 1856.

Resigned from office 6 May 1870.

Died at Shrewsbury 15 January 1888, at the age of 81.

John Davies

A native of Welshpool. Joined the Shrewsbury Borough Police Force December 1851. Promoted sergeant 15 May 1856.

Appointed Chief Constable of Shrewsbury 13 May 1870.
Resigned his office 7 May 1881. Retired to Liverpool.

Joseph Harrop

Appointed reserve sergeant and clerk of the Middlesbrough
Borough Police Force 14 January 1873.
Promoted acting inspector and chief clerk 6 October 1880.
Resigned his post 10 June 1881.
Appointed Chief Constable of the Borough of Shrewsbury
June 1881. Resigned his office 27 May 1887.
Appointed Chief Constable of the Borough of Burnley 1
July 1887. Dismissed from office 27 July 1901.

George William Whitfield

A native of Wortley, Leeds. Height 6'-1".
Appointed 3rd class constable in the Leeds Borough Police
force 22 November 1872. Promoted 2nd class constable 21
March 1873. Promoted 1st class constable 20 March 1874.
Promoted second class sergeant 7 January 1876.
Resigned as chief inspector 25 April 1881.
  Appointed superintendent of the Monmouthshire Constab-
ulary 26 April 1881. Superintendent of the Pontypool
Division 12 May 1881. Resigned his post 11 July 1887.
Appointed Chief Constable of the Borough of Shrewsbury
June 1887. Resigned his office October 1888.
  Appointed Chief Constable of the City of York October
1888.
  Vice-chairman of the National Fire Brigades Union 1891 &
1892.
  Resigned as Chief Constable of York August 1894.

Henry Blackwell

A native of London. Articled to a London architect, he
was, after completing his engagement, employed as a draughts-

man at the Science and Art Department, South Kensington, where he was engaged in preparing designs for the International Exhibition of 1862.

In 1872 he joined the City of London Police Force, passing through various grades of the service, during which time he had been chosen to be in attendance on Shah Nasr Eddin of Persia on the occasion of his visit to the City of London, in the June of 1873, and also to the Sultan Abdul Aziz of Turkey and Czar Alexander II of Russia on their visits.

Resigned from the City of London Force in 1881.

Appointed Chief Constable of Newport, Isle of Wight 5 September 1881. Thanked by Queen Victoria for the services he rendered at Newport, on the occasion of her Majesty's visit to that town.

Resigned his office 12 November 1888.

Appointed Chief Constable of the Borough of Shrewsbury 19 November 1888. Resigned his office 31 January 1906.

Died in London 18 April 1906.

Arthur Baxter

Joined the Shropshire Constabulary 6 November 1890.

Promoted 2nd class sergeant 1 September 1893.

Resigned 31 December 1895.

Appointed Chief Inspector Shrewsbury Borough Police 31 December 1895.

Appointed Chief Constable of the Borough of Shrewsbury 31 January 1915. Retired 7 November 1915.

Herbert Frederick Harries

A native of Shrewsbury, born 5 May 1871. Educated at Shrewsbury School.

Member of the Shrewsbury Borough Council 1907–1915.

Chairman of Shrewsbury Watch Committee. Member of the Atcham R.D.C. & Board of Guardians. Chairman of the Eye Ear & Throat Hospital, Shrewsbury. Chairman of Shrewsbury

Free Library committee. Member of many local committees. Appointed Honorary Chief Constable of Shrewsbury 9 November 1915. Relinquished the post 1 March 1918.

Awarded the Order of the British Empire for his services with the Shrewsbury Borough Police Force during World War I. Died 20 December 1928.

Frank Davies

A native of Brecon.

Joined the Shrewsbury Borough Police Force January 1900.

Promoted sergeant 13 March 1914. Promoted Inspector 6 August 1915. Promoted Chief Inspector 23 May 1917.

Appointed Chief Constable & Chief Officer of Shrewsbury Fire Brigade 1 March 1918.

Originator of the 'Boots for Bairns' fund which supplied every winter hundreds of poor children with footwear.

Awarded the King's Police Medal January 1934.

Awarded the Silver Jubilee Medal (George V) 7 May 1935.

Awarded the Coronation Medal (George VI) 12 May 1937.

Retired from his post 31 March 1940.

Died at Shrewsbury, aged 78. December 1956.

George Harry MacDivitt

A native of Birmingham.

Served in the Coldstream Guards 1914 — 1918 War.

Joined Shrewsbury Borough Police Force 18 March 1921.

Promoted sergeant and chief-clerk 7 September 1934.

Awarded Coronation Medal (George VI) 12 May 1937.

Promoted inspector 1 April 1938.

Appointed Deputy Chief-Constable 3 March 1939.

Promoted chief-inspector 1 April 1939.

Appointed Chief Constable of Shrewsbury 1 April 1940.

Retired from office when the Shrewsbury Borough Police Force amalgamated with the Shropshire Constabulary 1 April 1947.

Died at Shrewsbury, aged 78. 18 December 1975.

AGREEMENT TO AMALGAMATE THE OSWESTRY BOROUGH POLICE FORCE WITH THE SHROPSHIRE CONSTABULARY. 1861.

It is AGREED this eighteenth day of March. One thousand eight hundred and sixty-one. BETWEEN Her Majesty's Justices of the Peace of and for the County of Salop in General Quarter Sessions assembled on the one hand and The Mayor, Aldermen and Burgesses of the Borough of Oswestry in the said County by the Council of the said Borough on the other hand as follows (that is to say)

That the Police Establishments of the said County and Borough shall from and after the First day of April next be consolidated into one Police Establishment pursuant to the Acts passed in the 3rd and 4th and 19th and 20th years of Her Majesty's Reign chapters 88 and 95.

SECONDLY. That upon the present Police Force ceasing to act on the said first day of April next four additional County Constables consisting of One Serjeant, one first class Constable, and two other Constables shall be provided so that the duty of preserving the Peace and protecting Property including Nightly Watch shall be properly discharged within the said Borough of Oswestry.

THIRDLY. That such Constables shall be selected by the Chief Constable and the name of every Constable so intended to do duty in the said Borough shall upon his nomination be transmitted to the Mayor of the said Borough and in case any objection to such Constable be made by the Mayor within one Calendar Month after such transmission he shall be removed by the Chief Constable and another Constable provided.

FOURTHLY. The said Borough shall contribute to the total cost of the Force (after deducting the Government allowance and receipts for discharge of Constable duties) such a proportion as the four additional Constables shall bear to the total average Number of the whole Consolidated Police Force (exclusive of the Chief Constable whose Salary is however to be included in the total cost) Such proportion to be paid by the Treasurer of the said Borough to the Treasurer of the said County in the following manner (that is to say) The amount of the Salaries or Pay to be calculated proportionable as aforesaid of the said four additional Constables doing duty in the said Borough shall be paid quarterly at Midsummer, Michaelmas, Christmas and Lady Day in each year and the remainder of the proportion to be paid on or before the first day of December in each year by the Treasurer of the said Borough to the Treasurer of the said County.

FIFTHLY. The said Borough shall also contribute and pay the like proportion towards any deficiency which may arise in the Superannuation Fund.

SIXTHLY. That the said Borough shall give up the Apartments in the Local Gaol upon the County finding a party to take charge of such Gaol.

SEVENTHLY. Should any difference arise between the said County and Borough relative to this Agreement the same shall be determined by the Government Inspector of Police for the time being.

NICKNAMES OF SOME OF THE MID 19th CENTURY OFFENDERS, WHO WERE REGULARLY BROUGHT UP IN THE COURTS.

SHREWSBURY.

William Cullis alias The Frankwell Beauty.
Sarah Anne Davenall alias The Great Western.
James Davies alias Young Pretty Patch.
Catherine Edwards alias Irish Kit.
Harriet . . . . . . alias Harriet the Match.
. . . . . Healy alias Drop the Pie.
James Jones alias Durras.
Richard Jones alias Dick o' the Hayes.
Thomas Lloyd alias Tommy Split.
Thomas Meredith alias Tatoe Tom.
Richard Owen alias Dolly Dick.
Edward Stedman alias Valiant.
Mary Williams alias Moll Merrylegs.
. . . . . . Blayney alias Blood 'Un.
Susan Edwards alias Pluked the Hare.
Richard Griffiths alias Dick the Pinman.
Thomas Gwillam alias Buck Urchin.
Esther Maria Jones alias Snuff and Duck.
John Jones alias Jack the Sweep.
William Thompson alias The Artful Dodger.
Jon Alcock alias Jack the Rat.
Frederick Jones alias Young Castlerag.
William Price alias Captain Flappets.
William Matthews alias Bowshut.

John Davies alias Dumble Dum Deary.
John Davies alias Dorrington Jack.
Richard Hughes alias Sixpenny Dick.
John Price alias Waterloo.
Thomas Roberts alias The Machine.
Mary Goold alias Molly O.
James Jones alias Buy a Bit.
Stockton Humphreys alias Romeo.
Richard Morris alias Skyver.
William Davies alias Smoker.
Sarah Pearce alias The Rose.
Richard Jones alias Dick the Miller. (a notorious poacher).
William Shakespeare alias Glory.
Benjamin Shakespeare alias Ben Battle alias Molly Brierley.
William Davies alias Ruffy.

BRIDGNORTH.
Benjamin Tipton alias Peeck for Peeck.
Thomas Jones alias Sailor Jones.
William Farmer alias The Dodger.
Samuel Rogers alias Henry Williams alias Harry the
traveller
George Rowley alias Plum Eyes.

COCKSHUTT.
John Jones alias The Lion.

IRONBRIDGE.
Richard Northall alias Dick the Devil.

LUDLOW.
George Robinson alias Corkey.
Henry Morrison alias Red White and Blue.
William Jones alias The Ram.

MARKET DRAYTON.
Eliza Farnall alias The She Bear.

254

William Farnall alias The Bear.
Arthur Hudson alias Sergeant Shee.
Richard Biggs alias Cinder Dick.
Mrs. Neild alias Frying Pan.

MUCH WENLOCK.
Frances Massey alias Bacca.

OAKENGATES.
William Davies alias Jim a Long.

OSWESTRY.
Edward Griffiths alias Ned Death.
Mary Hughes alias The Great Western.
Thomas Jones alias Tom the Coach.
Emma Roberts alias Down Derry alias Sugar.
Alfred Humphreys alias Young Coachey.
Daniel Powell alias Noble Dan.
William Salman alias The King of the Poachers.
Jane James alias The Crocodile.
Benjamin Williams alias Ben the Basket.

WELLINGTON.
Joseph Hughes alias Joe Thunder.
Robert Jones alias Limpy.
Edward Swinnerton alias Yoicks.
Thomas Worrell alias Squench.

CHAPTER ONE
1. Eddowes Salopian Journal, 6.7.1836. (abbreviated hereafter to E.S.J.)
2. Bridgnorth Borough Council Mins. 15.1.1836.
3. Ludlow Borough Council Mins. 10.8.1837.
4. Salop Quarter Sessions. Abstract of Orders. (Ptd) Vol. III. p.284.
5. E.S.J. 2.1.1839.
6. Do. 2.1.1839.
7. Life and Opinions of General Sir Charles James Napier. Vol. II. pp.15-56 (1857)
8. E.S.J. 16.10.1839.
9. Do. 16.10.1839.
10. Do. 16.10.1839.

CHAPTER TWO
1. Salop Police Committee Books. 4.3.1840. S.R.O. 1818/1.
2. Oswestry Borough Minute Book. 31.10.1840.
3. E.S.J. 13.1.1841.
4. Do. 6.1.1841.
5. Salopian Telegraph and Border Review, 6.11.1841.
6. Do. 18.12.1841.
7. Sutherland to H.O. dated 10.10.1841. H.O.45/57.
8. Do. dated 23.8.1842. H.O.45/258.
9. Salopian Journal. 27.7.1842.
10. Eyton to H.O. dated 19.8.1842. H.O.45/258.
11. Do.
12. Salopian Telegraph and Border Review. 27.8.1842.

13. Salopian Journal. 1.3.1843.
14. Do. 2.10.1844.
15. The Shropshire Conservative. 19.10.1844.
16. Shrewsbury Borough Council Minutes. 5.5.1845.
17. Do. 10.11.1845.

CHAPTER THREE
1. A History of Police in England & Wales. T.A. Critchley. (1978), p.113. (Abbreviated hereafter to H.P.E.&W.)
2. Shrewsbury Borough Council Minutes. 18.2.1856.
3. H.P.E.&W. p.117.
4. Shrewsbury Chronicle. Sept.1858. (Abbreviated hereafter to S.C.)
5. Salop Police Committee Books. 18.10.1858. S.R.O. 1818/2.

CHAPTER FOUR
1. Report of Inspector of Constabulary year ending Sept: 1860. pp.29-30.
2. Do. p.31.
3. Do. p.30.
4. Do. p.31.
5. Do. p.30.
6. E.S.J. 15.10.1862.
7. Letter. S.R.O. Q/Q. Box 108.

CHAPTER FIVE
1. E.S.J. 1.1.1873.
2. Shrewsbury Watch Committee Minutes. 6.5.1870.
3. Bridgnorth Watch Committee Minutes. 4.8.1870.
4. E.S.J. 1.12.1875.

CHAPTER SIX
1. E.S.J. 18.5.1881.
2. Shrewsbury Watch Committee Minutes. 18.1.1884.

3. Bridgnorth Chief Constable's Journal. 10.3.1863. S.R.O. 1868/1.

CHAPTER SEVEN
1. Shrewsbury Chronicle. 3.11.1893.

CHAPTER EIGHT
1. Wellington Journal and Shrewsbury News. 16.1.1900.
2. Shropshire Constabulary General Order. No: 837. 7.4.1902. S.R.O.1818/32.

CHAPTER NINE
1. Shrewsbury Watch Committee Minutes. 27.10.1911.
2. Do. 27.7.1914.
3. Do. 6.8.1915.
4. S.C. 18.2.1916.
5. Do. 3.3.1916. Police Review. 25.2.1916.
6. Do. 24.3.1916.
7. Do. 19.5.1916.
8. General Order. No. 1332. 1919. S.R.O. 1818/33.
9. The First Hundred Years. Roberts & Durnell. (1963), p.27.
10. Do. p.28.

CHAPTER TEN
1. General Order. No:1458. 1921. S.R.O.1818/34.
2. S.C. 11.11.1921.
3. H.P.&W. p.200.
4. General Order. No:1553. (1926). S.R.O. 1818/34.
5. Do. No:1554. (1926). S.R.O. 1818/34.
6. S.C. 12.5.1926.

CHAPTER ELEVEN.
1. S.C. 1.1.1932.

CHAPTER TWELVE
1. S.C. 5.4.1940.

2. Do. 1.12.1944.
3. Do. 28.3.1947.
4. Chief Constable's Annual Report. (Salop) March 1948.
5. Do.
6. S.C. 16.12.1949.

CHAPTER THIRTEEN
1. S.C. 27.4.1951.
2. Do. 17.4.1953.
3. Do.
4. Shropshire Star. 25.9.1980.
5. S.C. 16.4.1954.
6. Do. 14.10.1955.
7. Do.

CHAPTER FOURTEEN
1. S.C. 23.3.1962.
2. Salop Police Committee Report. 23.7.1966. p.39.
3. Do. p.40.
4. Do. p.41.
5. Chief Constable's Report. 1966.
6. One Policeman's Story. Sir Eric St. Johnstone. C.B.E., Q.P.M., (1978), p.267.

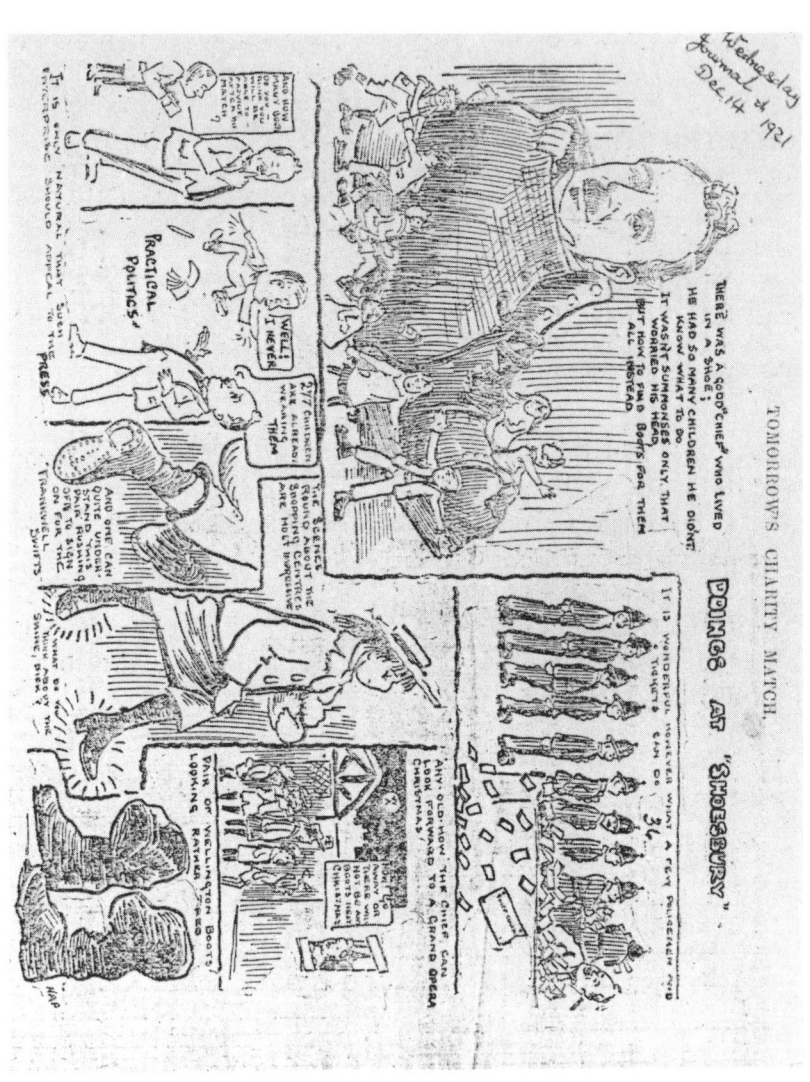

260

Index of Names

Index of Places